THE THUNDER & LIGHTNING'S OF

GOD

When GOD did Terrible & Wonderful things which I looked not For

Dr Michael H Yeager

NINETY AMAZING TRUE SHOCKING STORIES FROM THE AUTHORS LIFE!

ISBN: 9781092960137
Imprint: Independently published

DEDICATION

We dedicate this book to those who are truly hungry and thirsty to live in the realm of the super natural, and to those who have already tasted of the heavenly realm. We dedicate this to the bride of Christ, those who are called to go deeper, higher, and farther than they have yet experienced. It is only by the grace that comes by FAITH in CHRIST that we will be able to accomplish His will in this earth.

CONTENTS

ACKNOWLEDGMENTS

*To our heavenly Father and His wonderful love.

*To our Lord, Savior and Master —Jesus Christ, who saved us and set us free because of His great love for us.

*To the Holy Spirit, who leads and guides us into the realm of miraculous living every day.

*To all of those who had a part in helping us get this book ready for the publishers.

*To my Wife Kathleen and our precious children, Michael, Daniel, Steven, Stephanie, Catherine Yu, who is our precious daughter-in-law, and Naomi, who is now with the Lord!

Introduction

The miraculous happenings, heavenly visitations, and divine deliverance's that you are about to read are all true. They have happened personally to my family and I. These experiences are recalled and shared to the best of our ability.

By no means do the following stories account for all the visitations and miracles of God that we have experienced in our lives. If we would recount every single answer to prayer, and every wonderful miracle and blessing, there would be no end to this book! Both my wife and I, including our children, have had numerous supernatural dreams, visions, healing s and experiences. In some of our heavenly encounters, God gave us specific information which has come to pass, as well as visions and dreams which have yet to be fulfilled.

What we are about to share with you in this book are simply some highlights of what we have experienced in the Lord. Some of these experiences will seem to be incredulous, however, they are true. This is not a testimony of how spiritual we are, but how wonderful and marvelous the Father, the Son, and the Holy Ghost are! We share these experiences to the best of our recollections and understanding. Not every conversation we share in these experiences are exactly word for word. We would love to name every person that was a part of these wonderful occurrences, but privacy laws do not allow this. If you are reading this book and you saw, experienced, or were a part of these events, please do not be offended because your names were not mentioned.

At the end of this book there will be a brief teaching on how you can enter into a position where God will supernaturally begin to speak, lead and guide you in your life. It is God's will that all who follow Him would enter into this realm where all things are possible. What God has done for us, He will do for everyone. He is not a respecter of people.

GOD Said: You Better Not Lie, or You'll Die to!

One day I picked up a book by a well-known author. This book had come highly recommended by one of my favorite preachers at that time. The topic was about angelic visitations. This was something I was interested in, because of my many experiences with the supernatural. I began to read this book, and noticed immediately that there were experiences he said he had, which did not seem to line up with the Scriptures. I did not want to judge his heart, but we do have the responsibility to examine everything in light of God's Word. If it does not line up with the word of God, then we must reject it, no matter who wrote it.

As I was pondering the stories in this book, the Spirit of the Lord spoke to my heart very strongly. It was as if He was standing right there next to me, speaking audibly. What He spoke to me was rather shocking! The Lord told me that the writer of this book would be dead in three months from a heart attack.

I asked the Lord why He was telling me this. He said the stories in the man's book were exaggerated, and judgment was coming. He told me that the man had opened the door for the devil to kill him. The Lord warned me that day that if I were ever to do the same thing would come to me. I did not realize that the Lord would have me to be writing books, many them filled with my own personal experiences. Now I know why he spoke this to me, telling me that I better not exaggerate my experiences.

When the Spirit of the Lord spoke this to me, I turned and told my wife. I held the book up and said, in a very quiet whispering, trembling, wavering voice, "Honey, the man who wrote this book will be dead in three months from a heart attack." Plus, I told her why the Lord told me this. I wish I had been wrong. Exactly 3 months later, the man died from a heart attack. God can speak to us through the positive and the negative circumstances of life. We better take heed to what he is saying

CHAPTER ONE

The Why of This Book

These stories, testimonies that I'm about to share with you are absolutely true. Many of them will seem exaggerated or fictional, but they're not. (Liars will go to hell) No doubt you will agree with me once you're done reading my book that I have lived an amazing extraordinary life.

Now, you might ask, why you brother Mike? I guess maybe you could say about me like what was said about Nebuchadnezzar. That God was going to demonstrate who He is and what He can do by using someone as an illustration.

You might ask me: why did you call the book: The **Thundering's and Lightning's of God**? It's based on what I experienced when the Lord, by an angel took me into heaven back in 1975. Whether in the Body or out of my body I could net tell!

In this visitation I found myself upon the sea of glass looking upon the throne of God. I will share a part of that with you at this moment, but then I'll share the whole story with you a little later in this book.

The Throne of God

Next I found myself in an immense never-ending realm. So

large was this place that I could not see an ending. Above me, behind me, to the left and the right just seemed to be a never-ending horizon. The floor under my feet was like a sea of crystal glass radiating and pulsating with ever-changing colours that flowed through it like an incoming wave of the ocean. In the distance, I saw lightning and extremely bright flashes of light proceeding from one point.

Not knowing what else to do, I began to move toward this phenomenon. As I drew closer, I heard thunder echoing off in the distance which sounded like mighty trumpets. The sea of glass under my feet shook with every peel of lightning. And with every step I took toward this phenomenon, my heart beat faster. It was as if the hair on the back of my neck and up my arms and head were standing straight up.

In the far distance I could see that I was approaching what looked like a huge throne. In front of the throne and around it, there seemed to be some type of activity that was transpiring. As I got closer I began to discern the most awesome creatures I could have ever imagine. Yet my attention was not on them.

The Scriptures declare that there are four of them altogether, full of eyes before and behind. The first is like a lion, the second like a calf, the third has the face of a man, and the fourth beast is like a flying eagle. They each have six wings and on the inside of the wings they are full of eyes. When I was still a great way off, even before I saw them, I heard these beasts declaring with a loud voice, "Holy, holy, holy, Lord God Almighty, Who was and Who is and Who is to come."

I only had eyes for the One on the throne. I could tell that the throne was amazing, but even more majestic and splendid than the throne was the One who sat upon it. He appeared like the brightness of translucent diamonds. A light shined out of the One on the throne that was of such an intensity and holiness.

"And in the midst of the seven candlesticks one like unto the Son of man, clothed with a garment down to the foot, and girt about the paps with a golden girdle. His head and his hairs were white like wool, as white as snow; and his eyes were as a flame of fire; And his feet like unto fine brass, as if they burned in a furnace; and his voice as the sound of many waters. And he had in his right hand seven stars: and out of his mouth went a sharp two edged sword: and his countenance was as the sun shineth in his strength" (Rev. 1:13-16).

Before HIS Throne

I knew without a shadow of doubt that I stood before God the Father and His Son, Jesus Christ. Around about them and stretching over the top of them shone numerous emerald rainbows much clearer and colourful than the natural mind could conceive.

"After this I looked, and, behold, a door was opened in heaven: and the first voice which I heard was as it were of a trumpet talking with me; which said, Come up hither, and I will shew thee things which must be hereafter. And immediately I was in the spirit: and, behold, a throne was set in heaven, and one sat on the throne.

And he that sat was to look upon like a jasper and a sardine stone: and there was a rainbow round about the throne, in sight like unto an emerald. And round about the throne were four and twenty seats: and upon the seats I saw four and twenty elders sitting, clothed in white raiment; and they had on their heads crowns of gold. And out of the throne proceeded lightning's and thundering's and voices: and there were seven lamps of fire burning before the throne, which are the seven Spirits of God.

And before the throne there was a sea of glass like unto crystal: and in the midst of the throne, and round about the throne, were four beasts full of eyes before and behind. And the first beast was like a lion, and the second beast like a calf, and the third beast had a face as a man, and the fourth beast was like a flying eagle. And the four beasts had each of them six wings about him; and they were full of eyes within: and they rest not day and night, saying, Holy, holy, holy, Lord God Almighty, which was, and is, and is to come.

And when those beasts give glory and honour and thanks to him that sat on the throne, who liveth for ever and ever, The four and twenty elders fall down before him that sat on the throne, and worship him that liveth for ever and ever, and cast their crowns before the throne, saying, Thou art worthy, O Lord, to receive glory and honour and power: for thou hast created all things, and for thy pleasure they are and were created" (Rev. 4:1-11).

I fell as one dead before the throne, quivering and shaking before the presence of my Lord. Then a voice spoke forth as if coming from everywhere. It filled my mind and heart with shaking and trembling. This voice was filled with absolute complete and total authority and holiness.

I knew it was the Father's voice that was speaking to me. As I lay on my face before the throne of God, I heard unspeakable words that could not be uttered with human vocabulary. It was literally as if streaks of lightning were hitting my body with every word that He spoke. **As His words hit my body they would explode in me like the soundings of thunder.**

My whole body literally shook and vibrated uncontrollably at these thundering's. **These thundering's flooded my body and took a hold of me.** It had to be God supernaturally strengthening me in order to keep me alive through this experience.

I am convinced that if you had been standing at a distance you would have seen streaks of divine lightning and fire striking my body. **This divine lightning and fire** was not meant to destroy me but to some extent was meant to impregnate me with God's divine purposes and abilities.

I knew that my inner man was drinking deep of the mysteries and divine plans of God. I remember the tears flowing from my eyes, down my face as I listened to the Word of the Lord. The glory of God was all around, upon, and in me. My body was enveloped in a glistening cloud of energy.

Through this whole experience I laid there weeping and whispering **"Thank you, Jesus. Thank you God"** over and over. I did not truly understand with my mind what was transpiring, but I knew in my heart that God was speaking to me divine truths and mysteries, that which was to be accomplished and would shortly come to pass.

I knew that He was supernaturally imparting into me the grace that was necessary to accomplish His purposes for my life. This seemed to go on forever. Then as quickly as it had started it was over. The Spirit of the Lord whisked me instantly away from the throne room of God.

God Shows up Extraordinarily in Order to Reveal Himself

As you study the Scriptures from Genesis to Revelation, you'll discover that there are times when God will just Suddenly show up in an amazing, mind-boggling, heart-stopping, beyond the imagination kind of way.

Let me just list some of these amazing visitations from God. **#1** Noah's Flood, **#2** Sodom and Gomorrah destroyed, **#3** Joseph taking over Egypt, **#4** The Burning bush on Mount Sinai **#5** Moses Delivering Egypt by Mighty Signs and Wonders **#6** The Red Sea Splitting, **#7** God Revealing Himself on Mount Sinai **#8** The Earth Opening and Swallowing the Enemies of Moses **#9** The Walls of Jericho Falling Flat **#10** Sampson Destroying a Thousand Philistines **#11** Samuel Calling down a Fierce Thunder Storm **#12** David killing Goliath and the Philistines **#13** Salomon Given Amazing Wisdom That Confounded the World **#14** Elijah Praying That It Would Not Rain, and Then Prayed It Would Rain **#15** Elijah Calling Fire down from Heaven **#16** Three Hebrew Children Could Not Burn **#17** The Lion Could Not Eat Daniel .

These are just some of the examples in the old covenant of God bringing Shock and Awe to the human race.

Isaiah 64:2 as when the melting fire burneth, the fire causeth the waters to boil, to make thy name known to thine adversaries, that the nations may tremble at thy presence! 3 When thou didst terrible things which we looked not for, thou camest down, the mountains flowed down at thy presence. 4 For since the beginning of the world men have not heard, nor perceived by the ear, neither hath the eye seen, O God, beside thee, what he hath prepared for him that waiteth for him.

God does this in order to wake up the human race to the reality of who he is. He will not only do this for a people, a nation, a world, but even a person. A good example of this is the apostle

Paul as he was on the road to Damascus in order to persecute Christians.

Acts 9:1 And Saul, yet breathing out threatenings and slaughter against the disciples of the Lord, went unto the high priest, 2 and desired of him letters to Damascus to the synagogues, that if he found any of this way, whether they were men or women, he might bring them bound unto Jerusalem.

3 And as he journeyed, he came near Damascus: and suddenly there shined round about him a light from heaven: 4 and he fell to the earth, and heard a voice saying unto him, Saul, Saul, why persecutest thou me? 5 And he said, Who art thou, Lord? And the Lord said, I am Jesus whom thou persecutest: it is hard for thee to kick against the pricks.

6 And he trembling and astonished said, Lord, what wilt thou have me to do? And the Lord said unto him, Arise, and go into the city, and it shall be told thee what thou must do. 7 And the men which journeyed with him stood speechless, hearing a voice, but seeing no man. 8 And Saul arose from the earth; and when his eyes were opened, he saw no man: but they led him by the hand, and brought him into Damascus. 9 And he was three days without sight, and neither did eat nor drink.

Please notice the shocking way in which God used to get Saul's attention. My salvation to some extent with similar to what happened to Paul. The difference was that I was in the midst of taking my own life because I was a manic depressant.

The beginning of my spiritual walk

Take hold of grace by faith. Faith is the victory that overcomes the world. The sins that we must overcome by grace through faith is revealed in Galatians 5 and many other scriptures.

*Just a little example: Before I was born again I was addicted to pornography, drugs, alcohol, smoking tobacco, smokeless tobacco, violence, ungodly music, hate.

My favorites when it came to addictions were marijuana, vodka, Southern comfort, ripple wine, and Pabst blue ribbon beer. My music was Dr. Hook and the medicine band, the Grateful Dead, Pink Floyd, and America.

You name it, I had it. I had tried desperately to quit these things with my own power until I finally got discouraged, gave up, and was in the process of committing suicide.

As I was about to slit my wrist, the fear of God fell upon me. I fell to my knees crying out to Jesus. He came gloriously into my life at that very moment. At once, faith in Christ took hold of grace and set me free from everything I just listed. I'm telling you; Jesus set me free! I have never bragged or boasted about my ability to overcome. For almost 40 years I have always given Christ the glory.

Have I arrived? No! But do I do the things that I used to do? No! Have I fallen short at times? Yes! Do I repent and get back up? Yes, I do by true grace, through faith, by hiding the WORD in my heart, JESUS gives me victory over the world, the flesh and the devil. Thank you, Jesus,!

*Jude 1:4 For there are certain men crept in unawares, who were before of old ordained to this condemnation, ungodly men, turning the **grace** of our God into lasciviousness, and denying the only Lord God, and our Lord Jesus Christ.*

Committing Suicide February 18th

Supernaturally one night, God stepped into my life, instantly and radically changing me forever! My last three months of military life was so amazingly transformed that I was put in charge of working parties and details from time to time. God instantly delivered me from all of my devices including all of my foolish behaviors. I was a new creature in Christ! Christ had supernaturally set me free from the tormenting demonic powers that had possessed my life for so long!

Here is what happened! On my 19th birthday, I was overwhelmed with a demonic spirit of self-pity and depression. I decided to end it all by slitting my wrist! I went into the bathroom with a large, survival hunting knife. I put the knife to my wrist with full intentions of slitting my artery.

I was determined to kill myself. I held the knife firmly against my wrist and took one more last breath before I slid it across my wrist. I was going to make sure that I was going to go all the way down into the bones of my wrist. We had a young man who tried to cut his wrist in boot camp. All he succeeded in doing was messing his hand all up.

Blanket of Fear

All of a sudden, invisible presence came rushing down upon me like a blanket. It was a tangible, overwhelming presence of mind-boggling fear. It was the fear of God, and it overwhelmed me! Instantly, I realized with the crystal-clear understanding that I was going to hell. I deserved hell; I belonged in hell, and hell had a right to me. Furthermore, I knew if I slit my wrist, I would be in hell forever.

And great fear came upon all the church, and upon as many as heard these things (Acts 5:11).

Overwhelming Love

I walked out of that little military bathroom to my bunk. I fell on my knees, reached my hands up toward heaven and cried out to Jesus with all of my heart. All of this was supernatural and strange. I did not ever recall any time when anyone ever shared with me how to become a Christian or how to be converted. I knew how to pray.

I cried out to Jesus and told Him I believed He was the Son of God, had been raised from the dead, and I desperately needed Him. I not only asked Him into my heart but I gave Him my heart, soul, mind, and life. At that very instant, a love beyond description came rushing into my heart. I knew what love was for the first time in my life.

At the same time, I comprehended what I was placed on this earth for—I was here to follow, love, serve, and obey God. A deep love and hunger to know God grabbed my heart. I was filled with love from top to bottom, inside and out—inexpressibly beyond belief. Jesus had come to live inside of me!

Rivers of waters run down mine eyes, because they keep not thy law (Psalm 119:136).

Completely Delivered

I was instantly delivered: from over three packs of cigarettes a day, from worldly and satanic music, from chewing tobacco; from cussing and swearing, from drugs and alcohol, and from a filthy and dirty mind.

Some might ask why my conversion was so dramatic. I believe that it's because I had nothing to lose. I knew down deep that there was not one single thing worth saving in me. The only natural talent I ever possessed was the ability to mess things up. At the moment of salvation, I completely surrendered my heart and life to Jesus Christ.

I am crucified with Christ: nevertheless I live; yet not I, but Christ liveth in me: and the life which I now live in the flesh I live by the faith of the Son of God, who loved me, and gave himself for me (Galatians 2:20).

Blood upon the Cross
(1963)

There was only one other time I could remember up to this time having experienced a supernatural visitation from God. I was about seven years old. Even during those years, I had caused my parents all kinds of heartache and sorrow. I was always getting into trouble, yelling, screaming, cursing, and disobeying.

I caused my mother, Shirley, so much heartache that once, in utter frustration, she told me that I had to be the devil himself. She never knew how those words deeply affected me. No matter how hard I tried to be good, I just got worse. I remember as a little boy I would get up on the sink in our little bathroom, look in the mirror, and run my hands through my hair. I was absolutely positive that I could feel two large lumps beginning to form on my skull. I was almost positive that I was the devil himself.

One night during this time I had gotten up to go to the bathroom. It was a cold winter night, and there was at least a foot of snow on the ground. The house was very quiet because everyone else in my family was sleeping. The light of the moon was shining through the bathroom window. The window was made of milk-colored, perforated glass.

11

As I looked through it, a shiver ran from my head to my feet. There in the milk-colored glass I saw three crosses. The middle one seemed to be three-dimensional. An overwhelming sense of love radiated from the middle cross. Then as I looked at it very intently, I thought there was a figure of a man hanging on it. I saw blood flowing from his hands and feet and his head. The next thing I knew, I was crying. I wept uncontrollably and did not understand what it was all about. Yet somehow I knew that God had touched me.

For the next two weeks, I was totally different, almost a saint. I believe it was because of this experience that I began to have the desire to be a Roman Catholic priest. My mother was completely amazed at the change that overtook me.

I became very polite, kind, and helpful. No one had to ask me to help; I simply did it. And even when the other children mocked me, I just ignored them instead of fighting back. I even quit aggravating my sister, Debbie. But I'm sorry to say that this did not last very long. Before I knew it I became worse than I was before. This spiritual experience as a child, this encounter that I had with God, was forgotten as if it had never happened.

Word of Knowledge & Gift of Healing
His Hernia Was Instantly Gone

One night, I was at a fellowship gathering with other believers from our little church. Chief Officer Lloyd, and his wife, Bonnie, had invited us all to their house for fellowship.

As I was standing in their front room, enjoying the fellowship, a kind of foggy image came floating up from my heart into my mind. In this semi-foggy vision, I saw a bulge in the lower stomach area of the man standing directly across from me. I did not know that this bulge was actually a hernia. I had only been born again for about a month, and not yet been taught on the gifts of the Holy Ghost. This was the word of knowledge, operating by a vision, inspired by the Holy Ghost.

As I saw this image in my mind's eye, I said to the Lord in my heart: "Lord, if this image is really of you then let that brother come over to me." The very moment this little prayer left my heart, this navy chief, Frank, looked up and walked over to me. I walked towards him, and we both reached out our hand, to shake hands. He introduced himself as Frank. As we were making small talk, I brought up the image I had seen.

He looked rather surprised, and he informed me that he was indeed having a terrible time with a hernia. The doctors had operated on it three times, up to this point, but it had torn loose after each operation. I asked if I could pray for him and he gave me permission. I explained that I wanted him to put his hand over the hernia and I would place my hand over his.

Then I simply prayed, but it was a long prayer. I spoke very quietly to this hernia, telling it to go away in the name of Jesus Christ, and for his stomach muscles to be healed. The moment I finished praying, it disappeared. The hernia was instantly and literally sucked back into his abdomen - it was gone!

We both just stood there. We were wonderfully surprised and rejoicing in the miracle that God had just performed! How this miracle came to pass is that God had given me "a word of knowledge and operating with the gift of faith and healing." Afterwards, Frank and I became good friends. At times, we would go fishing on the Bering Sea, for halibut, but that is a whole other story.

For to one is given by the Spirit the word of wisdom; to another the word of knowledge by the same Spirit; to another faith by the same Spirit; to another the gifts of healing by the same Spirit (1 Corinthians 12:8-9).

My First Exorcism

My first encounter with a demon possessed man was in 1975. I had only been a Christian for about two months, and I was in the Navy at the time. I was stationed on a military base on Adak, Alaska. One night (at about 8 pm) I was witnessing in my dormitory room to three men doing a bible study with them.

While sharing biblical truths with these three men, another man entered my room. We called him TJ. This individual had always been very different and strange. He was kind of out there. I had never even spoken to him up to that time, except one night when he showed a nasty movie to the guys in his dorm. I had walked out of his room not being able to handle his level of filth!

When TJ entered my room, he took over my bible study and began to preach some weird off-the-wall things about the devil. He said he was from California where he had been part of a satanic church. He showed us the ends of his fingers in which some of the ends were missing from the first joint out. He told us that he had eaten them for power, and that he had drunk human blood at satanic worship services.

As he spoke, an invisible power began speaking through him. An evil and demonic darkness descended upon us in my dormitory. A invisible demonic power took him over right in front of our eyes, and his eyes filled with a malevolent glow! One of the guys who were in my room, Hussein (who was a Muslim) declared this was too much for him, and left the room. The other two, Bobby and Willie, sat and listened.

I had never encountered anything as sinister and evil as this e before. I honestly didn't know what to do at that time, so I went downstairs to the barracks right below me. There was a fellow Christian I had the opportunity of working with who lived right below me. After I had given my heart to Jesus Christ, Willie, the cowboy told me that he too was a born again, Spirit-filled Christian.

I had yet to see the evidence of this in Willie's life, but I didn't know where else to go. I went down to his room and knocked on Willie's door. When he opened the door, I explained to him what was happening in my room. I was able to get him to come to my room upstairs.

Willie stepped into my dormitory and stopped. We both saw that TJ was now up on a stool that was made from a log, and he was preaching under the power of satanic spirits. At that very moment cowboy Willie turned tail and ran out of my room. I went after him. He told me that he had no idea what to do and that he could not handle this. He left me standing outside by my door alone.

I went back into my room and did the only thing I could, I cried out to Jesus Christ. The minute I cried out looking up towards heaven, I'm telling you that a bright light from heaven shone right through my ceiling. It was one of those Shock and Awe situations! It was a **B**eam of light that was about 3 feet wide, an all glistening bright light, shining upon me. I do not know if anyone else in my room saw this bright light. All I know is the Spirit of God rose up within me, and I was overwhelmed with God's presence.

My mouth was instantly filled with an amazingly powerful and prophetic word from heaven. I began to preach **Jesus Christ** by the power of the spirit! As I began to speak by the spirit, the power of God fell in that room. The next thing I knew was that TJ had dropped to the floor like a rock.

TJ began to squirming just like a snake with his body bending and twisting in I an impossible way. I am not exaggerating in the least! There was no fear left in my heart as I watched this demonic activity. There was nothing but a Holy

15

Ghost boldness and divine inspiration flowing through me at that time like a mighty river.

Now during this divine encounter of Heaven both Willie and Bobby had fallen on their knees crying out to Jesus to save them. At the same time they gave their hearts to the Lord, and they were both instantly filled with the Holy Ghost! The next thing I knew I found myself kneeling over the top of TJ as he was squirming like a snake. I placed my hands upon him as squirmed. Willie and Bobby came over at the same time joining me and laid their hands upon TJ also.

With a voice of authority inspired by the Spirit, **I commanded the demons to come out of the man in the Name of Jesus Christ**. As God is my witness, we all heard three to five different voices come screaming out of TJ! The voices were full of pain with an eerie reverb.

After the demons were gone it was like TJ breathed a last long breath like that of a dying man, and grew completely still. After a while, he opened up his eyes that were now filled with complete peace. He began to weep. At that very moment, he gave his heart to Jesus Christ. I led him into the baptism of the Holy Ghost right then and there. The presence of God overwhelmed all of us as we gave praise and thanks to the Lord. The next Sunday these three men went with me to church.

Shock & Awe When God Sent Me to Hell

Because these were Shocking experiences I will share my whole experience of going to Hell and Heaven!

My journey to hell and to heaven took place even before I knew what the Bible had to say on either subject. If either one of these or any of the other experiences I have had through the years had been contrary to the teachings of Christ or the prophets, I would adamantly reject them, turn my back on them, and declare that they were not of God.

A God-given vision of heaven or hell or any other visitation would never contradict Scriptures. I am not sharing with you something I made up out of the figment of my own imagination for the purpose of selling books or to make a name for myself. Please understand that when God gives visions, dreams, and divine encounters that many of these experiences could be revealed by shadows and illustrations of spiritual truths that He wants us to grasp and understand.

How This Experience Happened!

*Now I was stationed on an island in the Navy in the Aleutian chain on an island called Adak, Alaska, which is known for its many earth quakes. This island is where I was stationed in the military as an electrician's mate third class. The Navy base had a top-secret military installation and was used as a harbor for submarines and ships.

The top-secret installation was so hush-hush that most of us on the base did not really know what was taking place there. When I first arrived on the base, I quickly had to get used to the tremors and continual earthquakes. There were times I experienced tremors and quakes so strong they would wake me out of my sleep. My bed would shake so violently that I thought I was going to fall out of it.

I remember one night when I first arrived I was sleeping very soundly. All of a sudden my bed not only began to shake, but it was literally bouncing up and down like a rubber ball. I thought it was the men in my barracks playing a newbie trick on me. I automatically began to yell for them to stop before I opened my eyes. But when I opened my eyes and looked around no one was there. That was how much the building shook.

My Journey to Hell Begins

Now, one night I was deep in prayer with Willy, (I had only been saved for about two months) an African American brother in my barracks. I had the privilege of seeing Willie come back to Christ. At one time, previously he had walked with the Lord but had backslid. Before and after he was saved our nickname for him was "Willy Wine" because now he was filled with new wine.

As we were praying together, something very strange and very frightening began to happen to me. At the time of this event there was a gathering of some men in our battalion. They were having a party in the common area right outside our sleeping quarters where we were praying. The party they were having was quite loud with music and laughter, but it did not hinder us from crying out to God for souls.

As we were praying, I could sense that something was about to happen. The hair on the back of my arms and neck stood up on end. It was as if electricity was filling the very atmosphere around us. I sensed a strong tugging to go deeper in prayer. I gave myself completely over to the spirit of intercession, crying out to the Lord.

I began to cry out in prayer to God intensely, asking Him to allow me to have a supernatural experience of hell. I wanted this in order that I would have a greater and deeper compassion, a deeper love, a deeper understanding for the lost. I truly wanted to know the pains, the sorrows, the torments, the fears, and the agonies of those in hell. I wanted to weep and wail, to travail with a broken heart over the unconverted to reach them more effectively.

Please understand that I believe God put this desire, this prayer, into my heart for the love of souls. I began to pray in a realm that I had never been in before when suddenly an overwhelming and tangible darkness descended upon me.

"And when the sun was going down, a deep sleep fell upon Abram; and, lo, an horror of great darkness fell upon him" *(Gen. 15:12).*

A frightening darkness enveloped me. Everything around me disappeared. I no longer heard the music or the party that was taking place. Even though Willie was right there with me, I did not hear or see him. And it seemed as if time itself had come to a stop. To my utter shock, amazement, and horror, the floor and the building around me began to shake more violently than I had ever experienced before. Usually when we did get a quake (Adak Alaska) it would only last a matter of seconds. But in this situation the shaking did not stop as it normally did, rather it increased.

The Floor of the Building Ripped Open

All I could do at this moment was to try to hug the floor and hang on for dear life. The darkness lifted, but I could not see Willie anywhere. Then a terrible ripping and grinding noise filled the air. I saw the floor of the barracks ripple like that of a wave on the sea. The very floor of the barracks that I was laying upon began to tear and rip apart. I watched in stunned amazement and horror as the floor tiles popped and stretched. The concrete and steel within the building began to twist and rip apart. And the floor I was laying on began to split and tear open right below me.

I immediately began to look for a way to get out of the building. Everything was shaking so violently that I could not get up off the floor to make a dash to escape. The dust and dirt in the room was so thick and heavy that I could hardly breathe. Now this rip in the floor began to enlarge and became an opening.

I would call it more like a hole. I began to slip and fall into this hole; I tried desperately to reach for any kind of handhold that I could find. I began to scream and yell for help. But there was no one to help me. I became increasingly desperate trying to grab hold of something, anything that I could get my hands on. Objects around me began to fall through this hole in the floor. I watched as physical objects slipped past me into this hole. And I could feel myself sliding more and more.

No matter how desperately I was trying to cling to and hold on to items to prevent my falling, there was nothing that I could do. Finally, I slipped and fell backward as if falling off a ladder. As I was falling, everything seemed to go into slow motion like film that is slowed for a preview.

I was falling with parts of the crumbling building all around me. I watched as I fell past twisted steel beams, concrete floors, walls ripped into pieces, plumbing, and heating pipes, and sparking electric wires. I went past the underground tunnels that connected the buildings together.

The next thing that I knew I was falling past the ground and rock of the island. This terrible rip in the earth, this hole that I was falling down began to take on the form and similarity of that of a well, like an endless tube, an ever- proceeding pit. It became approximately three feet wide. As I was falling, I was desperately trying to grab hold of the rocks that were protruding from the sides of this deep dark pit, but my descent was too fast. None of the rocks seemed to protrude far enough for me to get a good handhold.

Even as I was falling down this hole I was not experiencing any fear of going to hell or fear of dying because I had a calm assurance that I knew my heart was right with God. I was ready to meet my Savior. Don't misunderstand; I am not saying that I had no fear! Though I knew in my heart that I was right with God, I was still filled with the absolute horror of not knowing what was happening to me. At that moment I did not have any idea whatsoever that I was plunging into hell.

I kept trying to figure out how I could stop my descent into this hole. What I was experiencing was mind- boggling because to me it was truly physically happening. I could feel, touch, smell, hear, and see everything that was happening to me. Actually everything seemed to be amplified beyond my normal five senses.

Through the years I had experienced dreams, nightmares, and hallucinations from drugs and alcohol which I had taken, but none of them came anywhere near to what I was experiencing at that very moment. My mind kept screaming, How can I stop my descent into this hole? I just kept on falling down and down into this really deep dark hole. Deeper and deeper I fell—down, down, down. I must have fallen mile after mile.

"He hath said, which heard the words of God, which saw the vision of the Almighty, falling into a trance, but having his eyes open" (Num. 24:4)

Terrible Stink of Hell

Now as I was falling down this deep dark hole, a violent and overwhelming hot wind began blowing from somewhere at the bottom of this shaft and hitting me in the face. It was a suffocating, nauseating, stinking wind. It smelled of rotting eggs and sulfur. It became almost impossible for me to breathe. I tried to use my shirt as a mask to filter out the stinking smell. But it was to no avail.

"Their slain also shall be cast out, and their stink shall come up out of their carcases, and the mountains shall be melted with their blood" (Isa. 34:3).

21

Actually this experience in and of itself should have been enough to kill me. I kept trying to get a breath of fresh air, but there was none to be had. As I was desperately trying to breathe I continued to fall. How long I fell down this hole I do not know. But it seemed to me to have no end, to be bottomless. Or was it? As I looked down in the direction that I was falling feet first, I looked between my feet. I began to see a very small and very faint orange, yellowish, reddish glow. It began extremely small, but as I continued to fall toward the light it became brighter and brighter.

Never-Ending Cavern of Hell

Before I knew it I was out of this black hole, this tunnel. I had entered into a humongous and gigantic, seemingly never-ending cavern. I could see no end in sight. It was as if I had fallen into a whole different world, an underworld. I was falling like a skydiver. Now, I was tens of thousands of feet above an ocean of liquefied, swirling lava and blazing fire.

Thousands of feet below me was a frightening, boiling lake of fire. It was burning, churning, and bubbling, almost similar to that of a pan of overheated boiling molasses on a stove. I could see that it was extremely aggravated and violent. It was almost as if it was filled and possessed with an aggressive, living fury. Fire and brimstone were exploding upon its surface in every direction sending flames rising thousands of feet into the air.

The flames darted here and there like a huge blazing gasoline fire. It would appear one moment in one area, vanish, and then appear somewhere else. At the same time there were air- shattering explosions, like volcanoes erupting across this vast surface of liquefied lava. It was like a living, swirling, obsessed whirlpool of fire, brimstone, and lava. It glowed different colors of red, orange, and yellow.

Perhaps a better description would be that it pulsated and radiated like hot charcoal in a furnace, with molten steel, liquefied stone, and swirling gases. Fire danced across the top of its surface like miniature tornadoes spinning violently out of control. They would spin until they ascended up into the black nothingness of the cavern I was falling in.

Intense Heat in Hell

As I continued to descend toward the surface of this ocean, this endless lake of liquid fire and lava. It seemed to me that I was about ten thousand feet above the surface of this ocean. And even at ten thousand feet, the heat that was hitting me was so intense that my very flesh felt as if it was withering, melting, and burning.

It felt as if it was being ripped off of my hands, my face, and my body. In the past I have received minor burns whether it was from cooking or from building a fire to keep the house warm. But that was minor—a mosquito bite compared to what was happening to me now.

As I looked at my skin and flesh it was beginning to bubble and blister. My whole body was beginning to burn. My clothes were catching on fire, and I could not put them out. My shoes were melting to my feet. My hair caught on fire like the wick on a candlestick. It was as if someone had doused me with gasoline and then threw a match on me. I began to scream like a madman.

At the beginning of this book, I asked how could anyone truly have experienced what I am sharing with you and yet not be shaken to the very core of their being every time they retell their story? I'm telling you that as I recount to you what transpired, my heart is filled with dread and trembling.

At that same time my lungs felt like they were going to be burned out of my chest. I needed cool fresh air, but there was none to be had. Can you imagine what it would be like to be roasted alive slowly over an open burning pit with red hot coals? This is what I was experiencing.

Dreadful Screams of Hell

In the midst of this overwhelming pain and agony, my ears began to be filled with a strange, eerie sound—a humming sound, like a throbbing deep, moan that never stopped. As I was falling closer and closer to the surface of the burning lava, this humming, groaning, moaning sound increased in its intensity.

It became an ear-piercing, overwhelming, never- ending sound that grew louder and louder. It was as if my head was surrounded by a huge hive of angry bees. As I continued to fall toward this churning, massive ocean, the sound that I was hearing became more distinct and clear. It contained ear-piercing highs and incredible heartbreaking lows with many other pitches in between that are too numerous to describe to you.

I remember asking myself in my pain and torment, "What in the world can this sound be that I am hearing? What could be causing such terrible heart wrenching, horror-filled sounds?" And then at that very moment I believe that the Spirit of the Lord opened up my understanding to what was happening to me. It hit me like an eighteen-wheel truck slamming into my body.

The sound that I was hearing was not coming from equipment, machinery or something from nature. But it was coming from human beings, my friend. The sound that was coming to my ears was from human beings who were screaming, wailing, groaning, and moaning with an incredible, intense, overwhelming pain. They were in unbelievable agony with unbearable torments. My ears were filled with the terrible screams of damned souls.

"Therefore I will wail and howl, I will go stripped and naked"

(Mic. 1:8).

"And shall cast them into a furnace of fire: there shall be wailing and gnashing of teeth"(Matt. 13:42).

I remember my whole body began to shake violently almost as if I were having convulsions. It was like rivers of absolute dismay and complete horror. The bitter lamentations of suffering humanity engulfed me. Oh how their sorrows flooded my very being. Even as I retell this story to you it is as if my heart is being ripped out of my chest. And the agony and pain that I am experiencing right now is nothing compared to the agony that God is experiencing. You see, it is His will that none should perish. But all should have eternal life.

CHAPTER TWO

Headed to Hell

I had not understood or realized what was really happening to me. The Spirit of God must have been keeping my mind and heart blind to what was happening in order that it might create a greater impact upon my life. But now, at this very moment and second with a mind-numbing shock, I realized that God had heard my prayers. God had, for some strange reason, answered my cry quite literally. There was no turning back. There was no stopping what had begun. At the terminal velocity of124 miles an hour I was headed straight for the unbelievable torments and sufferings of hell—the terrible lake of fire which was right below me.

"And the smoke of their torment ascendeth up for ever and ever: and they have no rest day or night" (Rev. 14:11).

"If anyone's name was not found in the book of life, he was thrown into the lake of fire" (Rev. 20:15).

"Therefore hell hath enlarged herself, and opened up her mouth without measure: and their glory, and their multitude, and their pomp, and he that rejoiceth, shall descend into it" (Isa. 5:14).

Like Bobbing Corks in Hell

At about two thousand feet above the surface of the ocean of hell, the pain that was hitting my body was over whelming, unbearable, unbelievable, and all consuming. My lungs were on fire. My eyes felt like they were being burned out of my sockets. My clothes had burned and melted to my flesh. I was beyond third-degree burns.

And yet, incredibly I was still fully aware of everything that was transpiring around me. If anything, my five senses were more alive than ever before. I believe that God must have supernaturally increased my capacity to experience all that I was going through.

I was looking down in the direction in which I was headed. I could see upon the surface of the lake of fire what looked like little black objects violently bobbing up and down like fishing corks in the orange and red glow of the burning, churning, bubbling ocean of hell.

As my eyes became more focused (by the grace of God), I could see thousands upon tens of thousands of these objects dotting the surface. They were everywhere. As I looked upon them, I found myself possessed by an overwhelming curiosity. I lost interest in everything else that was happening to me.

Even though I was experiencing tremendous and unbelievable pain and agony, I was still able to focus my mind and attention upon these objects. My mind was very clear and sharp. The only way to describe my curiosity was that it was supernatural.

This curiosity gripped my mind and heart. And as I fell closer and closer, I could see that these objects were actually oblong, not round as I had thought. But they contained limbs at both ends. And these limbs were waving back and forth, back and forth, in a frantic jerking type of motion.

Out of my innermost being, I let out a deep, tormented groan as

I suddenly realized what I was looking at. These black, bobbing objects were nothing less than human beings! People! They were masses of humanity from every nation, culture, tribe, and tongue. And they were screaming, moaning, and yelling as they were being turned and tossed about, head over heels, carried along in the swirling lava of the burning, churning, undercurrents of hell.

Now, in my past I have heard people weeping and wailing, crying over the death of a precious loved one. I have experienced this myself when our four-and-a- half-year-old little girl, Naomi, died. That same year my mother died. I wailed and wept and cried. But never had I heard crying like this, such agony, such screaming, such sorrow.

The wailing and howls of pain broke my heart. It still breaks my heart to this day as I think upon this experience. I could not tell by looking upon these burning blackened masses of humanity who or what they were. It was only by the Spirit of God that I discern these truths. For when their physical body hit the flaming fires of hell they lost their sexuality. They lost their nationality, their race and color of skin. No longer could you determine what their age was. For hell makes all people equal.

Dreadful Screams of Hell

These are souls forever damned. These are souls with no hope, escape, help, or relief from pain. Maybe these are people you and I have known—dads and moms, brothers and sisters, aunts and uncles, neighbors and friends who have died without loving Christ. Their hearts were full of the cares and lusts of this world. Their lives were full of selfishness and sin. They had no time for God or His Word. They spent their lives pursuing the useless pleasures of this world, filling their minds with vain and useless amusements, foolish entertainment, ungodly movies, involving themselves in immoral activities. The Apostle Paul warned us:

"Know this also, that in the last days perilous times shall come" (2 Tim. 3:1).

Because God is a righteous God, He must judge sin. By the time that these people discovered this truth it was too late. For they died and woke up in a dreadful, boiling lake of brimstone, sulfur, and fire. They have no way of escape, no relief from pain, and no hope for the future. These people have nothing to look forward to except endless torment, loneliness, and pain. Their bodies burned black like burnt chicken that had been overcooked on a barbecue pit. The unquenchable flames of a never-ending hell blackened their souls. Those down there looked like living and moving pieces of charcoal.

Into the Lava of Hell

Because I was so caught-up in the stark reality of what was going on before me, I did not realize that I was still falling closer and closer to the surface of the lake of fire. Suddenly, I plunged into the lava. It was like burning mud and quicksand. Immediately it sucked me in with a frightening ferocity. It engulfed me, pulling me down, swallowing me up in its hideous stomach of endless suffering and pain.

It covered me over and filled my mouth and my nose, ears and my eyes with an overwhelming, intense burning pain. The flaming sulfur of hell came into my mouth. It went down my throat, into my stomach, and filled my lungs. I was immersed in a baptism of absolute horror. My eyes felt like they were being consumed out of my sockets. And yet they were still there. My whole body was on fire and burning like a marshmallow dropped into the red coals of a campfire.

I came to the absolute bleak truth that in no way could hell ever be exaggerated. Everything I had ever heard or read about the eternal destiny of the lost and the damned, those who do not love

God, does not sufficiently describe what I was experiencing right at that moment.

No words could exist to describe the intense pain, the heart wrenching sorrow, the absolute agony, and the everlasting torments of hell. Hell is totally deaf to the cries and agonies of those who are swallowed up and wallowing in its belly.

"And death and hell were cast into the lake of fire. This is the second death. And whosoever was not found written in the book of life was cast into the lake of fire" (Rev. 20:14-15).

Swallowed Up in the Darkness of Hell

Now at that very moment excruciating pain overtook me. It penetrated my mind, and inflamed every fiber of my being. It stuck to my flesh like melted black tar. The lava was like burning mud that sucked me into the very depths of hell. Deeper and deeper I sunk. It pulled me down like a whirlpool. I wish I could be more graphic in how it felt.

How deep I sunk I do not know. The depths of the oceans of this present world are nothing in comparison with the depths of hell. For it is called the bottomless pit. I could not resist its current. It pulled and sucked at me like quicksand. I gave up all hope of ever coming to the surface. I was covered and engulfed in total darkness. I could not see anything. Now you understand that my eyes were not burned out of my head. I could still see. And yet I could not see, because there was no light.

The Bible declares that there is no light in hell to be had. There is no light of the sun, the moon, the stars, or even a flame. It is the darkness of eternal midnight. When I began this journey, and throughout it, for the most part I could see what was taking place.

God allowed me to see because He wanted me to behold what

was happening in the underworld of the lost. For those who are eternally lost in hell this is not normal. They will never see light again because they have rejected the light of Jesus Christ. They will never have the privilege of seeing the glorious lights of creation again.

"But the children of the kingdom shall be cast out into utter darkness: there shall be weeping and gnashing of teeth" (Matt. 8:12).

Can Not Die in Hell

Now, as I was sucked deeper into the lava, brimstone and sulfur, the burning mud of hell was in my mouth, and I could not breathe. My lungs were collapsing. I kept trying to suck in oxygen, but I could not. I was suffocating, and yet, I did not die. My flesh was burning, and yet, I did not die.

My brain was being ripped apart from the pain and sensations in my body, and yet, I did not die. The flames of hell were burning my eyes, my tongue, my hands, and my belly from the crown of my head to the soles of my feet, I was in excruciating pain. The burning, boiling, searing, brimstone and sulfur of hell were penetrating every fiber of my being, and yet, I did not die. I am not in the least exaggerating my experience, if anything I am under-rating it.

As I was going through these terrible sensations, I felt an upward thrust pushing me toward the top of the lake of fire. A strong type of current was dragging me along. And then I came to the surface. I began bobbing up and down as I was being moved along, turning, end over end, head over heels, rolling and tumbling with the swirling masses of those around me in the violent waves and currents of hell.

By now, you would think that all of my feelings would have

been gone, burned out into nonexistence, that all of my five senses would have been seared into nothingness. You would think that I would have gone into absolute and total shock, that I would have been virtually and completely numb. But that was not the case. Every one of my five senses was still very much alive.

I could touch, taste, hear, smell; I could see the torments of hell. Now I can tell you, my friend, by personal experience that the most extreme and bizarre torments that a person could ever experience on Earth is nothing compared to the never-ending torments of hell.

ETERNITY IN HELL

There seemed to be no end to this nightmare called hell. A second dragged into an hour. A minute turned into a year, and an hour became an everlasting eternity. This was just the beginning of forever. There is no end to this place called hell. There is no escape. There is no exit. There is no way out. Hell is eternal; it is forever. Some would have you believe otherwise. You and I both know without a shadow of a doubt that God is eternal.

"For I am the LORD, I change not" (Mal. 3:6a).

"Jesus Christ the same yesterday, and today, and forever" (Heb. 13:8).

His Word is eternal; heaven and earth shall pass away. If God is everlasting, His Word is everlasting, and heaven is everlasting. Then so is the wrath, the anger, and the judgment of God everlasting.

"And the smoke of their torment ascendeth up for ever and ever: and they have no rest day or night" (Rev. 14:11).

Some believe that when Christ died upon the cross that the sacrifice that Jesus made changed the Father. But that is an utter and horrendous lie. What Christ did on the cross was never meant to change God the Father. For God does not need to be changed.

"Every good gift and every perfect gift is from above, and cometh down from the Father of lights, with whom is no variableness, neither shadow of turning" (James 1:17).

But Jesus' death on the cross was meant to change you and me. Have you ever stopped to think who spoke hell into existence? Who created hell? The Scriptures clearly declare that everything that was created was created by Jesus Christ. You heard correctly, the Scriptures clearly declare that God the Father created all things by the hands of Jesus.

"All things were made by him; and without him was not any thing made that was made" (John 1:3).

"For by him were all things created, that are in heaven, and that are in earth, visible and invisible, whether they be thrones, or dominions, or principalities, or powers: all things were created by him, and for him: And he is before all things, and by him all things consist"(Col 1:16-17).

Our blessed Savior and Redeemer, He who shed His precious blood for our redemption, gave His life and gave His all for humanity, brought hell into existence. Therefore hell must need to exist for the safety and good of all creation. Hell was not created for man but for the devil and his angels. Jesus longs to rescue the human race from this terrible and horrible place.

NO LOVE IN HELL

If you can imagine in the midst of the pain and agony, another even much greater and terrifying torment began to flood my soul. It was emotional, spiritual, psychological, and mental. Here in this place, this bubbling, boiling slime pit called hell, there is absolutely no love.

It is totally void of all love. Even when I was a sinner, I was surrounded by the love of God, His goodness, provision, and blessings. I may not have recognized or even realized it. Whether I knew it or not, God was watching over me. He was protecting, helping, and reaching out to me, even though I was not serving Him or loving Him. A guardian angel was there all the time, though I could not see him. Jesus said:

"Take heed that ye despise not one of these little ones; for I say unto you, That in heaven their angels do always behold the face of my Father which is in heaven" (Matt. 18:10).

Nature, birds, animals, and all of creation display the unfathomable love of God. The shining sun, the green grass, the budding flowers, the blue gray waters of the sea, the light blue skies, the glowing moon, and the sparkling stars at night. They all declare God's awesome love for His creation.

The beautiful fragrances that float upon the wind and the singing birds with their beautiful songs declare His love. God has blessed us and revealed Himself to us by His awesome creation according to Scriptures on God's goodness.

"Or despisest thou the riches of his goodness and forbearance and longsuffering; not knowing that the goodness of God leadeth thee to repentance?" (Rom. 2:4).

"That ye may be the children of your Father which is in heaven: for he maketh his sun to rise on the evil and on the good, and sendeth rain on the just and on the unjust" (Matt. 5:45).

We need to understand that unconverted, unregenerate man has accepted and believed the lies of evolution. But it is a lie from the satanic realm.

"In whom the god of this world hath blinded the minds of them which believe not, lest the light of the glorious gospel of

Christ, who is the image of God, should shine unto them"(2 Cor. 4:4).

For God is the Author, Creator, Maker, Architect and Master Designer of all of creation. God gave us the breath we are breathing, the clothes we are wearing, the food we are eating, the body we are living in; it all comes from God. He gave us all of the talents and abilities we have in order to put within our hands these possessions.

All that we have that is good and beautiful, lovely and beneficial, comes from God. It is God's divine marriage proposal, a divine romance. For you see, God is calling, pleading, imploring, and asking us to follow Him into light everlasting.

"Behold, I stand at the door, and knock: if any man hear my voice, and open the door, I will come in to him, and will sup with him, and he with me" (Rev. 3:20).

"We love him, because he first loved us." (1 John 4:19).

Jesus paid the ultimate price for the hand of His bride. He bought us with every drop of His precious blood in His body. And He longs for us to follow Him down the wedding aisle to the throne of His Father, to be one with Him forever.

You see, my friend, God is striving to lead us to a place of turning our backs upon our selfish lives, to crucify and mortify the corruptible and damnable seed of selfishness, which is the very nature of the devil and his fallen angels—the demonic horde. We must believe on the Lord Jesus Christ. We must walk in His divine nature of love so that we can be one with Him forever.

"Every good gift and perfect gift is from above, and cometh down from the Father of lights, with whom is no variableness, neither shadow of turning" (James 1:17).

Are you taking carelessly God's abundant goodness, His kindness, His patience, and the fact that He has suffered a long

35

time waiting for you? Do you not grasp that His kindness is meant to cause you to turn away from selfishness?

Our number one desire should be to love Him with all of our hearts. True Christianity is simply striving to love God with all of your heart, spirit, soul, mind, and body. We love Him because He first loved us. Love our neighbors as we love ourselves. We need to respond to His amazing love.

All of creation will be our jury, and they will declare us guilty of the most perverse wickedness and corruption if we do not. To think that we would turn down such a wonderful and awesome gift from God is unfathomable.

The reality is that Jesus is offering us to be made one with Himself simply by acknowledging our wickedness and by forsaking all in order to follow him. Yielding to the divine grace of His nature within us. While we have an opportunity, we need to respond to His unspeakable and amazing love.

But in that God-forsaken, burning slime pit called hell there is no love whatsoever. The goodness of God, the long-sufferings of God, the kindness of God, the blessings of God, and the mercies of God are all gone, eternally lost because people refused to listen. Masses have refused to obey. Multitudes have refused to love Him, even though He invited them to be His bride, His beloved companion for eternity.

All Alone in Hell

A loneliness and emptiness beyond description descended upon me. Even though I bumped into many others, there was no communication. You have no recognition of friends and relatives. Those in hell are tormented devils and souls. They are filled with dreadful shrieks, screams caused by the fierceness of their pains.

There are fearful blasphemies against God's power and justice who keeps them there. The torments of fellow sufferers do nothing to relieve you of your miseries. It only increases them. And every soul that you lead into hell with you will only magnify your sorrows a hundredfold. Dad and mom, pastor and preacher, teacher and politician, Can you live with yourself knowing your taking some you love to hell with you?

There are many who think that hell will be party time. They laugh, they mock, and they scoff at the reality of hell. They laugh at them who tell them of a place called hell. Their destruction is their own fault, and they will never forget it. And in life they refused to be one with God in order to continue to be one with the world. In hell they are all alone forever. Just this thought should cause us to turn from our selfish ways.

"But be ye doers of the word, and not hearers only, deceiving your own selves" (James 1:22).

Please, listen to me. This book could be an answer to someone's prayers for you, someone who knows you and is pleading for your soul. And if you reject this message, throughout eternity you will be screaming and crying, begging and pleading for water and all of your other desires. The rich man cried out for water, but it was too late.

And you will be tormented forever with both natural and sinful, unfulfilled desires. Your natural and spiritual selfish thirst will never be fulfilled, never satisfied. Your thirsts will never be quenched, and the agony of it will never end.

Endless Pain in Hell

In hell there is no relief, no freedom from pain. One's body does not go numb; rather, the pain intensifies. Every part of the soul, body, mind, emotions, and our total being is tormented at once. The human body is a wonderful and marvelous creation.

"I will praise thee; for I am fearfully and wonderfully made: marvelous are thy works; and that my soul knoweth right well" (Ps. 139:14).

And yet, amazingly the soul of man also has a body. The natural eye cannot see the body of the soul, but that does not mean it does not exist. Your soul in this life looks exactly like your physical body. But in heaven, if you die in Christ, you will receive a glorified body, a body that is glorious and amazing. There'll be no natural blood that flows through your new body.

But the very Spirit of God Himself flows through your veins. We will never need sleep. This new body can endure any kind of harshness or atmosphere or environment. It will be absolutely indestructible, eternal, and immortal. According to the Scriptures the unrepentant sinner Himself shall also receive a new body. This body will be cast into the lake of fire with the devil and his angels

(John 5:28-29, 1 Thes. 4:16, and Dan. 12:2).

God must put an end to the sinful shenanigans of the satanic nature. The pain, suffering, agony, and torment of eternal damnation restrain and hinder the satanic nature. But it cannot cleanse the human heart, soul, mind, will, and emotions from the seed of sin. Only through the sacrificial work of Jesus Christ and loving Him can our hearts be cleansed from this dreadful seed of sin.

How long I had been in hell, I do not know. It seemed like an eternity. I had been crying out in pain and agony unconsciously, screaming and wailing like the rest of the damned. And yet my cries were of a totally different nature. Their cries were cursing, profanity, wickedness, begging, and promises of repentance if given another chance. Curses were only to be followed by more curses.

The realm of hell is filled with the noise of the damned, weeping and wailing and crying. They were shouting and screaming and yelling and moaning in terrible overwhelming pain. And yet those who are in hell now understand their spiritual condition and that their punishment is just and proper. They understand that they alone are to blame for their present situation and eternal damnation.

Cry for Help in Hell

Now my cries were to God, justifying, praising, worshiping, and acknowledging that from God came my help. I remember screaming in pain that God is righteous in His judgments and that He is true and faithful and worthy of all glory and honor. From my heart and soul, out of my mouth came a nonstop flow of love and devotion, praise and worship to the Three in One.

It might be hard to believe that someone filled with such overwhelming pain and agony could be worshiping and praising the One who was causing such horrible afflictions, and yet that's what I was doing. The Scriptures declare for out of the abundance of the heart the mouth speaks. Then from somewhere within I cried out for deliverance.

"Though he slay me, yet will I trust in him: but I will maintain mine own ways before him" (Job 13:15).

"A good man out of the good treasure of his heart bringeth forth that which is good; and an evil man out of the evil treasure of his heart bringeth forth that which is evil: for of the abundance of the heart his mouth speaketh. And why call ye me, Lord, Lord, and do not the things which I say?" (Luke 6:45-46).

God Heard Me in Hell

In the midst of my prayers, I heard a voice that seemed to come from heaven. It was A majestic thunderous and awesome sound. This voice completely overwhelmed all of the sensations I was experiencing at that moment. It literally grabbed hold of me and placed me in a protective bubble. All of my blistered and burning flesh was instantly healed and made whole. My hair, clothes, and body were returned to their original condition just as they were before my journey began. The love and goodness of God came rushing back in to my heart and mind.

The sorrows and woes of hell disappeared. This voice had an amazing effect upon hell. It shook the very foundations of the lake of fire itself. I heard the audible voice of God say,

"Let My Servant Go."

The bowels of hell twisted and turned as if in torment. They ripped apart like the Red Sea must have when Moses stretched forth his rod. Hell had no choice but to obey the voice of the Lord of heaven, earth, and hell.

"And said, I cried by reason of my affliction unto the LORD, and he heard me; out of the belly of hell cried I, and thou heardest my voice" (Jonah 2:2).

"The sorrows of hell compassed me about; the snares of death prevented me; In my distress I called upon the LORD, and cried to my God: and he did hear my voice out of his temple, and my cry did enter into his ears. Then the earth shook and trembled; the foundations of heaven moved and shook, because he was wroth. There went up a smoke out of his nostrils, and fire out of his mouth devoured: coals were kindled by it. He bowed the heavens also, and came down; and darkness was under his feet" (2 Sam. 22:6-10).

Out of Hell

At that very moment, it was almost like hell itself vomited me out. Incredibly it felt like I was being shot out of a canon. The next thing I knew, I was standing on the edge of a high and steep cliff. No longer was I in hell, but I was standing on the lip of a cliff looking straight down into the ocean of torment I had just been suffering in. The ocean of hell was still bubbling, boiling, and churning. And I could feel some of the heat of it hitting my body. The stench of it was still suffocating.

I would say that the cliff was probably over a thousand feet high. As a looked around, I noticed that the land around me was virtually flat, with no vegetation. It all looked like it was compacted brownish, gray soil, with rocks and boulders.

As I looked behind me there seemed to be a mountain range on the far horizon. As I looked to my right side, I noticed that in the distance there was what looked to be a wide, dark, slow-flowing river. It was pouring its contents like Niagara Falls over the edge of the cliff into the yawning mouth of hell.

But there was something very strange and eerie about this river. I did not want anything to do with this river. Actually there was this overwhelming desire in my heart to run as far away from it as I could. I knew that there was something very wrong about what I was seeing.

In my heart I sensed that whatever the river was, it would bring to me tremendous pain and sorrow perhaps even more so than what I had experienced in the bottomless pit of hell. And yet, with this knowledge, this foreboding and dread in my heart, I knew that I must go to this river.

The Spirit of God was prompting me to go and investigate. So instead of running away from this river, I found myself walking along the edge of the cliff, toward the river. As I got closer and closer, I began to tremble and shake. I could barely breathe. I had

41

to take short gasps of breath. I could not believe, and I did not want to believe what I was seeing before my very eyes.

Broad and Wide Road

This broad and wide, Dark River was not flowing with water, as I had supposed. It was made up of multitudes and multitudes of people. Masses of humanity without number.

"Enter ye in at the strait gate: for wide is the gate, and broad is the way, that leadeth to destruction, and many there be which go in thereat" (Matt. 7:13).

I could see that there were those of all nations, tongues and peoples. I saw the dress of every religious group you could imagine. Upon this road there was a range of people who were both young and elderly. And by looking at their mannerisms and dress, you could determine to some extent what their livelihoods were.

There were people of all professions—doctors, nurses, plumbers, professors, pastors, teachers, housewives, factory workers, policemen, farmers, milk men, bankers, military personnel, politicians, and world rulers.

"And he saith unto me, The waters which thou sawest, where the whore sitteth, are peoples,and multitudes, and nations, and tongues" (Rev. 17:15).

"Multitudes, multitudes in the valley of decision: for the day of the LORD is near in the valley of decision" (Joel 3:14).

As I drew nearer and nearer to this river, I could see that the people were walking on what looked to be a very wide asphalt road that made its winding way as far as my eyes could see into the horizon. Every inch of the road was packed to capacity with humanity, like sardines in a can. It seemed almost impossible for people to be packed so tight and so close together.

Now this road came right to the very edge of the cliff. At the cliff it broke off with jagged edges hanging over emptiness. It looked like a road would if an earthquake had transpired with the earth dropping out from underneath a major highway! And below this broken highway was the yawning, never-satisfied mouth of hell.

Headed to Destruction

As I came closer to this river of humanity I found myself unconsciously looking deep into the faces of those who were walking on this broad and wide road. None of them, I literally mean that none of them seemed to be in the least bit concerned at all about where they were headed. They did not seem to be concerned about their future or where they were going.

They did not seem to question the direction in which they were walking. Many were laughing and jesting. Others simply engrossed in conversation. Others caught up in their own problems. As I looked upon their faces I could perceive in my heart who they were and what they were going through.

I knew in my heart that by the Spirit of God I was experiencing their sorrows, pains, loneliness, and depression. I also perceived the hopes, dreams, and visions that they had in their hearts, that which they had not yet apprehended or achieved.

But not one of them seemed to be concerned about what was about to happen. Or where they were going. It was as if they were sleepwalking, like they were slumbering not realizing the danger that was just before them. It was as if they were blind to their eternal damnation.

"And the cares of this world, and the deceitfulness of riches, and the lusts of other things entering in, choke the word, and it becometh unfruitful" (Mark 4:19).

"And he spake a parable unto them, saying, The ground of a certain rich man brought forth plentifully: And he thought within himself, saying, What shall I do, because I have no room where to bestow my fruits? And he said, This will I do: I will pull down my barns, and build greater; and there will I bestow all my fruits and my goods. And I will say to my soul, Soul, thou hast much goods laid up for many years; take thine ease, eat, drink, and be merry. But God said unto him, Thou fool, this night thy soul shall be required of thee: then whose shall those things be, which thou hast provided? So is he that layeth up treasure for himself, and is not rich toward God" (Luke 12:16-21).

At about twenty feet from the end of the road a small handful of them would seem to begin to wake up. At that moment it would become a totally different story. The reality of the situation seemed to finally dawn upon their faces. As they were pushed forward they began to try to push back against the oncoming masses.

And the more they were pushed forward, the more frantic they became. They began to scream and cry and yell for help. But it was too late; they could not detach themselves from the masses. They were pushed forward, inch by inch, foot by foot. Those on the very edge of the cliff would seem to lose their mind in absolute terror as they saw more clearly what was awaiting them at the bottom of the cliff. It was as if their eyes were popping out of their head.

Never have I seen faces so contorted with absolute horror and fear. I knew they could not believe what they were seeing. They began to push back with all of their might, clawing, hitting, scratching, trying to crawl over the top of those who were unwillingly pushing them to their destruction and damnation.

Screams of unbelievable horror came from their lips as they would try to hang on. Shouting and screaming with such deep desperation that it breaks my heart retelling it to you. It did not seem as if those who were only a few feet back could hear or see what was taking place until it was their turn. Or maybe they simply chose to ignore the commotion, because it did not yet involve them. They were so caught up in their daily living until destruction came upon them without warning.

"For when they shall say, Peace and safety; then sudden destruction cometh upon them, as travail upon a woman with child; and they shall not escape" (1 Thess. 5:3).

Into the Abyss of Hell

As the people on the broad and wide asphalt road fell over the jagged edge, I watched them dig their fingernails into its unyielding surface. Not being able to hold on, they would continue to claw at the rough cliff walls. Leaving trails of their precious human blood.

The cliff wall was covered and matted with human blood, flesh, and bones. You could hear their pitiful screams for help as they tried to stop their descent into hell. As they plunged toward hell I would watch them spinning and tumbling head over heels. No horror flick ever made could express the absolute terror and horror I was watching take place before my eyes. These peoples' worst nightmares were coming to pass— nightmares that would last throughout eternity.

When their bodies hit the burning, liquefied lava of hell it would create a splash like that of a rock dropping into a puddle of mud. For a few seconds I could see them struggling, still floating on the surface of the lake of lava, like a leaf on the water. Their clothes would catch on fire. Their hair would go up in flames and be consumed. Their identities were lost. No longer could you tell that they were male or female.

Their nationalities, their ages, even the color of their skin was devoured in the burning torments of hell. Oh you cannot believe the terrible, heart-wrenching screams as they hit the surface and began to burn. They would slowly sink into the burning mud of hell, swallowed up in the never-ending undercurrents of this ocean of damnation. These were men and women, young and old, grandmas and grandpas, and teenagers. These were people of all nations and cultures from every diverse aspect of life. For hell is not a respecter of people.

God's Heart Broken

As I watched these masses of humanity falling into the bottomless pit of hell I literally could not handle it. I ran from the edge of the cliff alongside this road of damned humanity like one who has lost his mind. I wanted to escape the sight of the pain and agony etched in peoples' faces as they were falling over the cliff. My heart felt like it was totally and mortally wounded.

I felt like I was being stabbed with a huge knife that was slowly twisting and turning inside of me in my heart. My heart felt like it was being torn out of my chest. Now, if I felt this way, can you imagine how God feels?

People believe that after Jesus suffered on the cross that He no longer suffers. But this is a sadly mistaken assumption. For the Father, Son, and the Holy Ghost are still in deep agony and pain over the fate of humanity. God's heart is broken over the loss of humanity and of the angelic realm that disobeyed and rebelled against Him.

I Have to Do Something

I ran from the dreadful scene before my eyes. I ran until I could run no more. Out of breath I finally slowed to a walk. As I continued to walk, I realized that I must do something about these masses and masses of people that were headed straight to hell.

I was still walking alongside this wide, broad, river of humanity but away from the cliff. So I began to shout to them, pleading and begging them to come off the road. I warned the people with all the compassion of my heart, with tears cascading down my face, flowing like a river, weeping, and pleading nonstop.

"Oh that my head were waters, and mine eyes a fountain of tears, that I might weep day and night for the slain of the daughter of my people!" (Jer. 9:1).

"Rivers of waters run down mine eyes, because they keep not thy law" (Ps. 119:136).

I tried everything I could, knowing that every minute that passed more and more people were falling over the cliff. And because I had experienced the pains and torments of hell I knew what they were about to experience and that they would never get out. I was preaching the thunder and the lightning of heaven. Then I would speak the love and mercy of the goodness of God. I preached the reality of Jesus and His atoning sacrificial work. With all the truths that I had available I declared God's kingdom that I might rescue some.

They Would Not Listen

Many of these people on the road would stare at me as if I had lost my mind. Some would yell back at me, telling me to mind my own business. Some yelled that they were Christians, and that they were going to heaven. And others would seem to listen, with tears flowing down their cheeks. They would say that they wanted to come off of the broad and wide way, but they could not, that their hearts were too addicted to sin.

They did not believe that Jesus had the power to deliver them, that they were beyond hope. Some said that they had blasphemed the Holy Ghost and therefore there was no salvation available for them. Others declared that they loved sin too much to let go of it. The demonic hordes were whispering in their ears, lying to them that God would not forgive them, that they were too far gone, or that hell was just a make-believe imaginary place.

"But if our gospel be hid, it is hid to them that are lost: In whom the god of this world hath blinded the minds of them which believe not, lest the light of the glorious gospel of Christ, who is the image of God, should shine unto them" (2 Cor. 4:3-4).

Laborers Few

I knew in my heart that the work before me was too great for one person alone. I desperately needed help to reach these this multitude of lost souls. One person by himself could not make barely a dent in evangelizing this ocean of humanity. I began searching to find someone, anyone, who could help me reach all these people.

Clusters of Saints

As I looked out across the flat plateaus, I could see clusters of objects in the distance. I could not make out what they were, but they seemed to be shining with a brilliant white. They were not on the broad and wide road but directly off to the side of it. As I moved farther up the road I saw that these white objects were in what appeared to be small and large groupings.

And as I looked out over the plain, I noticed there were more of these clusters. Not just one or two but hundreds of them were scattered across the horizon. Some appeared to be extremely large, others were very small with many different sizes in between. As I drew closer to the first one, I discerned there was some type of movement taking place in these brilliant white clusters. As I drew closer it became apparent to me what they were.

These clusters were made up of people wearing glistening white robes. They were all grouped together in circles, facing inward, sometimes back to back. Their backs were to the river of humanity walking on the broad and wide road and to all else. The closer I came near these clusters, the more it became clear what was happening.

Many of those within these clusters had their hands lifted up toward heaven. As I got closer I could see smiles of joy radiating from their faces. Tears were running down their cheeks. They were singing amazing and beautiful songs of love for Christ. At times one or more would break out in what seemed to be a prophetic Word.

From what I could hear, most of these songs were about how much God loved them and about the blessings that would overtake them in their walk with the Lord. These songs said that they were precious and important to Jesus and to the heavenly Father. I realized automatically who these people in white must be. They were fellow believers and saints in Christ—brothers and sisters in Jesus Christ. All of these clusters of saints seemed to be lost in their devotion to and for God.

But they seemed to be lost, totally and completely oblivious to the masses of humanity that were just a few feet away from them being led to an everlasting, never-ending, eternal damnation. They were enraptured in their own little spiritual experiences. They were enthralled with singing songs of praise and worship.

There was no denying the sincerity; it was evident in their involvement and enthusiasm. But what good is sincerity, blessings, joyful spiritual experiences, and Holy Ghost parties if you are not concerned about anyone else except your own little group. It's what Scripture refers to as sounding brass and twinkling cymbals.

"Though I speak with the tongues of men and of angels, and have not charity, I am become as sounding brass, or a tinkling cymbal. And though I have the gift of prophecy, and understand all mysteries, and all knowledge; and though I have all faith, so that I could remove mountains, and have not charity, I am nothing. And though I bestow all my goods to feed the poor, and though I give my body to be burned, and have not charity, it profiteth me nothing" (1 Cor. 13:1-3).

A divine and supernatural urgency rose up in my heart. I tried to push my way into one of these clusters. And as I did I found myself yelling and pointing to the river of humanity. It was not anger, self-righteousness, or disgust that moved me but God's love. It was His overwhelming love and compassion that was being shed abroad in my heart by the Holy Ghost. It was love for the unconverted, lost, and blind sinners.

I desperately needed help to reach the lost masses upon the road of destruction. I knew in my heart that the heart of God was being broken because His people were not having compassion upon those who had not yet come to love and know Him, those who had not yet been converted and become new creatures in Christ Jesus.

This is Not Our Cross

When I was finally able to get one group's attention, they looked at me as one who looks upon a lunatic. "Look. Look," I said, pointing toward the broad and wide road. "Millions upon millions of men and women, young and old, are only a short distance from your cluster. And they are headed right for hell. We have got to do something. Please, please help me to reach them!"

The worship and praise stopped. No one in the group moved. It was like they were in a stupor. Since it seemed like I had their attention, I continued with my exhortation for them to help me reach the lost. Finally, one of the men spoke up. "Excuse me, brother, but God has not given us a spirit of condemnation. It seems to us that you are trying to bring us into bondage with this legalism. Whom the Son has set free is free indeed.

You're putting this heavy guilt trip on us, and that definitely cannot be God. And to be quite blunt with you evangelism is not our ministry." For a moment I was totally dumbfounded. Surely this brother in Christ had to be joking. There is no way that anybody could be that ignorant of God's Word and God's heart. For a minute I was in such shock that I could not answer them. The Holy Spirit rose up within me, and out of my mouth came Scripture after Scripture.

"And Jesus said unto them, Come ye after me, and I will make you to become fishers of men" (Mark 1:17).

"For the Son of man is come to seek and to save that which was lost" (Luke 19:10).

I kept pleading and imploring them to help me pull humanity from the flames of hell. But no matter what I said, they did not seem to understand what I was saying. I could not get them to move. I remember standing there completely frustrated, weeping, and crying uncontrollably. Not only for the damned but for those who called themselves believers.

Somehow the enemy of our souls has deceived the majority of the church into a place of spiritual complacency and pacifism. Now, there is no denying that there is some small measure of concern for the lost. But there's not the red-hot fervency and overwhelming love for souls that we should have. It is so sad that it seems that those within the body of Christ do not believe in hell themselves. God's number one concern is for souls to be saved.

"And he said to them all, If any man will come after me, let him deny himself, and take up his cross daily, and follow me" (Luke 9:23).

In the Harvest Field

I fell to my knees on the ground under tremendous sorrow and the heavy burden that was upon my heart, surrounded by these brothers and sisters in Christ. I closed my eyes as I wept with heavy sobs praying that God would open the eyes of humanity and of His church. I prayed that God would forgive me for my lack of concern and love. I prayed that the Lord of the harvest would raise up laborers for the harvest field. How long I prayed, I do not know. When I finally opened up my eyes, I found myself back in my barracks upon my knees in prayer.

Willie Wine was on his knees right off to the side of me. I saw a strange expression on his face. Neither one of us said anything for a while. I noticed there was no music or sound of the men in the background. I asked him what was going on. He told me that they heard me screaming, crying, and wailing in the most unbelievable, heartrending and horrifying ways. He said they were all scared and ran for it.

Willie asked me what had happened. During all the hours that I was experiencing this supernatural visitation from the Lord, Willie had been in prayer right at my side. I tried to describe to him everything that happened. Partly due to this visitation, a miniature revival hit our military base.

From that moment forth an overwhelming burden came upon me. My love for Christ and souls went way beyond what I had experienced before. I became extremely desperate to reach souls for Christ. On the streets and highways, malls and shopping centers, Laundromats, and bar rooms. Wherever I could reach people, I was there.

Compassion for the Lost

After this particular experience, an overpowering love began to possess me! My heart was filled with immense concern for the lost and unsaved. I looked for men up and down the hallways and in the tunnels of our military facility.

One time when I witnessed to a man about the reality of heaven and hell, he basically said he did not want to hear it. God's love was so strong within me I instantly dropped to my knees and wrapped my arms around his legs. I begged him to give his heart to Jesus. I did not want to see him lose his soul and spend eternity in hell.

CHAPTER THREE
Angel Took Me to Heaven

My visitation from an angel and my journey to heaven took place even before I knew what the Bible had to say on the subject. If any of these SHOCKING experiences or any of the other experiences I have had through the years had been contrary to the teachings of Christ or the prophets, I would adamantly reject them, turn my back on them, and declare that they were not of God.

A God-given vision of heaven or hell or any other visitation would never contradict Scriptures. I am not sharing with you something I made up out of the figment of my own imagination for the purpose of selling books or to make a name for myself. What you are about to read truly happened to me. Please understand that when God gives visions, dreams, and divine encounters that many of these experiences could be revealed by shadows and illustrations of spiritual truths that He wants us to grasp and understand.

This divine, angelic visitation happened approximately one month after I had gone to hell. This time I was all alone once again **praying and crying out to God** in our dormitory. I had been walking around with my hands in the air **praying**, singing, and talking to the Lord. Suddenly, my room was filled with an overwhelming presence of the Lord. It was so real that I fell to my knees and tears began to flow freely from my eyes. I found myself lying flat upon my face totally caught up in this overwhelming presence. My face was buried into the floor. I was weeping, crying, and **praying**.

The Spirit of the Lord in the spring of 1975 began to take me into deep and fervent intercessory prayer. He began to teach me how to stand in the gap on behalf of others, to walk the floor for hours on end for souls. He taught me how to lay upon my face in His presence until there was a breakthrough. He showed me how to submit my body as an instrument, a vessel He could pray through.

Every believer, every child of God is called to intercede and travail for souls. It has been said that there is power in prayer. I know what people mean when they make that statement, but it's not exactly accurate. There are many religions in which people pray obsessively. But of course it brings no good results. The power does not come from the prayer, but the power comes from the One that we are crying out to! Jesus declared: Amazingly God did answer this prayer of wanting to experience the realities of hell. You can read this experience in my book: Hell Is for Real.

My Journey to Heaven

The description of my journey to heaven is much briefer than that which I experienced when the Lord sent me to hell. The reason for this is that there are many things the Lord spoke to my heart and revealed to me, things that are "not lawful" for me to share on this side of Heaven.

"How that he was caught up into paradise, and heard unspeakable words, which it is not lawful for a man to utter" (2 Cor. 12:4).

"And the vision of the evening and the morning which was told is true: wherefore shut thou up the vision; for it shall be for many days" (Dan. 8:26).

This divine, angelic visitation happened approximately one month after I had gone to hell. This time I was all alone praying and crying out to God in our dormitory. I had been walking around with my hands in the air praying, singing, and talking to the Lord. Suddenly, my room was filled with an overwhelming presence of the Lord. It was so real that I fell to my knees and tears began to flow freely from my eyes.

I found myself lying flat upon my face totally caught up in this overwhelming presence. My face was buried into the floor. I was weeping, crying, and praying. All of a sudden the room I was in was filled with an intense bright light. I lifted my head to see what in the world was going on. There in front of me was a portal. It was like an opening into another world. It was not square like a regular door opening.

This doorway was circular on the top like an archway. The light coming from this portal was so bright and brilliant that I could not really even look at it. This was not my imagination playing tricks on me. There literally was a brilliant, shining portal into another realm right there in my military dorm.

I was completely petrified and did not know what to do. It felt as if I was frozen to the floor and unable even to move a muscle. A holy fear gripped my whole body, my mind, and my five senses. I could see that someone was walking toward me through this tunnel of light. To my shock and amazement out of this glorious portal of light stepped a figure of a man. This was no ordinary man. He was about seven feet tall with a broad chest and shoulders with a slender waist. His flesh blazed like the burning of an arch welder, and he had dark short hair.

His face did not seem to have ever been shaved. In other words, there was no stubble on his face. He had the stature of a body builder only more solid and almost unearthly. He wore a glistening, brilliant, white gown with a slightly transparent belt around his waist that glowed of gold. I was not able to move or talk in his presence. When this angelic being finally spoke to me his voice seemed to fill the whole room. He said to me, "Fear not; for I have come from the presence of the Almighty to show you things that must come to pass."

I remember asking him with great trembling, "What is your name?" He replied, "My name is of no importance. I am but a messenger sent to you with a message and a mission that is greater than I." Inwardly, I wondered what kind of purpose could there be in this visitation. As I reflect upon this experience, I can tell you that parts of it are completely missing from my memory.

It's not that it was not real or substantial, because it was just as real as the flesh and blood world that I find myself in right now. I believe the reason that parts of this visitation are missing is because it is sealed away in my heart, and I am not able or permitted to reveal or repeat all that transpired.

Revelation 10:4 And when the seven thunders had uttered their voices, I was about to write: and I heard a voice from heaven saying unto me, Seal up those things which the seven thunders uttered, and write them not.

This angel spoke to me and said, "Now you must come with me., For there are many things you must see." This angel stepped forward, leaned down, and took me by the right hand. He lifted me to my feet. The way he lifted me up I must have been as light as a feather to him.

It was as if he rippled with unlimited strength, and I was like a little child in his hands. I knew in my heart that he could easily have kill me without any effort. This was my first experience in a tangible way with an angelic being. From that time up to now I have been protected, provided through and helped by these amazing messengers of God. Up this date I have had ten angelic visitations.

Back to My Visitation

I remember holding this angels hand with my right hand. There was tremendous heat coming from it. It was not the same type of heat I had experienced in hell. It is literally impossible to explain to you the sensations and feelings I was experiencing at that moment. The fire I felt in his hand was a holy fire. It seemed as if the heat was a living thing. Power radiated from his body. I cannot remember the color of his eyes. This angel was not Jesus. He was simply a messenger sent to take me into the heavens.

"Who maketh his angels spirits; his ministers a flaming fire" (Ps. 104:4).

"Are they not all ministering spirits, sent forth to minister for them who shall be heirs of salvation?" (Heb. 1:14).

Portal to Heaven

I found myself being led by this angel into the portal doorway of brilliant light. As I stepped into this light, this light flooded my whole being. All of the filthiness of the flesh felt as if it just melted right off of me. For the first time in my life I felt completely pure and holy. At that moment I was literally transformed—soul, mind, and body! My mind became extremely clear and more comprehensive than I had ever thought possible.

A whole new world opened up to me spiritually, mentally, and emotionally. Another thing I noticed was that when I stepped into this portal, time itself seemed to come to a complete and total standstill; it became eternity. How I knew this, I do not know. It was something I simply knew without any shadow of doubt. Virtual truths began to flood my innermost being. As I stood in this light, things that I could not possibly have any way of knowing were imparted into my soul supernaturally.

Tunnel of Light

The light in this tunnel was just as bright, but it no longer hurt my eyes. Before me laid a seemingly never- ending corridor. The walls, floor, and ceiling of this tunnel were made of tangible light. I was literally walking on or in a beam of light. The walls and floor were actually real. This long corridor of light seemed to be headed upward on a slight incline toward the heavens.

The angel and I began to walk up this long corridor together with him holding my hand as if I was a little child. We seemed to walk together like this forever. It felt like a never-ending walk, yet I never got tired or weary. Actually it was an extremely pleasant walk. After what appeared to be a noticeable length of time the angelic being just disappeared. I did not know exactly when he disappeared. One minute he was at my side, and the next minute I realized he was gone. At the same time I did not feel disappointed, or upset that he was gone. I just knew in my heart that this was the will of God. Not knowing what else to do, I kept on walking.

Now even though the angel was no longer with me, I did not feel all alone for I could sense that God was right there at my side, maybe not in the physical form but by His spiritual overwhelming presence. Something else strange was happening. Even though I was walking at a normal pace, it seemed like I was moving extremely fast. It was like I was on a high-speed escalator. It makes me laugh now, but I think I was going at the speed of light. At the same time both my mind and heart were experiencing an overwhelming peace and joy.

There were no fears, cares, sin, or sorrow, just total harmony and serenity of spirit, soul, mind, and body. All of my past was gone as if it never existed. All of the struggles and wrestling, fears and anxieties, were gone. It was absolute heavenly bliss. I cannot describe how incredible I felt. In all of my imaginations I never thought someone could feel as good as I was feeling. In hell there is nothing but pain and suffering. But in heaven there is nothing but pleasure and awesome peace.

Garden of Eden

The next thing I knew; I was out of this tunnel of light, and I found myself standing on a tall hill covered with emerald green grass. I had entered into a place so beautiful and incredible that it temporarily took my breath away. There, stretched out before me as far as my eyes could see, was a majestic and indescribable world. Right below me was the most perfect valley you could ever imagine.

What I was looking upon is beyond the comprehension of human description or understanding. There were snow-capped mountains just off to the left of me in the far distance, rolling hills to the right, and the valley that was below me was amazingly picturesque. In this valley was a beautiful river. In the distance straight ahead of me there was an incredible forest filled with trees greater than the redwoods in California.

"But as it is written, Eye hath not seen, nor ear heard, neither have entered into the heart of man, the things which God hath prepared for them that love him. But God hath revealed them unto us by his Spirit: for the Spirit searcheth all things, yea, the deep things of God"(1 Cor. 2:9-10).

Everywhere I looked there was an abundance of life! There were plants, animals, and insects. God is the Creator and Author of all life. Just by what He has created, you can tell He loves creativity and He loves life! In the first two chapters of Genesis we get a glimpse of God's perfect will.

I almost laugh every time somebody questions whether or not there could be life on other planets. If the Lord should tarry and we would have an opportunity to thoroughly examine the heavenly bodies, we will discover life even on asteroids. Granted it may be microscopic, but it would still be life. I could even believe that there is life living in the vacuum of space itself.

"And God saw everything that he had made, and, behold, it was very good. And the evening and the morning were the sixth day" (Gen. 1:31).

The grass upon the hill and much of the valley was a deep emerald green. It was the perfect length, not too short and not too high. Across the valley I could see wheat fields blowing in the wind. Upon the hillsides and plains were beautiful flowers growing in perfect uniformity, as if a gardener with the most exquisite taste had planted each and every one of them exactly what they needed to be.

There were amazing, beautiful bushes and hedges as well as plants of every description, size, and shape. Even though through the years I have loved and enjoyed nature, I have never been one to really memorize the names and types of trees, flowers, and plants. The mass majority of the things I saw I could not give you names for, but they were everywhere in abundance.

As I said, in the distance I could see that there was a large forest of trees that were gigantic in proportion. These were redwoods, but they were taller and wider than the redwood forests in Oregon or California, reaching towards the heavens above them. I have lived in California and Oregon, and there is no denying the beauty of the redwood forests located there. And yet there is absolutely no comparison between these redwood trees and the ones that are there.

All the plants, animals, and everything I beheld were absolutely perfect in their beauty and completeness. The greatest artist that has ever lived could never imagine what I was now seeing and experiencing.

As I gazed across the landscape, I saw animals large and small, too numerous to count. There were deer, rabbits, and lions eating grass. A small family of bears was splashing in the river, which seemed almost transparent. This river flowed down from a snow-white mountain range unlike any on earth. It was almost like a zoo, but with none of the cages and fences to keep you separated from the animals.

It may sound like it was crowded with the description I am sharing with you, but this was not the case. All of the animal and plant life was scattered across the horizon in such an amazing and splendid picturesque way. The river that tumbled its way down the mountainside created waterfalls here and there, until it found its way down to the valley seeking the lowest place of gravity. As the water fell from the side of this mountain, it created a half a dozen or so multicolored rainbows that stood out as if they were three-dimensional.

I have no words to describe the beauty of which I was seeing. I stood frozen in place, overcome with what lay in front of me. I was in a garden that must have been very similar to the Garden of Eden in the book of Genesis. Of course it has not been inhabited by the human race since they were expelled from it. Two cherubim were assigned to stand before its gates. They were to bar the entrance of man from coming back into the garden, in order to prevent him from eating of the tree of life.

Divine Orchestra

In this place called heaven, my hearing had become extremely sensitive. I had been so overwhelmed by what I was seeing, it had escaped my attention what I was also hearing. My ears seemed to be able to pick up sounds that were miles away. Not only could I hear everything, but also I could distinguish every sound.

I literally could hear the bees going from one flower to another collecting pollen. I heard a slight breeze blowing through the grass on the plains and a cow and its calf chewing their cud. A lion in the distance roared, not with the ferociousness of a vicious meat eater but of a lion that was relishing its existence in harmony with its other fellow creatures.

I could even hear rabbits skipping across the grass. I heard all of these distinct individual sounds, yet it was not annoying or confusing like the mad rushing about that goes on in the cities of men. It sounded more like a beautiful orchestra being conducted by a divinely gifted maestro. Such a symphony has never been heard upon Earth since the fall of man.

Supernatural Eyesight

At almost the same time, I noticed the vibrant and vivid colors. They were of such deepness, clarity, and brilliance. Everything was astonishingly three- dimensional. All of the artistic geniuses of this day and age could never even create on paper anything as near to perfection as this was.

After this supernatural experience, everything in this world seems to be dim and surreal to me. We may not be able to realize the fullest capacity at this moment, but the spiritual world is more real than the physical world that we live in.

Not only was there incredible supernatural clarity to my sight and hearing but also to my sense of smell, taste, and touch. It all seemed to be magnified a thousand fold. If you could compare these two worlds side-by-side, it would reveal the blandness, the ugliness of the natural world we live in. It is all because of the corruption of sin. The satanic seed that says "my will be done."

But this place of glorious beauty simply revealed the exquisiteness of all that God had created. The aromas that floated in the atmosphere filled my nostrils. The smells were very strong but not at all nauseating; it was quite the opposite. I could even taste to some degree through the sense of my smell.

It was one of many delightful experiences that I was encountering in this heavenly place. All of these things registered in my mind, and I knew that I was in heaven. In all of my imaginations of what heaven would be like, never once did it occur to me that it would be like this. Revelation knowledge flowed through my soul as I came to realize God's original plan for man. The earth was to be a miniature version of God's divine habitation.

But man's rebellion, his disobedience in yielding his soul to Satan, opened the door to disaster, pestilence, disease, perversion, and corruption. Which turned the earth into a tragic mockery of God's original plan. What was meant to be heaven on earth had become a hellish nightmare.

Upon a New Road

While pondering these thoughts, I noticed that there was a road that wound its way down through the valley. It was headed in the direction of the gigantic redwood forest. Instinctively my feet began to move me down the hill toward this road. When I finally arrived at it, I looked back from where I came from and realized that I had walked miles and miles.

Amazingly, I felt just as relaxed as when I first began, if not even more so. When I reached this road, I discovered that it was built with beautiful multi-colored flat stones, intricately laid together side by side. These stones look like highly polished marble filled with many gold speckles. The road glistened and simmered as if it was wet and slippery. Yet when I stepped upon it I discovered that it was not slippery or wet at all.

There were quite a number of different types of animals alongside as well as on the road. None of them fled from me as I walked past them. It was as if all creation was in complete harmony, and I was not a stranger. Rather, I was an intricate an intimate part of this heavenly place. There was absolutely no fear toward me in these animals that I walked past. Neither was there any fear whatsoever in my heart toward them.

It would've been so wonderful to stop and spend some time petting and playing with these animals. It also would have been nice to walk down through the meadows, to sit by the bank of the beautiful river that was flowing not too far from the road just to let my feet soak in the crystal clear waters. It would have been wonderful to sit down and watch all of the different types of fish that were probably swimming in this crystal-clear river. If only I could just stay right there forever.

Yet there was a deep urgency in my heart. There was something that must transpire while I was there. I knew I was not there just for a foretaste of the future. That God had brought me to this place to show me something pertaining to my purpose in life and humanity was certain.

I knew instinctively that what God wanted to show me was somewhere along this road that I was walking upon. I finally reached this majestic forest of redwood trees. The tops of these trees must have been reaching anywhere from two hundred to three hundred feet in the air. There were also smaller trees scattered throughout these giants of the forest. Their circumferences were anywhere from three feet to forty feet in dimension. It was simply mind-boggling.

I stepped into this forest walking upon the multi- colored road. As I came under the towering canopy of these trees, I felt myself being enfolded and wrapped up with comfort and security. How can I describe what I was experiencing at that moment? Without being misunderstood I would like to say that it was magical and mystical.

Walt Disney himself would be blown away. None of his children's movies ever came close to what I was experiencing now. Light filtered down through the branches here and there causing shimmering reflections of light to shine off of the leaves of other trees that were growing under the huge canopy. The ground, tree trunks, and large rocks and boulders were covered with many colors of moss. The moss was exquisitely placed as if by professional design. Ferns, some large and many small, stretched through the forest in perfect arrangement. I did not see any thistles or thorns. This place had never experienced the curse of sin.

The path led straight into the heart of the forest. There were no bends or turns as far as my eyes could see. It was as straight as an arrow flies. I walked down this path at an easy rate taking in as much as I could. It was as if I was walking on a cloud. It seemed to be dreamlike and yet it was tangible and touchable. Once in a while, there would be a stone bridge on the path.

The stone bridges were made of the same stones as the road itself. The bridges took me over bubbling, sparkling, and transparent water. At one of these streams I stopped for a moment and looked over the bridge into the water. As I looked into the water I could see schools of fish swimming by. They were bright and beautiful like coral reef fish back on Earth, but they were much more exquisite and stunning. The water was so clear that it looked like the fish were swimming in the air. As I continued to walk, my heart overflowed with love for the One who created all of this. As I recall this account, I still get spiritual chills flowing through me.

How far and how long I walked I could not guess. I do know that it was long enough to expect that the sun would be going down. However, there was no change in the light. It was just as bright as when I had first arrived. As I reflected upon this wonder, it dawned upon me that I had not seen the sun in the sky. That the light seemed to be coming from nowhere and yet everywhere! This light did not hurt my eyes. Actually, it was as if my eyes were drinking deep of the light. It was extremely strange and delightful. My eyes were absorbing and pulling in this wonderful light.

The Birds of Heaven

As I continued to walk, everything was so amazingly peaceful and tranquil. Majestic trees stood to the left and right of the approximately twenty-foot wide path. I found myself praising and worshiping God. I discovered that God also had transformed my voice. I could hardly believe how good I could sing. And with this new voice I began to sing with all of my heart my love for the One who meant everything.

I was so at home, at peace, and in harmony with this place that I never wanted to leave. I belonged here. I knew I was made to live here forever, that this was my natural environment. As I continued to walk, sing, and worship, the trees began to be filled with birds, thousands upon thousands of birds. The light filtering in between the trees glistened on these birds which were of such magnificent beauty and variety.

There were large and small birds of colors and species beyond count. Cockatoos, canaries, doves, parakeets, and finches came just to name a few. Their voices echoed throughout the forest. I knew in my heart that they were singing praises to God. It made you want to be able to join in with them. As I kept on walking, I was completely and totally surrounded by them. It was so overwhelming that I could not walk any further. I just stood there caught up in the majesty and the beauty of it all. They were all lifting their voices in praise, worship, adoration, and love for the Author of life.

Divine Commission

I was so caught up in the wonder and beauty of it all that I did not even notice the angel who had been with me at the start of this journey had returned. He was standing alongside me, gazing at the birds in the trees. The angel asked, "Do you see all of these splendid and beautiful birds?" Surprisingly, I was not at all startled or surprised by the return of this angel. In heaven there is no fear, sickness, or sin.

There is nothing but joy, peace, and tranquility beyond description. I turned and spoke to the angel not as a superior but as a fellow companion in the plan and purposes of God. "Sir," I said, "Do you not think that these birds are the most beautiful and amazing creatures you have ever heard or seen?" The angel asked, "Do you understand what it is the Lord God is revealing to you?"

When the angel said this to me, I turned once again and looked up directly into his face. I said to him, "What do you mean?" And then this angel said something to me that still overwhelms me to this day. As I share this part of my experience with you, I am almost to the point of weeping. Deep, deep feelings are stirring and moving in my heart. For God was about to reveal His divine commission for my life, the purpose for which Jesus rescued me.

"These birds you are looking upon and listening to are a type, and a shadow of those things which will come to be in and through your life. Even as these birds are of so many different species and colors, so in your future will you have an impact upon many cultures and tongues and nations."

At this statement my mind seemed to go numb for a moment. It just did not seem to make sense. I remember saying, "I don't understand what you mean." He replied, "Servant of the Most High, be it known to you that what you see is a shadow of the souls of men and women who will be brought into the kingdom because of your obedience and hunger for the Lord.

Many will be set free from the bondage of sin. Multitudes of many nations, tongues, and tribes will hear the glorious truth, and this truth will set them free. They in turn will go forth in the power and presence of the Holy Spirit and will take the name of Jesus, even as you have done and will do. They will drive back the forces of the adversary. For the day of the Lord is at hand, and a new day is about to dawn. Strengthen your heart. Be strong in the Lord and the power of His might. Hold up the arms of your brethren; wash their feet. Humble yourself. Be a servant, and the Lord will use you. Help those who are called and chosen but have none to assist them. Undergird and encourage them to fulfill the call of God upon their lives."

The words of this messenger of God penetrated my heart to its deepest core. I fell to my knees, then to my face, crying and weeping uncontrollably. God had spoken to me. I would never be the same again! The Lord did have a divine purpose for my life. I was called of God and sent forth by the Almighty to set others free. Instantly, in my heart I knew that it was not about me. I knew that I was only one small gear in the majestic machinery of God's divine plan. My heart was filled with joy unspeakable and full of glory. How long I lay there on that road and cried and wept, I do not know. The next thing I realized was that the angel was gone, and I was no longer in the woods.

The Throne of God

Next I found myself in an immense never-ending realm. So large was this place that I could not see an ending. Above me, behind me, to the left and the right just seemed to be a never-ending horizon. The floor under my feet was like a sea of crystal glass radiating and pulsating with ever-changing colors that flowed through it like an incoming wave of the ocean. In the distance, I saw lightning and extremely bright flashes of light proceeding from one point.

Not knowing what else to do, I began to move toward this phenomenon. As I drew closer, I heard thunder echoing off in the distance which sounded like mighty trumpets. The sea of glass under my feet shook with every peel of lightning. And with every step I took toward this phenomenon, my heart beat faster. It was as if the hair on the back of my neck and up my arms and head were standing straight up.

In the far distance I could see that I was approaching what looked like a huge throne. In front of the throne and around it, there seemed to be some type of activity that was transpiring. As I got closer I began to discern the most awesome creatures I could have ever imagine. Yet my attention was not on them.

I only had eyes for the One on the throne. I could tell that the throne was amazing, but even more majestic and splendid than the throne was the One who sat upon it. He appeared like the brightness of translucent diamonds. A light shined out of the One on the throne that was of such an intensity and holiness.

Had I not been in the spirit, it would have killed me, consumed me, burned me up, and evaporated me into nothingness. At the right side sat Jesus, clothed with a robe down to His feet, and about His chest He had a breastplate of glistening gold like that of a Roman general. His hair radiated like glistening white wool, more pure than the whitest snow. His eyes burned with divine love as if flames of fire. Streaks of lightning were flashing all around the throne. The roar of thunder continued.

Before the Throne

I knew without a shadow of doubt that I stood before God the Father and His Son, Jesus Christ. Around about them and stretching over the top of them shone numerous emerald rainbows much clearer and colorful than the natural mind could conceive.

"After this I looked, and, behold, a door was opened in heaven: and the first voice which I heard was as it were of a trumpet talking with me; which said, Come up hither, and I will shew thee things which must be hereafter. And immediately I was in the spirit: and, behold, a throne was set in heaven, and one sat on the throne.

I fell as one dead before the throne, quivering and shaking before the presence of my Lord. Then a voice spoke forth as if coming from everywhere. It filled my mind and heart with shaking and trembling. This voice was filled with absolute complete and total authority and holiness.

I knew it was the Father's voice that was speaking to me. As I lay on my face before the throne of God, I heard unspeakable words that could not be uttered with human vocabulary. It was literally as if streaks of lightning were hitting my body with every word that He spoke. As His words hit my body they would explode in me like the soundings of thunder.

My whole body literally shook and vibrated uncontrollably at these thundering's. These thundering's flooded my body and took a hold of me. It had to be God supernaturally strengthening me in order to keep me alive through this experience.

I am convinced that if you had been standing at a distance you would have seen streaks of divine lightning and fire striking my body. This divine lightning and fire was not meant to destroy me but to some extent was meant to impregnate me with God's divine purposes and abilities.

I knew that my inner man was drinking deep of the mysteries and divine plans of God. I remember the tears flowing from my eyes, down my face as I listened to the Word of the Lord. The glory of God was all around, upon, and in me. My body was enveloped in a glistening cloud of energy.

Through this whole experience I laid there weeping and whispering "Thank you, Jesus," over and over. I did not truly understand with my mind what was transpiring, but I knew in my heart that God was speaking to me divine truths and mysteries, that which was to be accomplished and would shortly come to pass.

I knew that He was supernaturally imparting into me the grace that was necessary to accomplish His purposes for my life. This seemed to go on forever. Then as quickly as it had started it was over. The Spirit of the Lord whisked me instantly away from the throne room of God.

Preaching the Gospel

The next place I found myself was on a sidewalk in what looked to be an alleyway of a low-income area of a large city. Coming down the street toward me were two large, rough-looking men. As they caught up to me, I found myself sharing the love and the Good News of Jesus Christ. I also shared the reality of divine judgment if they rejected the sacrificial work of Jesus.

As I continued to speak about the reality of Christ and that there is no other way to the Father but through Jesus, I noticed their faces begin to distort until they were filled with absolute, utter hate. Their eyes glistened with a hideous satanic appearance as if they were turning into demons right before my eyes. Before I could even raise my hands in self-defense, they began to hit me in the face and the chest with their fists.

After numerous blows, I finally fell to my knees. As I did, they kicked and stomped down on me. In the midst of this persecution, no hatred or malice emanated from my heart for these men that were trying to kill me. My heart and my mind seemed to be completely floating in a sea of love and peace. I found myself crying out loud for them. "Father, please forgive them, for they do not know what they are doing." And then everything went completely black.

When I came to, I found myself lying on the floor of my barracks. I looked around the room expecting to see the angel, but there was no one there but me. It was late in the afternoon. I think approximately at least five hours had come and gone since the angel had first appeared. My experience was not a dream.

The reality of everything that had transpired is still eternally embodied in my mind and my heart. I can see it all as clearly as if it had just happened. Whether or not I was in my body or out of it, I cannot tell. I can say this though: without a shadow of a doubt, God has placed a divine mission in my life to complete, a job to do, a purpose to fulfill.

By God's grace, nothing will rob me of the reality of it. With all my might, I am determined to fulfill God's will for my life. By God's grace I am not going to disappoint the One who has chosen me to be a soldier in His last day army. I hope you understand that you also have a divine mission and purpose in this life. I pray to God that you will be faithful to that divine call.

CHAPTER FOUR

Shekinah Glory Fills the Car
(1975)

I realize how preposterous and insane this sounds, but it's the truth. None of the stories that I share with you about my life are fake or exaggerated. There is a Scripture that says all liars will go to hell.

Revelation 21:8 But the fearful, and unbelieving, and the abominable, and murderers, and whoremongers, and sorcerers, and idolaters, and all liars, shall have their part in the lake which burneth with fire and brimstone: which is the second death.

Personally, I would not blame people for not believing this story. Most of my testimonies there were others who were present to verify exactly what happened. Now in this situation, I was all by myself coming out of Canada, driving my sister's Maverick.

I came out of the mountains of Canada Praying, singing and worshiping God in the Spirit as the sun was at its peak in the sky above me. I'm guessing it was right around 11 o'clock in the morning. As I continue to pray and worship God I began to be filled with an overwhelming love for the Father, and Jesus Christ. It felt like my heart was going to come out of my chest because of the greatness of God's love for me and my gratitude.

I was weeping, **praying** and crying as I drove along so much so to where I could not really see where I was going any longer. Suddenly the car began to be filled with the tangible presence of the Lord. The inside of my car was filling with a light, glistening, sparkly, light blue, green, silver, gold mist. I was so caught up in the presence of the Lord that without even thinking I raised my hands toward heaven, taking them off of my steering wheel.

In this place of deep intimate worship time came to at stand still. Here I was in my sister's 1973 red maverick driving through the rugged back roads of Canada with my hands lifted towards heaven, weeping and crying, and worshiping God. I was ushered into a supernatural, incredible, mind-boggling realm of the Holy Ghost.

I remember that after what only seemed a short time my hands came back to the steering wheel as this divine mist, the Shekinah glory was dissipating. To my utter amazement, I noticed that the sun, which had been in the middle of the sky when I began to experience the overwhelming presence of God, was just now barely peeking over the horizon and it was beginning to get dark. At that time I did not check the mileage of the car, but I know my car had gone hundreds of miles without me driving it. Someone had driven my car as I was caught up in this intense realm of worship!

This total experience could've possibly been 5 to 7 hours long. It had to be Angelic beings that took complete control of my vehicle as I was lost in the Spirit! My heart was filled with joy unspeakable and full of glory at this amazing miracle. To this day as I think about this experience, I can hardly grasp its reality.

Then a cloud covered the tent of the congregation, and the glory of the LORD filled the tabernacle (Exodus 40:34).

Truskowski Tries to Stab Me to Death

After being born again for a while, I perceived in my heart that

I needed to reach out and witness to the gang I used to run with right outside of Chicago. We were not a gang in the sense that we had a name or any entrance rituals that we had to go through. We were just a group of young men who were constantly involved in corruption, drinking, fighting, using drugs, stripping cars, and doing other things to horrible that I will not mention. One day, I was sitting in a car between the two instigators of most of our shenanigans, Gary and Claire. Both of these men were very large and quite muscular.

I had fervently shared Christ with them and the others to let them know how much God had changed me. They sat around drinking, using dope, and cussing while I shared the good news with them. I explained I was on a heavenly high that drugs and the world could never take them to. Most of them just stared at me, not knowing how to respond. They all had known the old Mike Yeager. The crazy and ungodly stuff that I had done. They had seen me many times whacked out on drugs and alcohol. Now here I was a brand-new creation in Christ preaching Jesus with a deep and overwhelming zeal.

Now Gary who was one of the main leaders was different in many negative ways than the other guys. He was like a stick of dynamite ready to explode at any moment. He had been up to the big house already and spent some time behind the bars of justice. He never did like me, but now there was an unspoken, seething hatred for me under the surface, which eventually exploded. We were coming out of Racine, Illinois, as Gary was driving the car we were in. Claire was sitting against the door on the right side in the front seat, with me in the middle. At that moment I did not realize why they had put me in the middle, but it became very obvious.

Before I knew it, Gary reached up and grabbed a large knife from the dashboard of the car. I believe the vehicle was an old Impala that had the old-style steel dashboard. The heating and air conditioning were controlled by sliders in the dash. The knife had been shoved down into one of the slots. He pulled the knife out of the dashboard with his right hand, jabbed it high up into the air, and drove it down toward me very fast, trying to stab me in the gut with this knife. I saw him reach for the knife, and at that very moment I entered into the realm of the Spirit when time seems to come to a standstill. This has happened to me on numerous occasions in such dangerous situations.

When I enter this realm, time slows down while my speed or movement seems to increase. You could argue whether I speed up or time slows down. I really can't say, though; it just happens.

The knife came down toward my guts in slow motion, and I saw my hands reaching up towards the knife and grabbing Gary's wrist to prevent him from stabbing me through the gut. I could not prevent the knife from coming down, but I was able to cause it to plunge into the seat instead. His thrust had been so powerful that the knife literally pierced all the way down through the Springfield car seat. He immediately pulled it out of the car seat and tried to stab me again. He continued to try to stab me as he was driving down the road. Every time he tried to stab me, I was able to divert the stab just fractions of an inch away from my privates and for my legs.

During this entire event the peace of God was upon me in an overwhelming way. I was not shaking or breathing hard in the least; neither was my heart beating fast. It sounds unbelievable, I know, but it felt as if I were in heaven. The presence and the peace of God was upon me in a powerful supernatural way. I know this might sound extremely strange and weird, but I was actually kind of enjoying myself as I was watching God deliver me from this madman.

During this entire time, it was like a slow-motion review of a movie. Up and down the knife came as he kept on trying to kill me. This large muscular man was not able to kill a small 5'8" skinny guy. I just love how God does the supernatural miracles. There was not one thing in my life in which that I knew I was out of God's will. I believe if I had been out of the will of God most likely Gary would've succeeded in murdering me. He kept on trying to kill me until up ahead of us a police car came out from a side road. Gary's car window was open and when he saw the policeman he threw the knife out the window.

Gary continued to drive down the road without ever saying a word about what had just happened. In this whole situation Claire who I had thought was a friend of mine, did not in any way try to help me. No one said a word as we drove down the road, but the peace of God was upon me like I have the invisible blanket.

Thou wilt keep him in perfect peace, whose mind is stayed on thee: because he trusteth in thee. Trust ye in the LORD forever: for in the LORD JEHOVAH is everlasting strength (Isaiah 26:3-4).

Truskowski Shoots Me with a Shotgun

About two days later I had to go to Gary's house. I really shouldn't have gone there, because there was just something satanic and evil about him. Just the day before, he tried to stab me to death! When I pulled up in my sister's red Maverick I was sitting on his porch. When he saw me get out of the car he grabbed a shotgun (I think it was a twelve gauge) which had been leaning against his house.

I walked toward him and he aimed it right at my stomach. What was there about my gut that he was so enamored by it? There was no fear in my heart at the least. I just kept walking toward him. I was about twenty feet away from him when the barrel of the gun jerked slightly to the right as the gun went off.

The sound of the gun echoed through the valley. Nothing happened to me! As I think back to that day, I firmly believe an angel nudged that gun barrel with his little finger. If there was bird shot in the gun, no pellets hit me, and if there was a deer slug in it, I did not feel it go by.

It must have missed me by a matter of inches. I was not shaking or breathing hard in the least; neither was my heart beating fast. It sounds unbelievable, I know, but once again it felt as if I was in heaven. I walked up the steps of the porch and walked up to Gary. I took the gun out of his hand, and leaned it back against the house. Gary just stared at me without saying a word. That was the last time I ever saw Gary. I have no idea what happened to him.

> *No weapon that is formed against thee shall prosper; and every tongue that shall rise against thee in judgment thou shalt condemn. This is the heritage of the servants of the LORD, and their righteousness is of me, saith the LORD (Isaiah 54:17).*

Yupik Indians Tried to Steam Me Alive

At the time as a 19 year old missionary living with the Yupik Indians in the Alaska bush it did not seem as if I had many results. However, the Word of God never returns void. I have been told by reliable sources that one of the young men I shared Jesus with is now an Assemblies of God pastor in the Dillingham area. When I was there, there was no Christian testimony in the community. But now there is an Assembly of God church right outside of Dillingham, Alaska. Now to the story of how I was almost steamed to death.

Steam baths were introduced to Yupik Indians by Russian fur traders and missionaries. The steam baths I experienced in the Bristol Bay area consisted of a dressing room, combination cooling room, and the hot room with very low ceilings that were only about four feet high. They were covered over with tundra to keep the steam and

heat from escaping. These hot rooms were called a maqili or
McQay.

The wood stove heater was an oil drum on its side with a
chimney. Rocks were piled on top of the oil drum. There was half of
a steel barrel full of water in the corner of the room next to the exit.
They had about four-and-a-half-foot long piece of wood with a
kitchen pan attached so they could scoop water out of the barrel,
stretch the pan over the top of the oil barrel stove and dump it on the
rocks. This sent forth a tremendous amount of heat and steam. They
packed the barrel completely full of wood for a steam bath. Steam
baths seem to be an area of great pride for the Yupik men.

They told stories how they would pass out trying to outdo each
other. They were known to have fallen on the rocks and burned to
death. They stayed in the steam bath as long as they could and then
go out and roll in the snow or jump in the river. They also had a
bench right outside where we would sit with nothing but a
washcloth covering our loins.

One day they invited me to take a steam bath with them. On that
particular day there were three young Yupik Indians and an older
man who looked like a walrus. The Spirit of the Lord spoke to my
heart and told me not to be fearful. They were going to try to steam
me out of the maqili /McQay. God said not to be concerned because
He was going to reveal Himself to them through this test. When we
were all in the McQay and had closed the door they all stared at me,
speaking in their native tongue to one another and laughing. Then
they dumped water on the red hot rocks.

The older gentleman had control of the scoop. As he continued to
splash water on the rocks, it began to get extremely hot. I had a wet
rag which they had given me, along with a pan of water at my feet. I
dipped the cloth into the water and put it against my face and nostrils.
I bowed my head and prayed quietly in tongues. I could hear the
water hissing as more and more water was thrown on the red hot

rocks. I could feel their eyes staring at me. The heat was almost unbearable.

The minute I stopped thinking about Jesus and praying it would feel like I was being steamed alive. Finally, I heard the door of the McQay open and close three times. At this point I looked up and there was only the old Yupik Indian and myself. He smiled at me with a toothless grin. I bowed my head once again and continued to pray knowing this was going to get extremely difficult.

I knew this was a fight for their souls. I wanted the Spirit of God to reveal Himself to them. They needed to understand this was not a white man's religion but Jesus is the living God and Savior of all men. All at once I heard a very large splash. The old Yupik Indian threw a whole scoop of water upon the rocks and ran out the door of the McQay.

I panicked. It felt like my flesh was being melted from off my bones. I ran for the door to open it, but either it was locked or they were holding it shut from the outside. I pounded on the door and at that instant the Spirit of the Lord arrested me and told me to go back into prayer.

I fell on my face directly on the wood plank floor and began to speak in tongues. The Spirit of God sent a cool breeze where there was no wind. A cold wind literally blew over the top of me. After what seemed to be a long time they let me out. I am sure they never understood how I could have beaten them at their own native hobby, or how I survived such tremendous heat. They never did ask me. They simply stared at me when I came out.

Glory at Abbot Loop Fellowship

Shekinah Glory

One Sunday while I was visiting Anchorage, Alaska, I decided to visit a church someone had told me about. I believe the name of it was Abbott Loop Fellowship. I arrived late because I had to hitchhike and walk my way there in twenty degrees below zero weather.

You might ask, why in the world would I go through such trouble to get to that church? It's called being spiritually hungry and thirsty. I entered the sanctuary and found a chair all the way in the last row. The worship was wonderful, and I found myself being caught up in the Spirit. I smelled a beautiful fragrance in the air which I had never experienced before. It smelled like some type of beautiful flower.

My eyes were closed during this time, but as I smelled this beautiful aroma I opened them. The same glistening fog that had filled my car when I was driving through Canada began to descend upon me. Before I knew it, I could not see anyone else. I became totally lost in worshiping and praising God. To this day, I do not know if anyone else saw, or smelled what I experienced on that particular day.

It came even to pass, as the trumpeters and singers were as one, to make one sound to be heard in praising and thanking the LORD; and when they lifted up their voice with the trumpets and cymbals and instruments of music, and praised the LORD, saying, For he is good; for his mercy endureth for ever: that then the house was filled with a cloud, even the house of the LORD; So that the priests could not stand to minister by reason of the cloud: for the glory of the LORD had filled the house of God (2 Chronicles 5:13-14).

Stabbed in the Face with a knife Multiple Times by a demon possessed women!

After I had arrived in Anchorage, it was quickened in my heart to stop at a small full gospel church that I used to visit. **The Neighborhood Full Gospel Church**. Now, It just so happened that an evangelist I had known while I was in the Navy on Adak, Alaska, was there. We spent some time reminiscing what had happened while we were in Adak.

He shared how the Lord had laid upon his heart to go to Pennsylvania to open up an evangelistic outreach center in a town called Mount Union, Pennsylvania. He invited me to go to Pennsylvania with him and his wife to open this evangelistic outreach.

I perceived in my heart I needed to go with them. I planned to fly back to Wisconsin where he and his wife would pick me up as they went through. However, before I left Alaska the spirit of God had one more assignment for me: a precious demon possessed woman needed to be set free.

One Sunday we decided to attend a small church along the road to Fairbanks. I was the first to enter this little, old, rustic church. When I went through the sanctuary doors, I immediately noticed a strange, little, elderly, lady across from me - sitting in the pews.

She turned her head and stared right at me with the strangest look I have ever seen. I could sense immediately there was something demonic about her. Out of the blue, this little old lady jumped up, got out of the pew, and ran out of the church. At that moment I perceived that God wanted me to go and cast the devils out of her.

When the service was over, I asked the pastor who that elderly lady was. He said she was not a member of his church, but she came once in a great while. He also told me that she lived with her husband in a run-down house on a dirt road. I asked him if it would be okay to go and see her? **(I knew in my heart that God had sent me there to help bring deliverance)** He said he had no problems with this, especially since she wasn't a part of his church.

We followed the directions the pastor gave us, and when we arrived at the house it was exactly as the pastor had described it to us. It was run-down, and the yard was overflowing with old furniture and household items.

It reminded me of the TV show "Sanford and Son" - but it probably had ten-times more junk in the yard! I do not know how the old couple survived the winters in Alaska in such a poorly-built house. As we got out of the car, a little old man met us outside. It was her husband. He was thanking God as he walked toward us, and said he knew we were men of God, and that we had been sent by the Lord to help his poor, tormented wife. He informed us that his wife was in their kitchen.

So, we walked up to the house, having to go down the twisting and cluttered junk-filled path. We entered the house through a screen door that led into their summer kitchen. When we entered the kitchen, we could see his wife over at a large utility sink. Her back was to us, but we could see she was peeling carrots over her kitchen sink … with a very large, scary-looking, butchers knife!! As I stood there, looking at the back of her head, I began to speak to her about Jesus.

Out of the blue, she turned her head like it was on a swivel to look at me. I could hardly believe my eyes! It was like I was watching a horror movie! This little lady's eyes were glowing red on her swiveled head.

I rubbed my eyes at that moment; thinking that maybe I imagined this. No … her head had swiveled - without her body moving - and her eyes were glowing red.

Fear immediately filled my heart as she looked at me with the big knife ... a butcher's knife ... in her hand. Immediately, I came against the spirit of fear in my heart by quoting the holy Scriptures:

"For God hath not given me the spirit of fear; but of power, and of love, and of a sound mind" *2 Timothy 1:7*. I shared with her about Jesus Christ.

The next thing I knew she was coming right at me - with her knife - as if she was filled with great rage. The knife was still in her right hand when she spun around and came at me. She leapt through the air onto me, wrapping her small skinny legs around my waist. How in the world she was able to do this - I do not know?

The next thing I knew, she was lifting up her right hand and hitting me in the face, very hard, multiple times. I could feel the pressure of her hitting me on the left side of my face. As she was hitting me in the face, out of my mouth came: "In the **Name of Jesus!**"

The minute I came against this attack **"In The Name of Jesus"** she was ripped off of me; picked up by an invisible power, and flung across the room about 10-feet or more. She slammed very hard against the bare wall of her kitchen, and slipped down to the floor.

Amazingly when she hit the wall, she was not hurt! I went over to her, continuing to cast the demons out of her In the Name of Jesus. Once I perceived that she was free, and in her right mind, I asked her how she had become demon possessed? She told us her terrible story.

Her uncle had repeatedly molested and raped her when she was a very young girl. She thought she was free from him when he got sick and died. But then he began to visit her from the dead, continuing to molest and rape her at night. To her, it was physical and real. She did not know it was a familiar spirit disguised as her uncle. This had probably gone on for over fifty years!

I led her to the Lord. Sweet, beautiful peace came upon her, completely changing her countenance. She was a brand-new person in Christ, finally free - after almost fifty years of torment. She and her husband began to go to church with us - until I left Alaska. I remember that we took them to see the Davis family at a local church, visiting Alaska on a missionary trip.

Years later, the evangelist who visited this lady with me, heard me retelling the story at a church; about how the woman kept punching me forcefully with her right hand. At the end of the service, he came and informed me that I was not telling the story correctly. I wondered if he thought I was exaggerating. He said that he was standing behind me when she jumped on top of me and began to hit me with her right fist.

But, he informed me, it wasn't her hand she was slapping me with … she still had the large butchers knife in her hand; and he saw her stabbing me in the face with this knife. Repeatedly!!

He said he knew that I was a dead man, because nobody could survive being stabbed in the face repeatedly, with a large butcher knife. He expected to see nothing but blood, but instead of seeing my blood everywhere, he saw that there was not even one mark on my face where the knife was hitting me. I did feel something hit my face repeatedly, but I thought it was her hand! Instead, it was her knife, and it could not pierce my skin! Thank God for His love, His mercy, and His Supernatural Divine Protection.

I am convinced that if I had not been walking with God in His holiness and obedience, the devil in that little old lady would have stabbed me to death. Many people in the body of Christ are trying to deal with demonic powers when they are out of the father's will. When we are moving in the Holy Ghost, obedience, and absolute love for Jesus Christ - there is no power in hell that can hurt us!

My God hath sent his angel, and hath shut the lion's mouths, that they have not hurt me: forasmuch as before him innocence was found in me; and also before thee, O king, have I done no hurt (Daniel 6:22).

How I Was HEALED of a Broken Back

I share these stories, my personal experiences, hoping that they will give you an insight in how to receive healing, even in the most difficult situations.

I do not share these stories with any pride. I simply am telling you what transpired, the steps, the process, the struggles that I have gone through to take what Christ purchased for me.

I am amazed at how many believers, I am talking about Pentecostal believers who do not know how to receive healing from God. Up to this moment I have written three books on the subject of healing. I'm not an expert on the subject, but I am not a novice also. This story happened back in 1978 as a 22-year-old man. If I had not known how to take my healing from Christ by faith I would've most likely been crippled for the last 41 years.

 Now in the winter of 1978, I was working at the Belleville Feed & Grain Mill as a 21 year old kid. My job was to pick up the corn, wheat, and oats from the farmers, and bring it to the mill. There it would be mixed and combined with other products for the farmers' livestock.

One cold, snowy day, the owner of the feed mill told me to deliver a load of cattle feed to an Amish farm. It was an extremely bad winter that year, with lots of snow. I was driving an International 1600 Lodestar. I backed up as far as I could to this Amish man's barn without getting stuck.

The Amish never had their lanes plowed in those days, and they most likely still do not. I was approximately seventy-five feet away from his barn, which meant that I had to carry the bags at least seventy-five feet. I think there were about eighty bags of feed, with each bag weighing approximately one hundred pounds. During those years I only weighed about 130 pounds.

I would carry one bag on each of my shoulders, stumbling and pushing my way through the heavy, deep snow to get up the steep incline into the barn. Then I would stack the bags in a dry location. As usual, nobody came out to help me. Many a time when delivering things to the farms, the Amish would watch me work without lending a helping hand.

About the third trip, something frightening happened to me as I was carrying two one-hundred-pound bags upon my shoulders. I felt the bones in my back snap. Something drastic just happened. I fell to the ground at that very moment almost completely crippled. I could barely move. I was filled with intense overwhelming pain.

I had been spending a lot of my time meditating in the Word of God. Every morning, I would get up about 5:00 a.m. to study. I had one of those little bread baskets with memorization scriptures in it. I believe you can still buy them to this day at a Christian bookstore. Every morning I would memorize from three to five of them. It would not take me very long, so all day long I would be meditating on these verses.

The very minute I fell down, immediately I cried out to Jesus, asking him to forgive me for my pride, and for being so stupid in carrying two hundred pounds on my little frame. After I asked Jesus to forgive me, I commanded my back to be healed in the name of Jesus Christ of Nazareth.

Since I believed I was healed, I knew that I had to act now upon my faith. Please understand that I was full of tremendous pain, but I had declared that I was healed by the stripes of Jesus. The Word of God came out of my mouth as I tried to get up and then fell back down.

Even though the pain was more intense than I can express, I kept getting back up speaking the name of Jesus, then I would fall back down again. I fell down more times than I can remember. After some time, I was able to take a couple steps, then I would fall again. This entire time I was saying, "In the name of Jesus, in the name of Jesus, in the name of Jesus."

I finally was able to get to the truck. I said to myself if I believe I'm healed then I will unload this truck in the name of Jesus. Of course, I did not have a cell phone in order to call for help and the Amish did not own any phones on their property. Now, even if they would have had a phone, I would not have called for help. I had already called upon my help, and His name was Jesus Christ. I knew in my heart that by the stripes of Jesus I was healed. I then pulled a bag off of the back of the truck, with it falling on top of me. I would drag it a couple feet, and then fall down.

Tears were running down my face as I spoke the Word of God over and over. By the time I was done with all of the bags, the sun had already gone down. Maybe six or seven hours had gone by. I painstakingly pulled myself up into that big old 1600 Lodestar. It took everything within me to shift gears, pushing in the clutch, and driving it. I had to sit straight like a board all the way.

I finally got back to the feed mill late in the evening. Everybody had left for home a long time ago with the building being locked up. I struggled out of the Lodestar and stumbled and staggered over to my Ford pickup. I got into my pickup, and made it back to the converted chicken house. I went back to my cold, unheated, plywood floor room. It took everything in me to get my clothes off. It was a very rough and long night.

The next morning when I woke up, I was so stiff that I could not bend in the least. I was like a board. Of course, I was not going to miss work, because by the stripes of Jesus I was healed. In order to get out of bed, I had to literally roll off the bed, hitting the floor. Once I had hit the floor, it took everything for me to push myself back up into a sitting position.

The tears were rolling down my face as I put my clothes and shoes on, which in itself was a miracle. I did get to work on time, though every step was excruciatingly painful. Remember, I was only twenty-one at the time, but I knew what faith was and what it wasn't. I knew that I was healed no matter how it looked, that by the stripes of Jesus Christ I was healed.

When I got to work I did not tell my boss that I had been seriously hurt the day before. I walked into the office trying to keep the pain off of my face. For some reason he did not ask me what time I made it back to work. I did not tell him to change the time clock for me in order to be paid for all of the hours I was out on the job. They had me checked out at the normal quitting time. (The love of money is what causes a lot of people not to get healed.)

My boss gave me an order for feed that needed to be delivered to a local farmer. If you have ever been to a feed and grain mill, you know that there is a large shoot where the feed comes out. After it has been mixed, you have to take your feed bag, and hold it up until it's filled. It creates tremendous strain on your arms and your back, even if you're healthy.

As I was filling the bag, it almost felt like I was going to pass out, because I was in tremendous pain. Now, I'm simply saying, "In the name of Jesus, in the name of Jesus, in the name of Jesus" under my breath. The second bag was even more difficult than the first bag, but I kept on saying, "In the name of Jesus."

I began on the third bag and as I was speaking the name of Jesus, the power of God hit my back and I was instantly and completely, totally healed from the top of my head, to the tip of my toes. I was healed as I went on my way. My place of employment never did know what had happened to me. That has been 38 years ago, and my back is still healed by the stripes of Christ to this day.

And from the days of John the Baptist until now the kingdom of heaven suffereth violence, and the violent take it by force (Matthew 11:12).

She's the One

I was standing outside The Mount Union Christian Center, on a ladder one day, putting up new letters on the marquee, when I heard behind me the sweetest voice I had ever heard. The voice said, "Praise the Lord, Brother!" I turned around on the ladder. And there before me I saw a beautiful, blue-eyed blonde. I said back in return, "Praise God, Sister!" Immediately the Spirit of God spoke to my heart and said: she is your wife! All I could think at the moment was, wow! To be honest, I was quite overwhelmed.

This blue-eyed girl and I spoke for a little while. She told me that her name was Kathleen, and that she was home taking a break from college. She was one of the lead vocalists for a Christian college in Phoenixville, Pennsylvania. Actually, she was not even really supposed to be home. God had arranged it. (She will share her story with you after this little intermission.) I did not tell her what the Spirit of God had said to me, until after we were married.

Proverbs 29:11 says, "A fool uttereth all of his mind, but a wise man keeps it in till afterwards."

When Kathleen walked away, I got down from the ladder and I went into the old movie theater. I was so filled with the spirit of joy that I jumped up upon the back of the old, unstable, theater chairs. I ran on the back of these chairs all the way down to the front, spun around, and ran back to the rear of the theater on top of the chairs again. As I was running, I was shouting, "She's the one! She's the one!" Five months later we were gloriously married.

And Adam said, This is now bone of my bones, and flesh of my flesh: she shall be called Woman, because she was taken out of Man. Therefore shall a man leave his father and his mother, and shall cleave unto his wife: and they shall be one flesh (Genesis 2:23-24).

Kathleen's story:

When I met Michael (Mike), it was a God-arranged appointment, because I wasn't supposed to be there—I was supposed to be in college! We met while I was attending my second semester at a college in Valley Forge. It was the end of March 1978, the week classes were supposed to start after Spring break. I may have never met him, had not the Lord arranged for me to be home during that cherished week of destiny. I was only nineteen years old at the time.

During spring or Easter break, I was on tour with the school's choir. Our schedule had been quite grueling, and who ever set up the itinerary made it so we would have to travel during the night to make it to many of our next destinations.

Because of the excessive traveling, we did not sleep very well. Many of the choir members lost their voices, and I was one of them! However, when it would come to the time of my solos, the anointing of God would take over and I would miraculously be able to sing.

At the end of the tour, I was both exhausted and totally without a voice. School classes were scheduled to begin the following Tuesday, but I really wanted to go home and rest.

Seeking the dean of women's permission to go home and miss four days of classes was not going to be an easy task. Nonetheless, I was willing to try. When I entered the dean's office, I could tell that she had already had a bad day. She could tell that I had very little voice left, as I tried to squeak a whisper of my request to skip a few days of classes and go home to rest.

Perhaps, my squeaking only irritated her frayed nerves, but she let me have it! In her tirade, she told me in no certain terms that all we students were alike, and I could not go home!

Instead of getting angry, I felt compassion for her, and gave her a big hug. I told her that it was alright. I told her that I knew she was having a bad day, and prayed that the rest of her day would go better. I thanked her for her time, and let myself out of the room.

Not much later, my den mother came to me and asked what I had done to the dean of women! My den mother said that she had gone to see the dean of women shortly after I left, found the dean of women sitting in her chair, with her mouth open, and tears running down her face.

My den mother told me that all she could get out of the dean was, "I just chewed that girl up one side and down the other, and she came over, gave me a hug, thanked me, and wished me a good day!"

My act of kindness did not go unrewarded, because, apparently after the dean regained her composure, she determined to find me and talk to me privately. When I saw the dean coming, she called out to me. I wasn't sure what to expect when she grabbed my arm and drew me close to her. She whispered in my ear, "I am not even sure that I am allowed to do this, and I might get in trouble, so tell no one. You may go home for a few days." I gave her another big hug and thanked her. I was going home!

When I arrived home, little did I know that God was at work to bring Mike, my future husband, and I together.

The first day home I slept all day, but the next day my mother and I ended up in Mount Union to go shopping. Before we left the house, I decided that I didn't want to be bothered. I put my hair down around my face, put my glasses on, and dressed in a knit polyester pant suit. I certainly was not dressed to attract any male attention!

As God would have it, before we went grocery shopping, we passed by an old theatre called the Mount Union Christian Center. There was a young man on a ladder, putting "Jesus the Ultimate Trip" on the marquis. My voice had miraculously recovered, and I said, "Praise the Lord, Brother!" and he responded "Praise the Lord, Sister!"

This afro-haired young man, was cute and on fire for God! We spoke together for a little while about the goodness of God and of how the Lord had saved and touched lives during my choir tour. Michael spoke of God's goodness and wonders, too.

I liked Mike from the start, and was hoping to meet again before I returned to school. Little did I know that I would see him again that night and have lunch with him the next day.

I have to add here: After meeting Mike at the theater/Christian center, a young girl came running into the grocery store to find me. She was insistent on telling me that Mike really, really, liked me and asked if I liked him. She must have seen Mike running on the back of the theater chairs shouting, "She's the one! She's the one!" I told her that I barely knew him, how could I tell if I liked him? Sure, he was nice, but I had not fallen for him—not yet!

However, she did spark a little more interest in me. So, that night, my mother, sister, and I came back to the center. Only this time I was dressed, perfumed, and ready for a little male attention— well one male's attention.

My mom was dating a man from the center, so I asked him to ask Mike if he'd like to go out with us, meaning my mom, my future step-father, and me. I was delighted when he accepted. This young man was beginning to win my heart.

Before I went back to college, Mike handed me a Laurel blossom; which I kept for years pressed within my college year book. The flower reminded me of the blossom of love that was beginning to bloom in my heart for this man of God.

Michael won my heart because he loved God. Our conversations were always centered on Jesus and God's Word. Had Michael been a forward person, I would have dropped interest in him immediately. I loved the Lord and only desired to serve Him. A man with any other desire would have turned me off instantly.

Consequently, by the time I went back to college to finish the semester, Mike was all I wanted to talk about, he had won my heart. The feeling must have been mutual, for I was back at school less than a day, when he called and spoke with me for over an hour. Michael wrote me long letters that were full of the Word of God. You could say, the Word of God within Mike's letters washed over me and made me one with him and God's Word.

I showed Mike's letters to my friends, because there was nothing embarrassing in them. They thought that he must be a baby Christian. I thought that to be a sad indictment on us "Bible" students! If it were only baby Christians who loved the Word of God and would fill their letters with scriptures, then we Bible students had lost our first love! When we lose our love for the Word of God, we are in trouble!

Mike and I kept in touch by phone calls and letters until I was to return home the first week of May. I had hoped to stay at the college to finish a short summer semester. (I reasoned that my feelings were better kept at a distance.) However, Mike was praying that God would bring me home, because he wanted to be with me!

I was stubborn, though. Had not my mom decided to get married May 6th, and wanted me there to sing and help her prepare for her wedding, I might have stayed at Valley Forge. My stubbornness to stay at college was not totally against Mike and spending the summer at home, but it was aimed at trying to make my mom wait to get married. I wasn't willing to give up my mom that easily to another man. My mom and I had been best friends for years, and while I was away at college she met a godly man and fell in love. For me, that was a hard pill to swallow. But God was in it!

Back home, our romance budded quickly, and by June we knew that we wanted to get married. Nonetheless, I wanted to go back to school for at least one more year. When Mike applied to go to a well-known Bible training center, I silently prayed that they would accept him for the following year, because I wanted to go along and attend too. Furthermore, I wanted to wait another year before getting married.

When Michael received his acceptance in July, I was torn. I wanted to go with Mike, but I wanted to wait! I only knew Mike three to four short months! I had earlier vowed that I would never get married unless I had dated at least two years! To add to my dilemma, we contacted this Bible school, and yes, they would accept me, too. They always tried to accept couples. I had some serious decisions to make.

Needless to say, we were married on August 19, 1978, and I had just met Mike around March 28! Besides accepting Jesus as my Lord and Savior, marrying Mike is the best thing I ever did. God had ordained that we would be together. Sure we've had rough times, but God has brought us through.

Looking back today, I believe that God had things go quickly, because I surely would have changed my mind if I had two years to think about it. Furthermore, the whirlwind of getting married, preparing for a wedding, and preparing to go to Oklahoma (which was far away from home) were only a foretaste of what the Lord had for me and Mike together.

If I couldn't take a fast-paced marriage, then I would never be prepared for the fast-paced life that we have lived!

I did not miss any of my college classes that spring when I came home and met my husband-to-be. Right after I left the school to come home for a rest, a snow storm hit Valley Forge and prevented classes from starting until the following week—the week I returned. God is a God of wonders! I did not have any classes to make up, and could sit starry-eyed, thinking about Mike, stress free!

Be kindly affectioned one to another with brotherly love; in honour preferring one another;...Bless them which persecute you: bless, and curse not......If it be possible, as much as lieth in you, live peaceably with all men.. (Romans 12:10, 14, 17,18, 21).

He Was Going to Rape & Murder My Wife

I was working for the Broken Arrow school district as a janitor while my wife and I attended a Bible school in Oklahoma. One night at about 7:00 p.m. while I was waxing and buffing the floors in a classroom, the **unction's** of the Lord came upon me mightily. It was a divine urgency that overwhelmed my heart and my soul. Immediately I stopped what I was doing. I began to pray fervently in the spirit and also in English. I asked the Lord what was going on. He spoke to me in an almost audible voice saying, there is a man at your house right now who is there to rape and murder your wife!

For the last couple months there had been a lot of rapes and murders going on in the Tulsa and Broken Arrow, Oklahoma area. There was literally a man hunt trying to find this man before he committed another atrocious crime. But up to this time they had been completely unsuccessful in finding him.

When I heard the voice of the Lord say this to me it shook me to the very core of my being. I did not have a phone to call her to see if she was okay. In those days there is no such thing as cell phones. And we did not have a phone in our apartment. I knew it would be too late by the time I got in my truck and drove home. I did the only thing I could I began to cry out to God for her deliverance and safety.

I took authority over the demonic powers that were operating in this man. I kept praying and interceding. If you would have walked into that classroom at that moment you would've seen a man completely consumed in prayer on his knees, and in deep intercession. This continued for quite a while until all of a sudden the peace of God that passes all understanding came upon me. At that moment I knew that I knew in my heart God had divinely intervened, and that she was okay. The peace that passes all understanding had come upon my mind and my heart.

I do not get off work until after midnight, so it was rather late when I walked through the door of our apartment. When I came through the door the first thing I said to my wife was "Who came to the house tonight?" She looked at me a little surprised. She told me a man came by who said he was from children's services. I asked her what he wanted. He said they were doing a survey, and that he needed some questions to be answered. He began to ask her numerous questions about her life.

It turns out while that at that very moment he was asking my wife these personal questions, I was in deep intercessory prayer in the classroom where I was working. During that time we had another couple staying with us temporarily in our apartment. The husband's wife, Pam, came out of the back room as the stranger was talking to my wife.

Now Pam is just a very small petite woman that nobody in their right mind would be at all intimidated or concerned about. This man seemed to get extremely nervous and fearful at that moment. He said he needed to get some literature from his car, and that he would be right back. He quickly left through the door of our apartment. Thank God he never did come back. My wife said they saw him driving his car away.

The next day I called the children's services to investigate what had happened. I told them precisely what had happened. They adamantly declared that they never send anyone out after five o'clock. They also said that they did not have any man working for them who go to people's homes and ask questions.

God had supernaturally and divinely intervened by placing within me a holy unction to cry out to him. Now it might be assumed that this man simply left because there is another woman in the house. Personally I do not believe this is the case. A man so possessed by devils could have easily intimidated both of the ladies, and taken advantage of them. Praise God for divine intervention and guidance.

.

CHAPTER FIVE

Famous Author Died Because He Lied

One day I picked up a book by a well-known author. This book had come highly recommended by one of my favorite preachers at that time. The topic was about angelic visitations. This was something I was interested in, because of my many experiences with the supernatural.

I began to read this book and noticed immediately that there were experiences he said he had which did not seem to line up with the Scriptures. I did not want to judge his heart, but we do have the responsibility to examine everything in light of God's Word. If it does not line up with the word of God, then we must reject it, no matter who wrote it.

As I was pondering the stories in this book, the Spirit of the Lord spoke to my heart very strongly. It was as if He was standing right there next to me, speaking audibly. What He spoke to me was rather shocking! The Lord told me that the writer of this book would be dead in three months from a heart attack. I asked the Lord why He was telling me this.

He said the stories in the man's book were exaggerated, and judgment was coming. The Lord warned me that day that if I were ever to do the same thing, judgment would come to me. I did not realize that the Lord would have me to be writing books, many them filled with my own personal experiences. Now I know why he spoke this to me, telling me that I better not exaggerate my experiences.

When the Spirit of the Lord spoke this to me, I turned and told my wife. I held the book up and said, in a very quiet whispering, trembling, wavering voice, "Honey, the man who wrote this book will be dead in three months from a heart attack." Plus, I told her why the Lord told me this. I wish I had been wrong. Exactly 3 months later, the man died from a heart attack. God can speak to us through the positive and the negative circumstances of life. We better take heed to what he is saying.

Victory over Tumors

I woke up one morning with tremendous pain in my lower abdomen. I lifted up my shirt and looked down where the pain was. There was a lump on my abdomen about the size of an acorn. I laid my hands on it immediately, commanding it to go.

I said "You lying devil, by the stripes of Jesus I am healed and made whole." After I spoke to the lump, the pain became excruciating and overwhelmingly worse. All that day I walked the floor crying out to God, and praising him that His Word is real and true.

I went for a walk on the mountain right behind the parsonage. It was a long day before I got to sleep that night. When I awoke the next morning the pain was even more severe. It felt like somebody was stabbing me in my gut with a knife. I lifted up my shirt and looked and there was another lump. Now I had two lumps in my lower abdomen.

I laid my hands on them, commanding them to go. Tears were rolling down my face, as I spoke the Word. I lifted my hands toward heaven and kept praising God that I was healed. Even though I did not see any change, I kept praising God. All the symptoms were telling me that God's Word is a lie, and that I was not healed by the stripes of Jesus. But I knew that I was healed. It was another long day. It seemed as if I could never get to sleep that night. The pain was continual and non-stop!

When I got up the next morning the pain had intensified even more. Once again I looked at my abdomen and to my shock there was another lump the size of an acorn. Now I had three of these nasty lumps and each were about the size of an acorn. I did not think that the pain could get any worse, but it was. Once again I laid my hands on these tumors, commanding them to go in the name of Jesus Christ of Nazareth.

I declared that by the stripes of Jesus I am healed! It felt like a knife sticking in my gut all that day and night. I lifted my hands, and with tears rolling down my face, kept praising God that I was healed.

By faith I began to dance before the Lord a victory dance, praising God that I was healed by the stripes of Jesus. I went to bed that night hurting worse than ever. All night I tossed and turned and moaned, all the while thanking God that I was not going to die but that I was healed. I got up the next morning, and all of the tumors and pain were gone. They have never come back.

And he said, Let me go, for the day breaketh. And he said, I will not let thee go, except thou bless me. And he said unto him, What is thy name? And he said, Jacob. And he said, Thy name shall be called no more Jacob, but Israel: for as a prince hast thou power with God and with men, and hast prevailed (Genesis 32:26-28).

Prayed Eight Hours for Eight Days

The Spirit of the Lord woke me up early one morning with a tremendous unction to pray. I went out into our little front room and began to pray in English and the Spirit. Before I knew it, I was lost in the Holy Ghost. When I finally quit praying, it seemed as if I had prayed for very brief time. I looked at my watch and to my amazement, **seven to eight hours** had come and gone. During that whole time my wife never bothered me, she is wonderful in that way. When I am trying to press my way into the things of the Spirit, she simply leaves me alone.

The next morning the Lord woke me early again in prayer. I travailed and interceded in the Spirit and English. I was praying like a house on fire with deep groaning's and urgencies in the Holy Ghost. When this burden partly lifted, it seemed as if I had prayed for only one or two hours. When I looked at my watch, another eight hours had come and gone! This continued for **seven or eight days where the Spirit of God rolled me out of bed with a deep unction to pray! Every time that I prayed it would only seem like an hour, and yet it was seven to eight hours had come and gone!** (I did not write down every day that this happened because I wasn't expecting it to happen.)

Revival in Joint Church Services

Right after this time of **Spirit-motivated intercession** we had a wonderful move of God. The local ministerial that I was a part of was conducting a week-long community revival in the little town's pavilion. They wanted ministers to volunteer to speak. I agreed to do one of the services. My wife, Kathleen, would lead the worship for this service and I would preach the message.

A lot of the local community came to these meetings. I was there every night to support the other pastors. I think our night was the last service. Kathleen and I had both had been praying and fasting believing for God to do a mighty work. The host of the meeting opened with prayer and gave some announcements.

He introduced my wife and me as the pastors of the Three Springs Assembly of God. My wife did a wonderful job in leading worship. Then it was my turn. As I stood up to the pulpit, I sensed a great unction of the Holy Ghost to preach. I remember what I preached about The Name of Jesus. I'm not exaggerating when I tell you what happened.

The Spirit of God arrested everybody in that meeting. It was like they were glued to their chairs. Their mouths were hanging open. The pastors looked like they were in shock. Then I gave an opportunity for people to be prayed for. The front of the pavilion filled with people wanting prayer.

After the service, the ministers came to me almost timidly. I was the youngest pastor among them. I was twenty-six years old at this time. Some of the older ministers seemed to be almost distraught. One of them said to me, **"No one ever taught me to preach like that!"** I told him it was the **Holy Ghost**. After that particular service people from the community began to flock to our church. People were getting filled with the Holy Ghost everywhere.

RED HOT SKILLET COULD NOT BURN ME

I was cooking breakfast one morning, having just put oil in a cast-iron skillet. I was making eggs, bacon, and hash browns. As I was busy making breakfast, there was a knock on the door. When I opened the door, one of my parishioners named Paul was there. Paul and I were very good friends and would spend hours together praying and witnessing. He probably was fifteen years my senior. I invited him into the house and we began to talk about the things of God. I had completely forgotten about the cast-iron skillet on the stove.

The next thing that I knew, my wife was screaming.

I went into the kitchen and saw that the oil in the skillet had exploded into fire, with flames reaching as high as the old kitchen cupboards.

I knew if I did not move fast the whole house would go up in flames. The house was a firetrap waiting to happen. I was not thinking. I yelled for Paul to open the outside door as I was running for the stove and the skillet. I scooped the red-hot skillet up into my hands, spun around, and carried it out the door. Paul was standing out of the way and my wife was watching everything as it happened. I ran outside and flipped the pan upside down on the ground.

After a while the flames went out. I was standing and looking down at the cast-iron skillet when I suddenly realized what I had done. I was in such a hurry that I did not even grab a towel or any kind of heat pads before I scooped up the frying pan. I had literally picked it up with my bare hands. I looked down at my hands in complete amazement.

They should have been severely burned all the way to the bones. All that happened was that they became a little red. Not only that, but why didn't the flames of the burning oil not burn me? In just a brief period, all the pain and the redness in my hands were gone. If my wife and Paul had not seen me do it, I would truly doubt it myself. But God and his word is amazing!

Who through faith subdued kingdoms, wrought righteousness, obtained promises, stopped the mouths of lions, Quenched the violence of Þ re, escaped the edge of the sword, out of weakness were made strong, waxed valiant in fight, turned to fight the armies of the aliens (Hebrews 11:33-34).

Alvin Raised from the Bed of Death

One morning I received a phone call from my good friend, Paul. He told me that he knew of a man who owned a logging company and lumber yard who was about to die. They were waiting for him to expire any day because his body was filled with cancer. Most of it was concentrated in his chest and it had spread throughout the rest of his body. He was located in the McConnell burg hospital. Paul asked me if I would be willing to go pray for him. I asked him to give me one day to fast and pray for this particular situation. I spent the rest of that day in prayer, fasting, and in the Word.

The next morning Paul came to pick me up. We drove up to the McConnell burg hospital, praying as we went. We walked into the foyer and up to the information desk. The nurse gave us the necessary information we needed. Paul said he would wait for me and that he would continue in prayer in the hospital's chapel. I found the room where they had put this gentleman, knocked on the door, and entered.

They had placed him in a very small room—just big enough to be a closet—that was off the beaten path, like they were just waiting for him to die. He was lying on a hospital bed and was nothing but skin and bones; he looked as if he had just come out of a concentration camp. His skin and the whites of his eyes were yellow. He was a rather tall man who looked to be in his late sixties. He was lying on his bed wide awake. I had no idea what his mental condition was. I began to speak to him and discovered he was totally aware of his surroundings, and actually, I was amazed at how clear and quick his mind was.

I began to speak to him by introducing myself. He almost seemed to take an antagonistic attitude towards me right away. I began to share Jesus with him, but as I was speaking to him, a smirk appeared on his face. He began to tell me stories of the things he had seen in church— supernatural things. He said one time he was in a wild church service where everybody was jumping and shouting.

It was quite a number of years ago, and they did not yet have electricity in this church. He said as he was watching people dance and shout, one of them jumped so high that he hit a lighted kerosene lantern, causing it to fall off of the hook. It came crashing down onto the floor and should have immediately broken into pieces and caught the building on fire. Instead, he said it almost acted like a ball. It never broke or went out but landed straight up. The people just kept on dancing and singing to the Lord.

After he told me this story he looked me right in the eyes and said to me, "If I did not get saved back then, what makes you think you are going to get me saved now?" I did not answer him. My heart was filled with deep sorrow and overwhelming love for him. I knew I could not help him, and if was going to get saved and be healed it was going to take God moving upon him supernaturally.

I stepped away from his deathbed, and I bowed my head and cried out to God. "Lord, touch this man, help me to reach him because I cannot do it within myself. Lord, You're going to have to touch his heart or he will lose his soul and end up in hell." As I was praying under my breath I sensed the awesome presence of God come flooding into that little hospital room.

Then the Spirit of the Lord rose up within me, and I walked back over to his bed. I began to speak to Elvin once again, but it was under a divine unction of great compassion. I know I did not say very much, but as I was speaking, all of a sudden out of the blue, he began to weep uncontrollably. In just a matter of seconds his heart was completely open to the gospel. He gave his heart to Jesus Christ right then and there. Then I laid my hands on him and commanded his body to be healed. I rebuked the spirit of death, and cancer in the name of Jesus Christ, commanding it to go.

When I was done praying, it seemed to me there was some immediate improvement in his countenance and body. I told him as I got ready to leave that I would visit him again in the hospital. After I left something wonderful happened, but I did not hear the story until later that day when I arrived home from the hospital.

Immediately Elvin felt healed in his body. His appetite came back, and the yellow jaundice disappeared completely from his skin and from the white of his eyes. The hospital personnel were amazed at this transformation. They took some new x-rays and discovered that the cancer he had in his body was almost totally gone. The cancer that was in his lungs which had been the size of a baseball was now the size of a cashew nut. In three days' time they released him from the hospital and sent him home. He was working at his sawmill with his son and grandsons within a week!

Jesus saith unto him, Rise, take up thy bed, and walk. And immediately the man was made whole, and took up his bed, and walked: and on the same day was the sabbath (John 5:8-9).

Well Known Preacher Will Fall to Prostitutes

One of the members of the church gave me a book to read from a well-known evangelist. This particular book was on the subject of faith. I was very interested in reading it because I wanted to see what he had to say on this subject as this was an area in my life where God had placed upon me a great demand. Over and over in the last seven years I had to move in faith in order to be healed, delivered, protected, set free, and for our needs to be met. As I was reading this book my heart was filled with sorrow. Some personal tragedies had taken place in this man's life and in the lives of those he had loved.

He had not seen his prayers answered the way he thought they should be. Based upon these experiences, he had been teaching a doctrine of faith which did not line up with the Bible. In the process of embracing his own self-made doctrine, built upon his experiences, he was cutting himself off from all that God had made available for him. Not only was he cutting himself off from wonderful experiences, but he was leading all of those who followed him into the same misguided and wrong philosophy.

I'm sharing this with you not to be critical of anyone, but Scripture says that if any man thinks he stands, let him take heed lest he falls. I'm sharing this to help people come into the place where they can experience a continual flow of the Holy Ghost and the miraculous. As I continued to read that book, the Spirit of the Lord spoke to my heart and said, that if this man ever fell, (not that he would fall into sin) it would be to prostitutes.

It is actually frightening when God begins to tell you specific things, especially when it comes to judgment or repercussions of disobedience. I told my wife what the Spirit of the Lord Had spoken to my heart. I am sorry to say that a number of years later it was revealed that he had fallen to prostitutes. Now what in the world would this have to do with this book? We need to connect the dots. What is the victory that overcomes the world? Read Hebrews chapter 11. Look at all of these great woman and men of God. How did they overcome? By faith! But faith in what, or whom? (Lord willing that's another book.)

For whatsoever is born of God overcometh the world: and this is the victory that overcometh the world, even our faith. Who is he that overcometh the world, but he that believeth that Jesus is the Son of God? (1 John 5:4-5).

You're a dead man

God's audible voice said, "You're a Dead Man!"

I was driving into Mount Union, Pennsylvania with my wife to do some grocery shopping. I was driving a 1976 sport Ford Granada with a 302 Engine. The urge came to me to put the pedal to the metal and let it roar. The Lord had already delivered me from speeding years ago, but at that moment it was as if I allowed a devil to take over me.

I willingly gave in to this urge as I mashed down the gas

pedal, all the way to the metal and began to increase my speed. Yes, I knew better, but I caved and gave into temptation. My wife looked over at me just shaking her head. (Someone else was watching our newborn son Michael so he was not with us.)

I ended up accelerating to over 80 miles per hour. Kathleen was praying out loud that if we had an accident, she would not be hurt because of my stupidity and then she began to pray faster in the spirit. I was coming around the corner on Route 747 right before you enter into Mount Union when I heard the **audible voice of God** say to me, **"You are a Dead Man!"** Instantly the fear of the Lord hit me like a sledgehammer.

The voice of God and the fear of God went right to the very marrow of my bones. Instantly I knew that I was in real big trouble. I saw just ahead of me a stop signs to the left and to the right. At that very moment, I slammed on the brakes of my car, instantly slowing down.

As I came almost to a complete stop a flash of white flashed past my left to the right. I mean right then and there I saw a totally white, souped-up Dodge charger come speeding through the stop sign from the left. He ran the stop sign without stopping or slowing up in the least. I mean he really had the pedal to the metal.

I'm convinced he must have been going over 80 miles an hour. If I would not have slammed on my brakes exactly when I heard the audible voice of God, his car would have slammed right into my driver's side door. There is no doubt in my mind or my heart that I would have been instantly killed. Thank God he still speaks to us today. Thank God for his long-suffering and mercy never ends.

Now you might ask: why would God have spoken to you **audibly**? I believe it was the only way he could spare my life in this situation. Notice I was not seeking for God to speak to me **audibly**, he simply did this out of his love, and mercy, even though I was completely out of his will.

1 Peter 5:8 Be sober, be vigilant; because your adversary the devil, as a roaring lion, walketh about, seeking whom he may devour:9 Whom resist stedfast in the faith, knowing that the same afflictions are accomplished in your brethren that are in the world. 1 Peter 5:8-9 (KJV)

Going Deeper in God

We were preparing to leave the church that we had been pastoring for two years. Because the church was bringing in new candidates for examination, they did not need me to preach the Word to them any longer.

As a result, I was able to spend many hours memorizing and meditating on the Bible. A sense of great expectancy grew within my heart. The air was charged with the tangible power of God. I would walk the mountain behind our parsonage praying and meditating all day long. This continued for a number of weeks. At the time, I did not realize that I was about to step into a deeper realm of the Spirit.

Mifflin FGBMFI Holy Ghost Meeting

My wife and I were scheduled to minister at a number of meetings, and I had been invited previously to minister at the Mifflin Full Gospel Businessmen's meeting located in Belleville, Pennsylvania. We arrived right before the meeting was to start.

As I sat at a table with my wife, I remember that I felt no particular quickening of the Spirit of God on the inside whatsoever. One of the members of the organization came over and asked me if I would like to pray with some of the members before the beginning of the meeting. I consented to do so.

They were standing in a circle holding each other's hands. I simply stepped into this circle and took the hand of the man on my right and left.

The Cataracts Just Melted Away

The men began to pray, and I prayed very softly, agreeing with them. During this time of prayer, I did not perceive in my heart that I should pray aloud. When we were done praying, the man on my right, an older gentleman, stared at me. He said, "What in the world was that?"

I said to him, **"What do you mean?"**

He said it was like a **streak of lightning** came out of my hand, and up his arm, through his face. You could tell that something really radical had taken place. I told him that I had not felt anything.

That was the beginning of a wonderful, strange and unusual night. This same gentleman came to me at the end of the service, crying. He asked me to look into his eyes. I still remember to this day, his eyes were clear, glistening and filled with tears. He said to me, **"My eyes were covered in cataracts. The minute you touched me, the cataracts literally melted right off of my eyeballs!"** Thank you Jesus!

Right up to the minute before I opened my mouth I had not felt a single thing spiritually. However, the minute I began to speak at the pulpit, the river began to flow. I do not remember what I said, but I do know I was speaking under a strong influence of the Holy Ghost. Then I flowed right into the gifts of the Spirit after the teaching of the Word. A very precise word of knowledge began to operate. I remember looking out over the people and beginning to call specific people out. Many of the women and men appeared to be Mennonite or Amish.

I began to point to specific people, and call them to come forward. As they came, I would tell them what it was that was going on in their bodies. When they would get within ten feet of me, (no exaggeration) they did not fall forward or backwards, but just begin to crumple like soft snow flakes to the floor. Up to that time I had never seen anything like it!

It was like they just simply, and very gently went down. As far as I know, all of them were instantly healed. I do not remember laying hands on anyone that night. The Father, Son, and Holy Ghost were in the house.

How God anointed Jesus of Nazareth with the Holy Ghost and with power: who went about doing good, and healing all that were oppressed of the devil; for God was with him (Acts 10:38).

Her Face Hit the Concrete

We were conducting special healing meetings in Huntington, Pennsylvania, where we had rented a large conference room at Juniata College. The meeting room had a concrete floor with no carpet. After I had ministered the message I began to move in the gifts of the Spirit.

In this particular meeting I was quickened by the Spirit to have everyone stand facing the front in a long line. Quite a number of people had either been called out or wanted prayer. I specifically told the men that were standing behind these people not to brush against anyone's back. The reality of the presence of Christ was very strong. I knew that if someone brushed against these people, they would fall.

One of my coworkers accidentally brushed up against a young lady of approximately eighteen years of age. I was probably twenty feet from her. I saw the whole thing in slow motion. She began to fall forward. I went to move toward her, but I knew I could never make it in time. She fell forward with her hands at her side. I watched as her precious face slammed into the concrete floor. The minute her face hit the floor, it literally sounded like a pumpkin smashing and breaking in half and everybody gasped in horror.

I walked up to where she was laying. Even though I had been in the Spirit, my flesh was filled with trembling. I was fully expecting there to be blood. As I looked around her head I did not see any blood! I knew I had to quickly step back into the Spirit. As I did, I had total peace, so I left her lying there. I started at the end of the prayer line, working my way down, one person at a time. We saw many wonderful things that night. God set many free.

After the service I looked for this young lady. She was standing about where she had originally fallen. I walked up to her very gingerly. I almost did not want to look at her face because I was afraid of what I would see. She was shaking a little and crying. When I came around to her front I looked at her face.

To my amazement there was not one mark. In the natural there had to be some damage. We all heard her head when it hit the concrete. The room was filled with the sound of a loud thump. But here she was with not one mark on her face. I asked her what happened when she fell forward. She said that when she hit the floor it felt like as if she was falling into a bed of feathers!

And he went up unto them into the ship; and the wind ceased: and they were sore amazed in themselves beyond measure, and wondered (Mark 6:51).

My Son would have Burned to Death
Michael Would Have Burned to DEATH with Out an Open Vision!

While we were in Germany we bought a used Audi 100, with which we crisscrossed all over Germany, Holland, and the outskirts of France. One day as we were driving on the autobahn (German highway), I had an open vision.

All of a sudden, right in front of my eyes I saw the back seat of our car exploding in fire, with our son Michael burning alive in his car seat. This was a very disturbing image. I remember shaking my head, thinking this can't be! I tried to ignore it for a little while, but I had the vision again! I told my wife what I'd seen. She informed me that she was also seeing the same thing; that is why she had her chair leaning back, so she could grab Michael. She also had been praying in her heavenly tongues.

We pulled off to the side of the autobahn immediately, and got out of the car with Michael. I began to search high and low over the car. As Kathleen held Michael I searched underneath, in the trunk, and inside out but I could find nothing wrong. Not knowing what else to do, we all got back into the vehicle, strapped Michael back into his baby seat, and went back onto the autobahn. Kathleen kept her seat back as far as possible, and put her hand on Michael.

As we were driving, the same vision burst in front of my eyes stronger than ever. The vision was so real that I could barely see what was in front of me. Now, without a shadow of doubt, I knew something was going on. That God was trying to save us from a terrible tragedy! At the same time my eyes began to water and burn from some nasty fumes.

This time I pulled over to the side of the road as quickly as I could. I turned off the car and we evacuated the vehicle like it was about to explode. After I had got Kathleen and Michael far enough from the vehicle, I once again began to meticulously comb the car, which again came up with nothing wrong. The last thing to try was to pull the seat out of the back.

Since all American vehicles have their back seats attached, I wasn't sure how to do it. Yet to my surprise and delight, I discovered that the backseat was removable as I grabbed it. As I pulled it out, I was instantly overwhelmed by acidic fumes. Right underneath where Michael was sitting was a large twelve-volt battery! Acidic fumes were rolling out of its open caps at an alarming rate, bubbling and boiling. It was obvious that this battery was about to explode at any moment!

We managed to get the vehicle to a mechanic shop to be repaired. The mechanic told us that the alternator was putting out way too much amperage, perhaps due to some malfunctioning diodes.

He also informed us that had we not stopped the car, the battery would definitely have exploded into flames, and our precious little boy, Michael, would have been burned to death. Many believers die early and some from tragic deaths because they are not sensitive enough to the signs from the Spirit. They are not living within what I call the Realm of Faith and obedience.

He hath said, which heard the words of God, which saw the vision of the Almighty, falling into a trance, but having his eyes open (Numbers 24:4).

Germans Falling Out Of Their Chairs

EVERYONE FELL To The Floor WEEPING as I Was Preaching!

I was ministering in a German-speaking church called The Industrial Center of Germany. This church was situated about five stories up in a high-rise office complex. They did not have a pastor in this church at the time. They had a board of elders, and I understood one of the men was an oil tycoon. He was the one who supported all the activities and outreaches of the church. I had an interpreter with us who was a famous German worship leader and singer.

When I preached at the church, I ministered a radical message on being one hundred percent, completely and totally sold out to Jesus Christ. I shared that there was a price to be paid to enter the deeper things of God and that you had to die to the flesh to live in the Spirit. Jesus gave His everything, and now it was our turn to give everything. About two-thirds of the way through this message, something amazing happened.

As I stood before the congregation to speak, the Holy Ghost began to move upon me in a mighty way dealing with the subject of being completely sold out 100% to Jesus Christ. The presence of God was manifested in a very strong and real way. Something amazing happened as I was about 35 to 45 minutes into my message.

All of a sudden, the **Spirit of God fell** upon that congregation in such a mighty way that everyone in that church **fell out of their chairs at once**. Instantly everyone in the congregation was on the floor weeping and wailing under the influence of the Holy Spirit. This was such a strange occurrence because neither my interpreter or I seem to be feeling or experiencing what everybody else was. This happened in such a synchronized way that the thought came to me that for some reason they had organized this as a church.

Because I no longer had their attention, I simply quit preaching, and got down on my knees, and started praying along with them. This continued for quite a while. Eventually, the weeping and crying stopped, and people began to get up and trickle away from the meeting. **No one was talking.** There was a Holy hush upon the whole congregation. One of the leaders of the church invited us with a whisper down to the next floor where there had been a meal prepared for us in the fellowship hall.

As we sat down to eat, I could tell that they were all looking at me in a strange way. As my wife and I ate the food that was prepared to for us nobody in the room spoke at all. I finally worked up enough courage to speak to the brother who was on my left. I simply asked the man if this happened very often?

He replied, **"Does what happen very often?"**

I said, **"Where all the people suddenly as one fall on the floor and start praying, crying and weeping?**

" He looked at me as if something was wrong. **He told me they had never seen or experienced anything like this before in their church services".**

This had been a divine move of the Holy Ghost that came about as I was preaching on being completely sold out to **Jesus Christ.** The end results of this meeting were that the leadership of this church was so moved that they offered my wife and me to become their pastors. They told us that our financial needs were not to be concerned about because one of the brothers was an oil tycoon. I told them that I could not speak German, and therefore I would not make a good pastor.

They said this would be no problem because they would provide an interpreter into I became fluent in their language. I got quiet before the Lord and asked him whether I should accept this offer?

The Lord very strongly spoke to my heart and said: No, I have other plans for you, and as it is not for you to pastor this church. I informed them that I could not accept their offer, but that I was truly grateful and humbled by their request.

And why call ye me, Lord, Lord, and do not the things which I say?(Luke 6:46).

The Angels Catcher Mitt

My Family and I Were Saved from Certain Death by Angels While on a Motorcycle! (1983)

My wife and I were pastoring two churches. One church was in Gettysburg, Pennsylvania and the other one in Chambers-burg, Pennsylvania. My wife was about seven months pregnant with our second son, Daniel, when this event I'm telling you about took place. (I have three sons. From the first day that we were married, I always said to my wife, "Mike and his three sons.")

We were out one-day doing house visitation to some of our parishioners. This really sounds stupid, but it's true. My wife, my son Michael, and I were all on a Honda 450. Of course, I was in the front of the motorcycle driving. Michael, who was two years old, was in the middle. Close behind him was Daniel and Kathee.

(Danny was still in a protective bubble called a womb). Thank God there was a sissy bar behind Kathee. We had been visiting a family from the church near Roxbury, Pennsylvania. After we had spent some wonderful time with this family, we got on the motorcycle and headed home.

We were now headed home on 997, or Black Gap Road headed for Highway 30. The sun was just beginning to set, and it was glaring in my eyes. I was looking for a shortcut that I knew about. This shortcut was a dirt road. (I'm notorious for my shortcuts). As I was going along, I finally saw it to my right, and so I thought.

It was getting dark, in the last fading light of the sun was shining in my eyes so I could not see the road very clearly. I slowed up a little bit, and then turned off onto this dirt road was a shortcut, and would save me a little bit of time. I was probably doing about forty-five miles an hour. The speed limit through this area on 997 was fifty-five, and I usually always try to stay at the upper end, endeavoring to keep the law.

However, when I turned off on this shortcut, I discovered to my absolute horror and dismay that this was not the shortcut road that I was looking for. It was a very shallow area that was long and narrow created for semi-trucks to pull over in case of emergencies. Now right in front of us were three major obstacles: #1 a heavy-duty steel guard rail, #2 a large pile of big rocks, #3 and a large wooden light pole.

These obstacles were only about twenty feet in front of us. I knew instantly there was no way I could ever stop. Slamming on your brakes in the gravel in the dirt at 45 miles an hour, trying to stop within 20 feet, with four people on the bike is not at all a good idea.

Even if I would have laid the motorcycle over on its side, we would still slam into these items at forty-five to fifty miles an hour.

It was clear with an overwhelming clarity that we were going to hit the rocks, guard rail, and telephone pole. I knew in my heart that in the natural my precious wife with our unborn child, and my two-year-old son Michael was possibly going to be not just extremely hurt but killed. I was not at all concerned about myself now.

Now, I did not even have time to put on my brakes because this happens so fast. I just simply cried out JESUS! (I know that what I'm about to tell you will sound insane, but this is what truly happened.) At the very moment I cried out JESUS, it felt like two large hands pressed against us on both sides, left and right.

I mean literally I could feel tremendous pressure, (and yet it was soft and gentle) to the left and the right of my body. Now, we were still heading for the rocks, but then we instantly stopped, I mean INSTANTLY. It literally felt like we had either run into a big, invisible, enormous heavenly fluffy pillow, or a very large and soft baseball catcher's glove. There was nothing visible in front of us to stop us. We simply ran into some invisible supernatural force.

We were completely stopped, and for a moment we were standing upright. We simply fell over on our right side. We fell over onto the gravel and rocks, but we really did not fall unto them. I know this sounds far-fetched, weird and strange. But it was like we fell onto another enormous heavenly and fluffy pillow! We fell into something extremely soft between us and the ground.

Now here we are laying in the dirt and gravel with an overwhelming peace, and even joy was upon us. What a miracle! Little Michael wasn't even crying; I think he was laying in between us sucking his thumb, as he liked to do. As we look back to the road, we notice there were no skid marks in the dirt whatsoever.

It simply showed our tire tracks coming up to the place where we were, and then right there our bike stopped instantly. I looked at my wife, and she looked at me. We were both in shock, and yet great joy and peace came upon us. Then my wife informed me that just before we had arrived at this area on 997, she had seen two large pillars of light fire, one to the left of us, and one to the right.

Kathee's Interjection:

Right before the accident I remember going through a little town which had no lights, but I saw two pillars of white fire, one right to our left, and one right to our right. The pillars were like brilliant, white laser lights shooting towards the heavens. I realized at that moment that they were two angels of God! I began crying and praising God while on the back of that motorcycle even before the accident.

I was thanking God for His protection and goodness as we were headed down 997, with little Mikey sitting between my wonderful husband. I was still praising God when I noticed that we had turned off onto a dead-end path. I knew in my heart that we were going to crash. HOWEVER, I had and an overwhelming peace.

Everything happened so quickly that I knew God was indeed with us! The next thing I knew we were laying on the sand, gravel, and rocks.

As we laid on the ground, the presence of God was so real and so thick that you could have cut it with a knife. Michael and I just laid on the ground crying, talking, and thanking God for his wonderful mercy and protection.

It was like we did not want to get up because it was such a holy moment. I do not remember for how long we laid there, but it was for some time. It was like we were just laying before the throne of our heavenly Father enjoying a precious moment with him.

And the angel of God, which went before the camp of Israel, removed and went behind them; and the pillar of the cloud went from before their face, and stood behind them: and it came between the camp of the Egyptians and the camp of Israel; and it was a cloud and darkness to them, but it gave light by night to these: so that the one came not near the other all the night (Exodus 14:19-20).

Go on TV audible voice

Right after my wife gave birth to Daniel, we had some good friends come and stay with us. They were our spiritual parents to an extent. Mary was helping my wife clean the house and care for Michael. I basically stayed out of their way. While they were cleaning the kitchen, I was upstairs in my **prayer** room spending time with the Lord in **prayer** and meditating on the Word. When I was finished, I got up and started to come down the stairs.

As I was coming downstairs, I heard the audible voice of God. This is what He said to me, and I quote, **"Go on TV!"** That's what I heard. The audible voice of God was so real, that I instantly fell to my knees. I said, "Lord, the church does not have the money to put me on TV!" Then He began to communicate with me in His still quiet voice. He spoke to my heart and said, **the church will not pay for your TV time. You will believe and trust Me for it!** I said, Yes, Lord! He then quickened to my heart that the first TV station I would be on would be Channel 25 out of Hagerstown, Maryland. The Spirit literally informed me about the specific time I would be on would be Sunday Mornings at 6:30 a.m. Once again, I told the Lord I would obey Him.

Now my wife is always very supportive of me. (Or maybe I should say she never tries to stop me!) She is a real trooper. In fact, she is so much of a trooper that she was up and about within twenty minutes of giving birth to Daniel.

After the Lord had finished speaking to me, I went downstairs to share this with her. When I told her this, she became very upset with me. I believe part of the reason is because financially we were already in need of some miracles. We did not even have money for fuel oil to heat our house. We probably only had enough fuel oil for one more day.

She was so upset with me that she went and told Mary. (Mary, by the way is an aggressive pioneer woman. To date, Mary and her husband Paul have done many wonderful works in other countries and in America. She is a mother of the faith. I'm sure it did not help that my wife was distraught and had just given birth to Daniel.)

My Wife Extremely Upset

When I entered the kitchen, Mary cornered me. She tried to speak some sense into me. She basically skinned me alive! Of course, I didn't blame Mary or my wife, but I had heard from God!

Humble yourselves therefore under the mighty hand of God, that he may exalt you in due time: Casting all your care upon him; for he careth for you (1 Peter 5:6-7).

Channel 25 Hagerstown Just for you

After hearing the Lord telling me to go on TV, the very next day I called Channel 25, WHAG in Hagerstown, Maryland, asking to be transferred over to their sales department. When someone else answered the phone, I told this person that I was interested in purchasing a half-hour slot on their channel. I did not tell them what day of the week or time I wanted.

I simply said that I was going to produce a half-hour program. (How I was going to produce these programs I did not know). The sales personnel was a lady who informed me that they did not have any time available, and did not know when another slot would be available. I asked her if she would go to their programming department and discuss with them if there was anything they could do. She said she would, even though she thought it would not make any difference because they had no time available.

Approximately three days later, the sales personnel called me back, telling me that they had called a special meeting to discuss my request. She informed me that normally they do not have their TV station on the air until seven o'clock on Sunday mornings, but they had unanimously agreed to bring their station on the air at 6:30 a.m. just for me! From the very first day of our broadcast we had a tremendous response. All the finances that we needed to stay on the air came in.

Eventually, we were on seven TV stations one day a week. Then I was on with Dr. Lester Sumrall's network five days a week. Dr. Sumrall later came to our church and ministered for us. Until the day Dr. Sumrall died, my ordination papers were with him and his ministry.

CHAPTER SIX

Jesus said: Tell My Children Who They Are

I was standing in my office during **prayer** one day looking towards the east, which was nothing but my office wall. To my shock and amazement, Jesus Christ stepped right through the wall and into my office! This happened so fast that it frightened me. I was only about four feet away from this wall. When He stepped into my room, He did not say a word to me, but just kept walking right toward me.

Pauls Prayer: *Ephesians 1:17 That the God of our Lord Jesus Christ, the Father of glory, may give unto you the spirit of wisdom and revelation in the knowledge of him:18 The eyes of your understanding being enlightened; that ye may know what is the hope of his calling, and what the riches of the glory of his inheritance in the saints,19 And what is the exceeding greatness of his power to us-ward who believe, ….*

The next thing I knew, Jesus walked right into my body. It was one of the strangest experiences I have ever had. My body did not resist in the least. It was as if my body was made for Him to dwell in. It was almost like when someone comes home to their house, opens the door, and simply steps in. When Jesus stepped into me, His face would've been looking out of the back of my head. I know this is hard to believe, but I literally felt Him turn around inside of me.

His arms and hands went into my arms and hands. His legs and feet went into my legs and feet. The moment Jesus was in His proper position, I instantly grew a hundred feet tall!

I was gigantic in size. My head and half of my body were outside of the building I was in and I was looking down upon everything. My whole being was filled with amazing power, authority, and knowledge. All the problems and difficulties of this world were to be laughed at compared to the One who was within me. All of creation itself could not compare to Him!

As fast as it had begun, it was over. The next thing I knew, I was back to normal size. Then the Spirit of the Lord spoke something to me that would change the course of my life forever. He said to me, Go tell my children who they are! They know not who they are! The reason so many Christians walk around defeated is because they've never had a quickening of the Spirit, which brings revelation of who Christ really is. They do not realize that the same Jesus who overcame principalities and powers, rulers of darkness, and spiritual wickedness in high places now lives in us. The very one who brought all things into existence now lives in side of us. Christ in us the hope of glory!

Pastors Life on the Line

The company providing the steel for our building called from South Dakota, telling us that the steel building was almost ready to be shipped. They said they could ship it: cash on delivery. When the building arrived, I would have to give them approximately **$49,000**. At the time, we only had **$1,000** in our building account - with no other means of finances. The representative from the steel company also informed us they could store the building for about $1,200 a month, or they could ship it out within six to eight weeks.

As I was listening to the man over the phone, I heard the Spirit of the Lord say to me: *"Tell them to send it!"* I became very still before the Lord, because I wanted to make sure that I had heard Him correctly. The Spirit spoke to me again: *"Tell them to send it!"* I told the man from the steel company to go ahead and send the building! He told me that would be fine, and they would prepare it to be sent.

He also informed me that I'd better be aware that if the building arrived, and I did not have the money, I would be breaking interstate laws (I believe he said there were five of them) and I would be going to jail: because I was the one who gave the approval for the building to be shipped! I got very quiet before the Lord and asked Him again, *"What I should do?"* The Spirit, once again, confirmed and quickened in my heart, to have them send it. So, once again, I told the representative to go ahead and send it. He gave me another warning.

The **Gift of Faith** was operating in my heart. I knew that it was done. After I got off the phone, a desire came into my heart to give away the **$1,000** in our building account. I was not trying to bribe God to do something for us. The **$1,000** we had was not going to do a thing for us, so why not give it away - out of faith? We took that thousand dollars and divided it up into ten different checks, sending it to ten different ministries.

That Sunday, I went before the congregation and told them this story. I told them the steel was coming, and if they wanted to, they could get involved. I also told them we had invested **$1,000** into ten other ministries. I did inform the congregation that if I was missing God, in this regard, I was going to have a prison ministry. I had put my life on the line …

Amazingly, I had no fear or anxiety whatsoever during the six weeks leading up to the steel arriving. Without any doubt, I knew the money would be there. The finances began to trickle in. To this day, I do not remember where it all came from. I did not beg, plead, or call anybody for money.

I received a phone call approximately six weeks later from the representative of the steel company. They told me that they were loading the steel up on their big trucks, and asked, was I ready to receive it? At that point we were still extremely short of the finances we needed. I told them to go ahead and send it. Within three days the truck pulled onto our property.

I met the truck driver at the construction site and he handed me the paperwork. There were certain documents which I had to fill out. I started filling out the paperwork, knowing that I was still **$15,000** short of the **$49,000** that I had to pay them in just a few short moments. As I was signing the papers, one of the men from our church pulled into the parking lot. He drove his car right up to me with his window rolled down. I could see that there was something in his right hand; he handed a check to me for **$15,000**! Thank you, Jesus!

I would just like to take a moment and tell you that the people in this story, who gave of their finances, were operating in a higher level of faith than I was. That may sound strange … but it's not. We're always exalting those who believe for the money. But what about the ones who make these sacrifices to give what they have? I have been on both sides of this equation, more times than I can count. I have both given - until it hurt - and gladly received, with unspeakable joy.

Not that I speak in respect of want: for I have learned, in whatsoever state I am, therewith to be content. I know both how to be abased, and I know how to abound: everywhere and in all things I am instructed both to be full and to be hungry, both to abound and to suffer need. I can do all things through Christ which strengtheneth me (Philippians 4:11-13).

Supernatural Education

We had approximately thirty volunteer men assembled, to help put the steel of the building up. Men who did not attend our church came to help us. The majority were not construction workers in any fashion of the word. The Lord had put in our hearts to use volunteers to get the job done. The man we had gone through, to purchase the steel building, was to oversee this work, and was there with us.

He had been consistent all the time. He helped us do the footers and concrete piers, and he did excellent quality work. The large crane we needed to put all the steel up was on the property, with its operator. I think the cost of the crane and the operator was over $150 an hour. The big machine was idling and waiting to go to work. Everyone was standing there waiting to work.

We all bombarded the leader with questions and asked for directions. He had the blueprints in his hands, and every time he went to look at them someone would approach him. The pressure on him was overwhelming. It was easy to see that he was getting extremely frustrated.

From what I understand, he had not put up a building like this before, and if he had it was many years ago. More and more people kept tugging on him. Next thing I knew, one of the brothers from the church said: "Pastor Mike! There goes so and so!" I looked to see where he was pointing. Sure enough, there was the leader, going down the road in his automobile. I did not hear from him, or see him again, for quite a number of years.

At the time of construction, it seemed as if this was a satanic attack. Actually, I can now say what Joseph said, that although this situation seemed as if it was meant for evil: God meant it for good. The Lord was stretching our faith. There I was, standing in front of all of the volunteer men, who were waiting to go to work.

The steel was lying on the ground and the crane was idling. I can still remember walking away from everybody, looking up to heaven, and crying out to God. I said: "***Lord, please show me how*** *to put this building up. I had never even built a doghouse, let alone a large steel commercial building!"*

At that moment, it was as if an invisible blanket came down upon me. Wisdom entered into my heart and I knew instantly what to do: moment by moment. I grabbed the blueprints, walked towards the crane operator, and began to tell him where to put the steel. The building began to go up! Through the process, we lost volunteers and gained volunteers. The Lord began to send us skilled labor. Not much of it … but just enough! Within three months we were in our brand-new facility. Within three months we were in our brand-new facility.

Except the LORD build the house, they labour in vain that build it: except the LORD keep the city, the watchman waketh but in vain (Psalms 127:1)..

Terrible Warts Gone Over Night

A poverty-stricken couple began to come to our church. We watched as Jesus set this couple free from drugs, alcohol, violence, and immorality. We helped install a new bathroom in their little house. The wife became one of the main workers in the church. She was always there trying to help people.

One day they brought one of their young daughters to us. They told us she had a problem they did not know how to resolve. They had taken her to the doctor, but there didn't seem to be anything they could do. The girl was hiding behind them so her mother brought her to the front. Then she had the girl hold out her little hand. It was terrible.

Her little hand was completely covered with warts front and back. We are not talking about twenty or thirty warts. It literally looked like hundreds of warts. We laid our hands on her little hand. We then commanded these foul warts to come off of her hand in the name of Jesus Christ of Nazareth, and for her hand to be completely healed.

As we looked at her hand, it did not seem as if anything happened. We told them that when you pray in faith, you must believe that those things you asked for in faith are done. We explained that what we need to do is begin to thank God that she is healed—that the warts are gone in the name of Jesus. Both the husband and the wife agreed that it was done. They took their little girl, got in their car, and left.

The next morning, I received a phone call from the mother. She was extremely excited and bursting with happiness. She told us that when her little girl went to bed that night nothing had changed. The warts were just as bad as ever.

When she went to get her the next morning, every single wart was gone but one. They brought the little girl back to us to look at her hand. Sure enough, in one-night God had removed every single wart but one, which was in the palm of her hand! The skin on her hand was smooth and normal just like the other one, as smooth as baby skin. We declared that the last remaining wart would have to leave also!

Flew My Plane into the High Lines

I was in the midst of receiving my airplane license. I had finished ground school and had completed all of my cross country flying. One day I was at the York airport doing simple go-arounds (That's where you land and you just keep going after you land, and take back off again).

I later found out that the Spirit of God had quickened my wife and told her to pray for me. She had already been really upset at me for wasting all of this money on flying. The Lord told her that if she did not forgive me and get her heart right, I was going to die. She repented, and cried out to God, and said, "Lord, I give it to you. Please protect him."

Everything seemed to be going okay as I did go-arounds, but as I was getting ready to land, the wind shifted to another direction. They called me from the tower and told me that they felt it should still be okay to stay in the same pattern one more time; and that the next time around I could land in the opposite direction.

As I made my approach for the runway I began to meticulously go through all of the processes of making a proper landing: I lowered my flaps, turned on my carburetor deicer, and began to bring my airspeed down to where I would be landing at about forty mph. I was still about 30 feet above the runway. Everything seemed perfectly normal.

As I began to pull back on the yoke to flare the plane, all of a sudden my speed indicator dropped to zero. As a young pilot, I did not realize what this meant. It was an indication that the wind was now coming in from behind me. This meant I had just lost all of my lift. I dropped like a rock and my plane slammed into the runway. I hit the runway very hard. I pulled back on the yoke.

The minute I slammed into the runway, I bounced back up into the air like a basketball. I made a terrible mistake: instead of going around, once again I pulled back on the yoke and tried to land my plane. Once again I dropped like a rock, slamming just as hard into the runway as the last time. Not being very intelligent, I tried to land once again. This time when I bounced I was really in trouble.

Now my plane was completely turned away from the runway. There was nothing but a grassy field ahead of me with electrical power lines. I gave the little Cessna 152 full power. I kept my flaps down, in take-off position. Yet, I made another major mistake by keeping my carburetor deicer on. This means, I did not have the full horsepower of my engine.

Now, I was headed right for the power lines! My airspeed was barely enough to keep me in the air. I knew that I could not turn away from the power lines. If I tried to turn away I was a dead man. Moreover, I knew that I didn't have enough skill to fly underneath them. In addition, I knew that I could not get over the top of them. If I pulled back too much on the yoke, it would cause the plane to go higher, but it would drop like a rock again, because my speed was way too slow.

At that very moment I knew I was a dead man. My whole life flashed in front of me in a matter of seconds. My heart was filled with thankfulness to God for all the wonderful things He had done for me in my life, for giving me my precious wife and four beautiful children. The second thing that hit me was tremendous sorrow and regret: I would never see my beautiful wife, Kathleen, again in this world—I would never be able to hold her in my arms, never be able to hold my three sons and precious little girl to my chest.

I desperately wanted to get on the radio and tell the tower operators to tell my wife and my children that I was so very sorry and that I loved them beyond expression. I wanted to tell my wife and kids that I wished I could be there to see them graduate from school and one day get married—to see my precious girl walking down the aisle to stand at the side of her groom. But **my time had run out**. I did not have time to say my good-byes. I was headed straight for the power lines.

As I approached my certain death, these electrical power lines filled my eyes. It was if the wires were magnified in size. They looked to be six inches wide in diameter. They filled the windshield of my plane.

I realize that the wires are not anywhere near that size, but as I approached them, that's how I saw them. At that moment, all I could do was cry out for Jesus. The next thing I knew, I was through the power lines. I went right through them! I did not go underneath them, and I did not go over the top of them.

As I flew my plane straight ahead, I was overwhelmed with amazement, thankfulness, and tremendous joy. I kept rehearsing over and over in my mind what had just happened. Could it really be? Did I really go through the power lines? I know I did. I was headed right into the wires. Amazing! The tower kept calling out to me over the radio, "Mike, are you there? Are you okay? Please answer!"

They had, to some extent, seen what happened. When they finally got me to respond, all they could get out of me was, "Thank You Jesus! Thank you Jesus! Thank you Jesus!" The airport radio frequency at that time was also picked up by three other airports. All the traffic controllers and radio personnel on that frequency heard me say over and over, "Thank you Jesus!"

After I landed, the mechanical personnel took the plane into the hangar. They had seen me slamming into the runway. In their thoughts, there is no way that this plane did not have structural damage. They went over it with a fine-toothed comb. Amazingly, they came back with a report that everything was absolutely fine.

(2 Chronicles 7:3).And when all the children of Israel saw how the Þre came down, and the glory of the LORD upon the house, they bowed themselves with their faces to the ground upon the pavement, and worshipped, and praised the LORD, saying, For he is good; for his mercy endureth for ever.

Kathleen's perspective:

My husband had disappeared early in the morning. He probably told me where he was going while I was still asleep, but I never remembered. As the day went on, I decided to call his cell phone to Þgure out where he was. After several futile calls, I called Debra, Mike's sister, who worked in our church ofÞce at the time.

Upon hearing that he had gone for flying lessons, my anger began to rise. My thoughts were, ***Who does he think he is, going off and spending thousands of dollars on flying lessons, when we have enough bills to pay, and we need things for the house, the children, and me!***

Immediately, the Spirit of God arrested me and rebuked me. Within my spirit came, *which is more important, the money, or your husband's life?* Brokenness clenched my soul, and I quickly repented. Asking God to forgive me for my selfishness, I told the Lord that my husband was more important than millions of dollars, and that the money wasn't worth Mike's life!

The devil had lost the battle to keep me bitter and unforgiving and the unity between us, as husband and wife, was not broken. Directly, a spirit of fear tried to grip my heart, and I knew that fear was another tool of the devil to bring division and destruction. An urgency to pray and to stand in faith made me stop everything!

To this day, I remember where I was sitting when I began to pray: right at our kitchen bar. As I sat on the bar stool reiterating my repentance of selfishness, I implored the Lord to spare Mike's life, keep him safe, and bring him back to me and the children. Little did I know that I was truly pleading for my husband's life!

Through my tears, I remember boldly declaring, "Lord, You've given Your angels charge over us, to keep us in all of our ways, even in our stupidity." My declaration continued, "In our pathway is life and there is no death. So, Father, I put Michael in your hands.

"I know you'll bring him home safely."

At this point, I made a covenant in my heart. I made my stand, "I trust You, Lord, because there is no one else to trust. If, I can't trust You to keep Mike safe, then I can trust no one. Thank You for bringing my husband back to me!" I refused to give into bitterness, fear, or worry. My hope was in the Lord who is always faithful.

The devil had lost the fight on my side to cause division, bitterness, anger, fear, and lack of peace. I did not fail to repent and intercede for my husband when the Spirit of God dealt with me. God's grace had helped me through the test. God's faith had brought victory and brought my husband home alive. When Mike came through the door of our home that day, he told me of his near-fatal flight.

My response was, "If the Lord hadn't dealt with my heart, you might have eaten those power lines!" I embraced Mike with a thankful heart and a grace in my heart towards the Lord's goodness and mercy. God surely knew what He was doing in both of our lives to keep us under His protection. If I had given into bitterness and fear, or failed to intercede and stand in faith, I may not have my husband today!

Be ye angry, and sin not: let not the sun go down upon your wrath: Neither give place to the devil (Ephesians 4:26-27).

God's Got Your Number

From Kens Gobs own words: I was driving on 1-75 near Dayton, Ohio, with my wife and children in our coach bus. We turned off the highway for a rest and refreshment stop. My wife Barbara and children went into the restaurant. I suddenly felt the need to stretch my legs, so waved them off ahead saying I'd join them later. I bought a soft drink, and as I walked toward a Dairy Queen, feelings of self-pity enshrouded my mind. I loved the Lord and my ministry, but I felt drained, burdened. My cup was empty.

Suddenly the impatient ringing of a telephone nearby jarred me out of my doldrums. It was coming from a phone booth at a service station on the corner. Wasn't anyone going to answer the phone? Noise from the traffic flowing through the busy intersection must have drowned out the sound because the service station attendant continued looking after his customers, oblivious to the ringing. ."Why doesn't somebody answer that phone?" I muttered. .I began reasoning. It may be important. What if it's an emergency? Curiosity overcame my indifference. I stepped inside the booth and picked up the phone..

"Hello," I said casually and took a big sip of my drink. The operator said: "Long distance call for Ken Gaub. "My eyes widened, and I almost choked on a chunk of ice. Swallowing hard, I said, "You're crazy!" Then realizing I shouldn't speak to an operator like that, I added, "This can't be! I was walking down the road, not bothering anyone, and the phone was ringing... "Is Ken Gaub there?" the operator interrupted, "I have a long distance call for him. "It took a moment to gain control of my babbling, but I finally replied, "Yes, he is here. "Searching for a possible explanation, I wondered if I could possibly be on Candid Camera!

Still shaken, perplexed, I asked, "How in the world did you reach me here? I was walking down the road, the pay phone started ringing, and I just answered it on chance. You can't mean me.". "Well," the operator asked, "Is Mr. Gaub there or isn't he?" "Yes, I am Ken Gaub," I said, finally convinced by the tone of her voice that the call was real. Then I heard another voice say, "Yes, that's him, operator. That's Ken Gaub. I listened dumbfounded to a strange voice identify herself. "I'm Millie from Harrisburg, Pennsylvania. You don't know me, Mr. Gaub, but I'm desperate. Please help me." "What can I do for you?".

She began weeping. Finally she regained control and continued. "I was about to commit suicide, had just finished writing a note, when I began to pray and tell God I really didn't want to do this. Then I suddenly remembered seeing you on television and thought if I could just talk to you, you could help me.

I knew that was impossible because I didn't know how to reach you, I didn't know anyone who could help me find you. Then some numbers came to my mind, and I scribbled them down.".
At this point she began weeping again, and I prayed silently for wisdom to help her. She continued, "I looked at the numbers and thought, 'Wouldn't it be wonderful if I had a miracle from God, and He has given me Ken's phone number?'.

I decided to try calling it. I can't believe I'm talking to you. "Are you in your office in California? "I replied, "Lady, I don't have an office in California. My office is in Yakima, Washington. "A little surprised, she asked, "Oh really, then where are you?" "Don't you know?" I responded. "You made the call." She explained, "But I don't even know what area I'm calling. I just dialed the number that I had on this paper.". "Ma'am, you won't believe this, but I'm in a phone booth in Dayton, Ohio!" "Really?" she exclaimed. "Well, what are you doing there?" I kidded her gently, "Well, I'm answering the phone. It was ringing as I walked by, so I answered it. "Knowing this encounter could only have been arranged by God, I began to counsel the woman. As she told me of her despair and frustration, the presence of the Holy Spirit flooded the phone booth giving me words beyond my ability. In a matter of moments, she prayed the sinner's prayer and met the One who would lead her out of her situation into a new life.

I walked away from that telephone booth with an electrifying sense of our Heavenly Father's concern for each of His children. What were the astronomical odds of this happening? With all the millions of phones and innumerable combinations of numbers, only an all-knowing God could have caused that woman to call that number in that phone booth at that moment in time. Forgetting my drink and nearly bursting with exhilaration, I headed back to my family, wondering if they would believe my story. Maybe I better not tell this, I thought, but I couldn't contain it. "Barb, you won't believe this! God knows where I am!"

To the Rescue on a Snowmobile

We had very heavy snowfall this particular winter. I owned an old John Dear snowmobile that I had made available to the local fire department if they ever needed my help. Eventually, they called me up during a terrible winter storm telling me that they had a heavy equipment operator that needed to be transported to Orrtanna.PA.

He first needed to be picked up at his house and then delivered about 6 miles away. I informed them I would be more than willing to do this for them, especially because I love adventures. Actually, I am a snow addict. I can never get enough snow. The snowstorm and sleet had not yet abated and was raging in all its fury. I told my wife Kathleen that the fire department had called with a job for me to do.

Mike to the rescue, or so I thought. I dressed up in all my winter trappings. I then went out and brushed the snow off my John Dear snowmobile and laid my hands on it, commanding it not to give me any problems. I should have prayed over myself first. I started the old machine up, revving the throttle as I headed out of the church parking lot. I turned to my right going down the deserted, main highway. There I was, having the time of my life and doing it for the fire department!

Received Healing for a Busted Kneecap

Mike to the rescue, or so I thought. I dressed up in all my winter trappings. I then went out and brushed the snow off my John Dear snowmobile and laid my hands on it, commanding it not to give me any problems. I should have prayed over myself first.

I started the old machine up, revving the throttle as I headed out of the church parking lot. I turned to my right going down the deserted, main highway. There I was, having the time of my life and doing it for the fire department! Here I was doing about 50 miles an hour or faster, when I hit a section that was nothing but black ice.

The snowmobile's back end spun to the right out of control. I went flying through the air as it threw me for a lopper. I slammed my right kneecap extremely hard on the asphalt road. I felt my kneecap rip, break and tear as I kept sliding down the road for quite a distance. The snowmobile had continued on its way, spinning out of control.

The snowmobile itself eventually stopped because my hand was no longer cranking the throttle. Fortunately, it was not damaged because there was nothing but snow in every direction. There I was, lying on the road in the snow and freezing wind, clutching my busted up knee, alone and in tremendous pain! Immediately, I cried out to Jesus and repented for being so stupid and for not using Godly wisdom.

My theology is that almost everything that goes wrong in my life is usually my own stupid fault. Even if the devil is involved in it, it is most likely because I first opened the door for him. After I was done repenting and confessing to the Lord, I went aggressively after my healing. I commanded my kneecap to be put back into its normal condition in the name of Jesus Christ of Nazareth. I commanded every broken part of it to be made whole. You see, I could grab my patella and move it all around. It was no longer attached to my knee. It seemed to have become completely disconnected, no longer restrained by its associated ligaments.

Probably at this juncture, most people would have called it quits when it comes to completing the mission they set out on. But that is not my mode of operation. If I declared that I was healed then I needed to act upon it. I discovered a truth a long time ago, God cannot lie!

So, I slowly crawled back over to my snow machine and pulled myself back into the seat. I painfully swung my right leg over the seat into its proper position. At that very moment, wave after wave of pain overwhelmed me. Years of experience walking in faith, however, caused me to declare that I am healed in the name of Jesus. In the name of Jesus, I am healed. I opened the throttle and proceeded on the way to pick up the equipment operator. I kept proclaiming the truth.

On the way, there were a lot of areas where my snowmobile just would not go. The snow was way too deep in some areas to go or the road was flooded with water in others. The storm had dumped a combination of rain, ice and snow. One would need a boat to go through some of the areas where I went. Admittedly, at times I took chances that I should not have taken. I would accelerate to a high speed and just zip across the flooded areas.

The back end of the snowmobile would begin to sink as if I wasn't going to make it. But, I would constantly revert back to the old trusted declaration: In the name of Jesus, in the name of Jesus, in the name of Jesus, I will make it. There are a lot of wonderful messages preached on faith but that's not what wins the victory. It is when the Word has been quickened in your heart that you know, that you know, that you know, that you know that God and His Word are true.

I cannot describe to you enough the immense pain and agony that I was going through, yet I did not merely think that I was healed, I knew that I was healed! Faith is not thinking, hoping, or wishing. It is knowing that you know, that you know, that you know. I finally reached my first destination. The township worker saw me pull up outside of his house. As he came to the machine, he could not see my face because of my helmet and my ski mask. I did not tell him that I had an accident and possibly shattered my kneecap.

I do not adhere to bragging about the devil or his shenanigans, lies or deceptions. This was no little man that I had to carry on the back of my machine either. He mounted up and we were on our way. It took major faith to keep on going. We had to take numerous detours before I finally got him to the big earthmover that he was tasked to operate. He jumped off my snowmobile and thanked me for the ride. I told him it was no problem as I opened up the throttle and headed home.

This time, I decided to take a different route because the last route was so bad. It took all the faith that I could muster to get back to the parsonage. I was cold, wet, tired and completely overwhelmed with pain from the shattered knee. When I got home, I just kept thanking God that I was healed. During the next couple of days, I refused to pamper my leg. I did not put any ice or heat upon it.

I did not take any kind of medication or painkillers. I did not call anyone asking them to please pray for me and to believe God for my healing. I know this may seem extremely stupid, but I knew in my heart that I was healed. It has got to be in your heart! My head, my body and my throbbing, busted kneecap were all telling me that I was not healed, but let God's Word be true and every symptom a lie. When the next Sunday rolled around, the roads were clear enough for people to make it to church.

During that time, you might have called me Hop-Along Cassidy because of the way that I was walking. I do not deny the problem, but I sure as heaven denied the right for it to exist! One of our parishioners, who was a nurse, saw me limping badly. She asked me what happened and I told her. She informed me that this was a major problem. She tried to explain to me in medical terms exactly what she thought I had done to my knee.

Medically, in order to reattach and repair my patella, I would have to endure at least one major surgical procedure. She recounted to me that she had once had a similar injury although it was nowhere near as bad as mine. She went on to elaborate that even after an extensive operation, her knee was still giving her major problems. I thanked her for this information and went back to trusting and believing that by the stripes of Jesus Christ, I was healed.

I sure as heaven was not going to let go or to give up on God's promises. I wrestled with this situation day after day, commanding my knee to be healed and to function as God had designed it to do. When the pain would overwhelm me, I would tell it to shut up, be quiet and work! When it seemed like my leg would not carry me, I would command it to be strong in the name of Jesus.

This went on for well over a month. One morning I crawled out of bed and my knee cap was perfectly healed. You would think that when the healing manifested that I would begin to sing, shout and dance, but I did not and I do not! You see I had already done all of my rejoicing in advance because I believe that the minute I prayed, I received!

19 God is not a man, that He should lie; neither the son of man that he should repent: hath He said, and shall He not do it? or hath He spoken, and shall He not make it good? Num 23:19

A Reprobate and an Outlaw

One Sunday morning, the Spirit of God moved in a powerful way. Many people came forward to be prayed for. In the prayer line was a young evangelist who had been attending our church for some time. This morning the spirit of prophecy was flowing. When I came to this young man, I laid my hands upon him, he immediately fell under the power of God. I continued to go down the line ministering to the people. When I was about three people down from him the Spirit of God took a hold of me. I found myself back at this man's feet. I ended up straddling him with my left foot on his right side, and my right foot on his left side.

Then I reached down and grabbed his shirt with my left hand. With my right hand I began to slap his face very hard. I must have slapped him at least five times, on both sides of his cheeks. When I was done slapping him, I went back to praying for the other people. After a brief period, the Spirit of God took me back to him once again. I spoke by the Spirit of God to him. The Spirit of the Lord told him, "Even as my servant has slapped your flesh, so you must slap your flesh. If you do not crucify your flesh, you will become a reprobate and a fugitive from the law!"

When the Spirit of God moves upon me that strong sometimes, I do not even completely remember the things that I say. After the service, I did not consider what had happened.

Three days later I received a phone call from one of the ladies in the church. She was weeping and said that her twenty some year old daughter had ran away with this particular evangelist, and that previously he had been having a sexual relationship with another lady in our church. I prayed with her over the phone.

Approximately one month later I received another phone call from this same lady. She informed me that this man had beaten her daughter, and that they had gone out one-night drinking, when they were pulled over by a policeman. This evangelist got in an argument with the officer, which ended up with him physically fighting this policeman. Before he knew what, he was doing, he had grabbed the police officer's revolver out of his holster and aimed the gun at the cop. He then left her daughter and the police officer, and ran for his life. Supposedly, he was headed for Canada. The last time I had heard, he was a fugitive of the law.

I therefore so run, not as uncertainly; so fight I, not as one that beateth the air: But I keep under my body, and bring it into subjection: lest that by any means, when I have preached to others, I myself should be a castaway (1 Corinthians 9:26-27).

Holy Ghost Falls in Wales

A good friend of mine who has gone to be home with the Lord, (Malcolm White) use to set up my meetings in Great Britain! He had me go to a church that was not Pentecostal, but did not tell me this!

I was preaching once in a very old rustic church in Wales. The church was filled with many elderly people the night I was there. I think they were celebrating eighty-nine years of ministry since the founding of the church. There were approximately thirty to forty people in the service.

These people looked to me as if they could have all been there at the founding of the church. (Maybe they did not look quite that old.) Their pastor was a young Spirit-filled man who I had spent the afternoon fellowshipping with. That's where I made my mistake.

Knowing that this pastor was Spirit-filled and excited about Jesus, I reasonably thought that this whole church had come into the experience of the Holy Ghost. I was about to find out that I was wrong! A very strong stirring of the Spirit gripped my heart, I preached with fire and compassion in the Holy Ghost.

As I was finishing the message, the Spirit quickened me and the word of knowledge began to flow. As I looked over the congregation, I could see what was specifically wrong in people's bodies. This does not always happen, but it is wonderful when it does.

I began to call specific people out of their chairs. They all seemed to be a little bit hesitant to come forward. I thought maybe they were simply timid. (The Welsh people tend to be that way.) I kept encouraging them to come as I called them. The first person I called was a little old lady. As she came towards me, she crumpled right to the floor about ten feet away.

This seemed to cause quite a commotion. These old men jumped up and began to hobble their way over to her. I told them that she was okay and that it was the Spirit of God upon her, making her whole. Then I called out another person to come forward. This man came hesitantly towards me. At about ten feet away from me, without me touching him, or waving my hands at him, he crumpled to the floor. The same old men who were trying to get this lady up divided into two groups now. One group came over to try to help the older gentleman.

As I continued to minister, more people were falling under the power. I was having a wonderful time. I was excited! God was really moving in a spectacular way in this meeting. But something seemed to be seriously wrong. After I was done ministering, it seemed like people were avoiding me like the bubonic plague. As I was getting ready to leave, I noticed that all of these old men had surrounded the young pastor.

I left the church shortly after the meeting. Someone later told me as a result of the move of the Spirit of God in this service, the board of that church fired the pastor. It turns out they had never seen a move of the Spirit. I really felt bad for this pastor being fired. I was told that the pastor had been hiding the fact that he was Spirit-filled because he did not want to lose the church. He eventually pastored a church that was hungry for the things of the Spirit of God.

A Brief Description of Faith:

When God, His Word and His will are Supernaturally Quickened to you by the Holy Spirit! These realities become more real to you than anything in life. It is a revelation of who Jesus Christ & God, the Father really are! What they have done and are doing.

 It is a quickening in your heart, when you know, that you know, that you know, that you know: if God is with you, then who can be against you? Christ Jesus, Himself, lives inside of you.
Your mind, your will, your emotions, and every part of your being is overwhelmed with the reality of Jesus Christ! And you enter the realm where all things are possible! This is where, by God's grace, it is my hope and desire to take you.

Vicky Instantly Delivered from Alcohol

I actually would rather have this precious sister tell her story, but because she is not here, I'll try my best to tell as much as I know about what happened to this sister in Christ in this particular service.

The summer of 1993 I was conducting a regular church service at our church in Gettysburg Pennsylvania. I noticed that we had a good handful of visitors that morning, including one particular lady who stood out above the rest because she was rather tall with dark hair. She looked like she was in her early to mid-30s. As I was preaching the word of God, I could see that the spirit of God was coming on her in a wonderful way, plus others.

After the message, I gave an altar call for those who needed to get right with God or needed a touch of the Holy Ghost. I still remember to this day, this particular lady coming forward for prayer. Before I even got a chance to pray for her, she began to shake under the power of the Holy Ghost. Something dramatic was happening to her by the spirit of God. I finally stood in front of her, laying my hands on her gently in the name of Jesus Christ of Nazareth.

I never, ever put pressure on people's heads when I pray for them. Some ministers I have watched put so much pressure on people's heads to where they're pushing them backwards. There are also ministers that I know who use their faith to get people to fall, thinking this is what they need, and it is a sign of God's presence. I never do this, because it's not the position of the body that matters to me, but what God is doing in their heart. I have seen people supernaturally touched in a powerful way, walking away transformed without ever falling under the power of God.

Now in this particular situation, I barely touched this sisters head when she just crumpled to the floor. She laid on the floor under the power of the Holy Ghost, shaking and quivering from head to toe. I moved on to the next person, never realizing until about fifteen years later what happened that day. This precious sister became a member of our church, with her sister and other members of the family.

It was about fifteen years later that my family and I were over at her family's house celebrating Thanksgiving together. As I was speaking to her about her life, she informed me what happened that day. Someone had invited her to our church service, and she came under the gentle urging of the spirit. Unbeknownst to me she was an alcoholic. She informed me that even when she came that Sunday morning, she had already been drinking.

She was standing there in our church service drunk under the influence of alcohol. As I was preaching, the Spirit of God began to move on her in a wonderful way. When I gave the altar call, she could not help but come to the front to be prayed for. The power of the Holy Ghost came on her in a mighty way. She found herself laying on the floor. Right then and there the Holy Ghost completely delivered her from alcoholism.

She informed me on that Thanksgiving Day fifteen years later that from that moment, she never drank another drop. Thank God for the Holy Ghost, and the wonderful delivering power of the name of Jesus. The unclean spirit for the desire of alcohol had come out of her the minute hands were laid upon her!

CHAPTER SEVEN

Committing Suicide & God Showed up

God is wanting to lead and guide us with peace and joy. This is a divine inner manifestation of God's presence. It is not based on your feelings, circumstances, or situation. I had a very close and good friend of mine (Dale) who shared with me how he first experience this amazing peace and joy. He told me that he was all wrapped up in drugs, alcohol, immorality and wild living.

One night he had just come home from a wild night on the town , and he was standing on the deck of his back porch at 11 in the morning extremely depressed and hopeless. He stood on the outside deck contemplating suicide because he was so stinking miserable. He hated his life and everything about it.

As he was standing there, he finally cried out to God from his heart, surrendering his life to Jesus Christ. As he gave his heart to Jesus, something wonderful and amazing happened. It seemed like all of nature was singing at once he told me! As he looked out over the valley behind his house, and it was like all of nature was singing to him. The peace of God overwhelmed him from head to toe, even to the ends of his fingertips he told me. The sky was bluer then he had ever seen it. The grass was greener, the trees were greener and more full of life, the flowers were more beautiful and brilliant than he had ever seen them. Christ had come into his heart and completely changed every perception that he had ever had.

One minute he was so tormented that he wanted to and his miserable life, and the next minute he was so full of life, love, joy and peace that he felt like he had died and gone to heaven. This is the wonderful and marvelous experience of the new birth. When you totally surrender your heart, your mind and your life to Jesus Christ, he comes rushing in like a mighty wind.

He did not realize it at the time, but this was the peace that passes all understanding, the peace that makes you feel like everything is going to be all right no matter what is happening.

God Asked Me: Will you die for me?

I heard the voice of God asking me: are you willing to die for me? It was as I was getting ready to leave for the Philippines. I had been to the Philippines on numerous occasions. I had been going into an area of the Philippines where the NPA was extremely active. NPA is the abbreviation for the new People's Army, which are part of a communist movement.

At that time, they were very active and they were extremely brutal and dangerous. Godly men which I have worked with in the Philippines had been murdered by them. I heard the Lord continue to say to me: if I can use your spilt blood like a seed planted into the ground to bring about a wonderful harvest, are you willing to die? When I heard the Lord say this to me, I took it very seriously. With deep sorrow in my heart and tears rolling down my face, I said yes Lord!

It was not that I was not willing to die for **Christ**, because I had been in many dangerous situations since I had been born again in 1975. I have had numerous encounters with people threatening and trying to kill me. A gang I used to run with out of Chicago tried twice.

Some Yupik Indians in Alaska had tried to kill me. A demon possessed woman had stabbed me multiple times in the face and yet the knife could not penetrate my skin. A radical Muslim kept on wanting to shoot me, as he yelled and screamed in my face, with his finger ready to pull the trigger which would have sent me off into eternity, but the Holy Ghost restrained him.

Yes, I was more than willing to die, but in truth I did not want to. I had a lovely wife, 3 sons and a beautiful little girl. But I said yes Lord, if this is your will! I still remember that morning as I was getting ready to drive myself to the BWI Airport to catch a plane to the Philippines.

I hugged my precious wife very tight and my four beautiful children as if it was like the last time I would ever hold them or hug them again on this side of heaven. As I looked at my little girl Stephanie she was sucking on her 2 fingers and I had lovingly nicknamed her two fingers Stephanie. My 2nd son Daniel I had nicknamed him the watermelon kid because he loved watermelon so much. I hugged my oldest son goodbye who we had nicknamed Mick which is short for Michael. my 3rd son Steven could never give enough hugs even to this day.

As I backed out of my driveway leaving my family standing on the front porch tears were rolling down my face. I said Lord you died for me, you gave everything for me, so the least I can do is to be willing to give up everything you've given me, if I can be a seed of revival for others to be born again. As I was driving towards the airport on the main highway I was weeping so hard that I could barely see where I was going.

I was thanking God for the years that he had given me with my lovely wife Kathleen. I was thanking God for my 3 sons and my daughter. I was thanking God for all the opportunities he had given to me to minister the word and help others. I was also reflecting upon the fact of how many times I should been dead like many of my former buddies who were now dead.

I thought back on the times before I was born again when I had overdosed, drank way too much booze, played chicken with oncoming trains, driving on the other side of the road headed right towards others. When I had been in a gunfight with a crazy man. Oh how many times God had spared me, and yet most of my worldly friends were now dead.

All of those times when God spared my life, he could've allowed me to die and go to hell. But God had rescued me, and now it was my turn to die for him, how could I say no? I remember landing in the Philippines. I was completely free from fear. In my heart of hearts, I was already a martyr for **Christ**.

Now to my wonderful amazement and my great surprise God spoke to my heart while I was over there in the communist infested area. He said: son you're not going to die! I said what Lord? He spoke to me again: you're not going to die! I remember crying with joy, I said why Lord?

He said I needed to have you prove your love for me. He said I needed to have you to know that I was number 1 in your life. Even as Abraham offered up Isaac, and I gave him back, so in a sense you have offered up your wife and your children, and I give them back to you.

That has been over 23 years ago when the Lord spared my life. I'm still going to areas at times that are extremely dangerous, but I have no fear, because I know that God is with me. What if he ever asked me to offer up my life again as a seed with the shedding of my blood? All I can say is that if it ever happens again, by God's grace I'll say, yes Lord! You gave your life for me, it's the least I can do.

Deliverance of Sarah of Tourette syndrome

Tourette syndrome (TS) is a neurological disorder

characterized by repetitive, stereotyped, involuntary movements and vocalizations called tics. I am completely convinced that it is a demonic affliction. How many would make the mistake of thinking that someone with this syndrome is demon possessed, but they are oppressed! These demonic spirits, come and go, just like many people who have seizures. This is not a onetime pronouncement of deliverance. This is a true story of one young lady who was delivered by a progressive application of spiritual truths and authority.

Three months before school was out in 1994 I received a phone call from a husband and wife from Carlisle Pennsylvania. They called, asking if we could help them. They had been watching my TV program which was aired on their local TV station. They knew from my messages on TV that we had a Christian school. They had a daughter who was ten years old, who desperately needed help. Not only did she have tics syndrome, but she had major emotional problems.

The principle of the public school that she attended was demanding they place her in to a mental institution. She was completely uncontrollable. Whenever they would try to discipline her, she would run from them, many times ending up in the parking lot, crawling under the cars. One time when she was in the principal's office, Sarah got so angry, that she completely wiped out this office.

They told me that she had gone completely berserk trashing everything in her sight. The principal of the school could not handle it anymore. The only other option this couple had was to see if somebody would take her into their school. Our school was over 30 miles away from where they lived, but they were willing to drive it every day. I told them that I would pray about it to see what the Lord spoke to me. I truly felt in my heart that we could help this young lady. A meeting was set up to meet the parents with their daughter Sarah.

I always like to pray before I make any commitments. I sought the Lord about this terrible situation with their daughter. As I spoke face-to-face with the parents, and with meeting Sarah for the first time, I perceived in my heart we could help her. First I told them that if we were going to help Sarah for the next three months, they would have to allow us to do what we felt needed to be done.

The very first thing that they would need to do was to take Sarah off all mind-altering drugs, which the public school had put her on. This is always one of our requirements for a child to come to our school. From 1985, up to this moment, in our school we never allowed any mind altering drugs. In every situation, we have seen God do marvelous things in a student's life.

The second thing I told the parents is that we would want them not to hang around at all at the school, once they drop their daughter off. I perceived by the spirit of God that a lot of Sarah's problem was that she was using her condition as a way to get attention from her mother and father. This proved to be correct, because every time her mother came to pick her up, the tics became much worse. When she first came to our school, her head would shake back and forth very violently all day long. It was extremely painful to watch.

I had a meeting with my teachers informing them that they were not to lift their voice, or yell at Sarah for any reason. We were not going to put her in a situation that would stir up the devils that were manifesting through her.

Many so-called Christians, especially the spirit filled ones, would have been trying to cast the devils out of her the minute they saw her because they would have thought she was demon possessed. Granted, there were devils at work, but she was not possessed. She was oppressed, depressed and at times obsessed. People who do not have a lot of wisdom immediately try to cast devils out without getting the mind of Christ.

The Spirit of God told me what we needed to do. Every morning when her mother dropped her off, I would take her with one of the female teachers of the school into an office. I would speak very softly to Sarah, telling her that we would like to pray with her before the beginning of the day.

I would simply speak in a very soft voice over her that which was the will of God. This prayer would usually only be about five minutes long. Then I would tell her that she was going to have a wonderful day. Off to her class, she would go. We did not treat her any different than the other students. Through the day if they began to have problems with her, they would simply send someone to get me.

Once again we would take her into an office (with a lady teacher), and I would gently pray over her in the name of Jesus Christ. I also came against the demonic spirits that were causing the tics syndrome. I never got loud, authoritative, or weird. I would simply take authority over them, in a quiet, gentle voice. Immediately there was a wonderful change in Sarah. Every day she was getting better. Not only did the tics syndrome cease eventually, but she became an A+ student. It was obvious to me at the beginning that Sarah was a brilliant girl, who was not being challenged at the school she attended.

By the end of the three months, Sarah was completely free. She was a happy, smiling, hard-working A+ student. We could not have asked for a better young girl. I am sorry to say that at the end of those three months we never saw Sarah or her parents again. I guess they had gotten what they needed, and off they went. This is very typical in my experience.

When the next school year rolled around, I received a very strange phone call one day from the Carlisle school district. The principal was on the phone wanting to talk to me. When I got on the phone with this principal, who was a lady, she asked me a question with a tone of absolute surprise and wonder. She said to me: what in the world did you do with Sarah? She is completely changed!

I said to this principal, who was over a large school district, "What we did with Sarah you're not going to be able to do!" I said to her: we began to pray over her very gently, every day, consistently in the name of Jesus Christ. You could hear a pin drop for the next couple moments. The next thing I heard was, OH, okay, goodbye! The principal hung up the phone!

Hit by a Ball of Spiritual Fire

I decided to go one more time to a Benny Hinn crusade, but I made a big mistake in how I went about this. What I did is that I kept saying to myself: when I go to this gathering, and Benny lays his hands upon me, (he announced that he would lay hands on ministers) I will receive a powerful anointing to pray for the sick, and needy!

I kept saying this to myself for over a month. I also decided to fast for three days before this meeting. As I drove to his meeting in Richmond, Virginia, I kept confessing that the Spirit of the Lord would overwhelm me as hands were laid on me! Do not think for a minute that what you say does not have a powerful affect upon what happens in your life! What I was doing was similar to the women with the issue of blood who touched the hem of the garment of Jesus!

Matthew 9:20 And, behold, a woman, which was diseased with an issue of blood twelve years, came behind him, and touched the hem of his garment:21 For she said within herself, If I may but touch his garment, I shall be whole.

When I arrived where the meeting was there was already a massive crowd of people waiting outside to get into this meeting. Once again I found my way to the end of this massive long line. There was still approximately four hours before they were going to open up the doors to the arena. As the time approached I kept saying to myself: when Benny lays his hands upon me, I will receive a powerful anointing to pray for the sick, and needy! My whole body felt like electrical currents were flowing through me before we even entered the facility!

By the time they called for the ministers to come to the stage my legs had literally felt like they had turned to rubber due to the presence of God that was flowing through me. When I stepped up unto the stage my legs began to wobble and felt like rubber bands from my feet to my waist! Finally my turn came to have hands laid on me. Now, the next thing I saw was a Giant Ball of white fire coming towards me across the stage.

Everything disappeared at that moment, including Benny, the stage, the crowd! All I saw was this massive ball of pure white fire rolling towards me. Benny was not even anywhere near me as far as I could tell. When this ball of fire hit me it was like a spiritual explosion engulfed me, and I felt myself flying through the air. I was so engulfed by this fire that all I felt and knew was this complete immersion in this white fire.

A person who was there with me informed me later on of what happened! She said: Benny waved his hand toward you and you flew up in the air like you were electrocuted. It took four men to carry you off the stage. Benny said to them: "get him off the stage, he can't handle the anointing". I was standing about four feet from you way up front! One minute you're standing there and all of a sudden you'll literally flying through the air like somebody hit you with a bowling ball. It took four men to carry me off of the stage with me jerking like I was being electrocuted!

What Benny did not know is the fact of the matter was not that I could not handle the anointing, but that I had spoken, confessed this experience into being for a month! My confession had created such a spiritual dynamic that when the time finally came for its fulfillment, it hit me like a ball of fire!

Calvary Road and Revival

I came across a book that had a wonderful impact on my life called **"CALVARY ROAD"**! It is about a mighty revival that God brought in an overseas mission. This book is by Roy Hession, and it very simply outlines personal revival (sanctification) through being filled with the Holy Spirit. As it says in 2 Thessalonians 2:13, the work of the Holy Spirit in our life is to save us "through the sanctifying work of the Spirit and through belief in the truth."

Rom. 8:4 tells us that "the righteous requirements of the law might be fully met in us, who do not live according to the sinful nature but according to the Spirit". In this little book, the process of sanctification, through surrendering all, is simply and clearly revealed for those who are willing to seek the Lord with all their heart.

I was so impressed and convicted by this little book that I ordered the book by the case. I took this book and distributed it to the whole congregation for free. I also gave this book to all our staff, including the teachers in our Christian school. We even gave this book to the older classes in our Christian school.

I began to preach along the line of repentance, prayer, and one hundred percent commitment to Jesus Christ; that there should be no hidden sin in our lives. The fire of God fell in our church. (Revival!) The Lord started working in such wonderful ways that the teenagers in our private school started weeping and crying in the classrooms.

We had to stop the classes when this happened. I walked into the sanctuary of the church one morning, and there were all the teenagers lying on the floor weeping, crying, and calling out to God! This wonderful move continued for a short season.

LIFE CHANGING OPEN VISION

I informed my staff that I was going to give myself to long hours of prayer and the Word. I began with the Book of Ephesians; starting with the very first chapter. I did not only want to memorize it, I wanted to get it into my heart. This took me close to three weeks, and countless hours to memorize.

The next mountain I climbed was the Book of Galatians. As I was memorizing the scriptures and chapters of the Bible, I was getting terrible headaches. But I kept working at it because I knew that without pain, there is no gain. When I had conquered Galatians, I moved to the Book of Philippians.

Brain Quickening Experience

One day, as I was into the second chapter of Philippians; something supernatural and amazing took place. I had what the Bible calls an "open vision." This happens when you are wide awake, and yet everything disappears around you - except what God is showing you.

In the open vision, right in front of me appeared a very large body of water. It was pure blue, with not one ripple upon it. It stretched as far as the natural eye could see, in every direction. The room I was in had completely gone - there was nothing but this gigantic blue lake. As I lifted my head to look into the light-blue, never-ending, and cloudless sky; I saw a large, crystal-clear raindrop falling down from the heavens, in slow-motion, heading towards the body of water. I watched in amazement as it slowly came tumbling down towards this lake. When it hit the surface of the body of water, it caused ripples to flow forth.

As the ripples flowed forth from the center of where the drop had hit, they began to grow in size and intensity. Then, as suddenly as the vision had come, it was gone. I stood in my office in complete amazement; not understanding what had just happened, or, indeed, why it had happened.

I knew that this experience was from God, but I did not know what the significance of it was. I knew in my heart that God eventually would show me what it meant. When the Lord gives me a supernatural visitation, I do not try to understand with my natural mind. I simply give it to the Lord knowing that in His time, He will show me what the experience means or what He was saying.

I picked up my Bible and went back to memorizing scriptures. I immediately noticed there was a change in my mental capacity. It seemed as if my brain was absorbing the Word of God like a dry sponge soaking up water. Within one-hour, I memorized a whole chapter of the Book of Philippians - as if it were nothing.

I was amazed! Before this, it took me days to memorize a chapter and yet, now I could memorize a chapter in an hour. I continued to memorize books of the Bible until there were nine books inside of me. This is not including thousands of other scriptures that I continued to memorize while dealing with certain subjects.

I honestly believe that I could have memorized the whole New Testament, had I not allowed the activities of ministry to overwhelm me, and keep me preoccupied. The enemy of our soul knows how to make things happen in our lives to get us sidetracked.

Why in the world would God open up my heart and mind in such a dramatic way to memorize the Word? Because it is by the Word of God that our minds are renewed, and we can discover His perfect will for our lives. The Word of God has the capacity to quicken our minds and mortal bodies.

God's Word is awesome, quick, and powerful. I believe there is an activation of the things of the Spirit when we begin to give ourselves one-hundred-percent to whatever it is God has called us to do. There is a dynamic principle of laying your life down in order to release the aroma of heaven.

2 Corinthians 12:2-4 I knew a man in Christ above fourteen years ago, (whether in the body, I cannot tell; or whether out of the body, I cannot tell: God knoweth;) such an one caught up to the third heaven. 3 And I knew such a man, (whether in the body, or out of the body, I cannot tell: God knoweth;) 4 How that he was caught up into paradise, and heard unspeakable words, which it is not lawful for a man to utter.

I'm sorry to say, though, that I became so busy running the church, Christian school, a small bible college, radio station, TV broadcasting and construction projects, twenty-five churches in the Philippines, not including other aspects of being a pastor, that I did not continue in memorizing the Bible.

Through the years though, I've had an insatiable hunger for the Word of God. God has allowed me to write over seven thousand sermons, 30 books, and to do many things that I never have been taught or trained to do. In the midst of all these activities I have earned a PhD in biblical theology and I received a Doctorate of Divinity. I believe it is all because of the divine supernatural visitations and quickening's of God's Holy Spirit. The reason why I believe we do not experience more of these visitations is because of a lack of spiritual hunger. If we would hunger and thirst, God would satisfy these desires.

God gave a Total Stranger a Brand-New Liver

One day I had to go visit one of my parishioners in the Gettysburg Hospital. When I make these visitations, many times I will wear a minister's collar because it is a recognized symbol of religious authority. It's amazing how a little piece of white plastic can have such an effect on medical professionals, this also includes policemen and others in natural authority. When I put on a minister's collar I look almost like a Catholic priest.

Many times through the years I have walked into a hospital room, with doctors and nurses present. In most situations, they will ask me to wait outside until they are done. But the Scripture says to be as wise as the serpent, as harmless as a dove. So I go in as one in authority. When I do this the doctors themselves submit to my religious authority. I ask the doctors and nurses kindly to leave so I can minister to the person. Surprisingly they bow their heads, walking out of the room.

One day I walked into a man's room who I did not know. I asked him what his problem was. He told me that his liver was completely shot and that he was dying. I perceived in my heart that it was because of alcoholism. I told him that I would like to pray for him and ask if that was possible. He agreed to my request. I laid my hands on him, commanding in the name of Jesus Christ for the spirit of infirmity to come out. And then I spoke into him a brand-new liver, in the name of Jesus Christ of Nazareth! I do not speak loud. I do not have to because I know my Authority in Christ when I am submitted to the authority of Christ!

I do not pray real long prayers or even dozens of scriptures. The Word is already in my heart! Now believe me when I tell you that if I wanted to pray real long prayers in those situations I easily could. I could stand over the person and quote the whole books of the Bible by memory. When you are moving in the realm of faith none of these things are necessary. Many times it is obvious that people are trying to work up faith. If you study the life of Jesus and his ministry he never spent a long time praying or speaking over people. The long hours of prayer, and speaking the word was done in private when he was up on the mountain.

When I was done, I simply said goodbye, and out the door, I went. I was to go see another sick person. It was three years later when I finally discovered what happened on that particular day. One of the members of my congregation was down on the streets of Gettysburg witnessing to those he met. He ran into this particular gentleman who was dying because he needed a new liver. This particular man said: I know who your pastor is! The parishioner asked: how do you know my pastor? He said: three years ago I was dying with a bad liver. Your pastor walked in and laid his hands on me commanding me to have a brand-new liver.

And God gave me a brand-new liver!

God gave her a NEW HEART

A precious sister from Jesus is Lord Ministries ended up in the Chambersburg hospital with an extremely dangerous heart condition. I went to the Hospital. I walked into her room. She had all kinds of medical equipment hooked up to her. It looked extremely serious.

The spirit of compassion was quickened in me, and I laid my hands on her. I commanded her HEART to be healed in the name of Jesus Christ of Nazareth. My prayer to Christ was not very long. I simply obeyed the Bible by speaking to my dear sister's heart. After I prayed with her and for her we spoke for just a little while and then I left her. Up to that moment, it did not seem as if there had been any change in her condition whatsoever.

She shared her testimony with me later. The minute I walked out of the Room she told me that the equipment that was monitoring her began to sound alarms. The nurses came running into her hospital room.

She told them everything was okay. That her pastor had just prayed for her. She told them that she believed that God had healed her of our heart condition completely. Of course, looked and treated her like she was crazy! They put her through all kinds of medical test, over and over they tested her.

She kept telling them God had done a miracle and given her a NEW HEART! After many tests, they had to finally admit she was completely healed. She was immediately released from the hospital. That was over 24 years ago. She has never had another problem with her heart. All praise and glory to God!

Kathleen's Prayers Set me on a 40 Day Fast

Where Is the Man I Married?

I began to grow a little bit cold and lukewarm in my spiritual walk with God. Now I still was very much active in the church, but I wasn't flowing in the Holy Ghost. My wife became very concerned about me. Unbeknownst to me, she began to pray and intercede on my behalf.

Kathee's Perspective:

My heart yearned for the man I married. Michael was not on fire for God like he once was. He had become burdened by the woes and cares of life and the church. He was miserable, and making us all miserable with him! My prayer to God was to bring back the man I had married, and make him more on fire for God. I began anointing everything that Mike touched with oil: his truck, his clothes, even his computer.

However, my prayers did not appear to be very effective, that is, until the day the Spirit of God came upon me! A supernatural spirit of travail overtook me. This time as I prayed, I anointed his pillows and things with my tears instead of oil. I had truly touched heaven, because that very night when Mike returned home, God was waiting for him!

Back to Michael:

When I came home from church, Kathee was already in bed asleep. I slipped out of my clothes and crawled into bed. The minute I laid my head upon my pillow, the overwhelming power of God's conviction hit me. It didn't seem fair! Kathee was sleeping peacefully, but I was about to lose my sleep, and so much more!

Immediately I began to weep and cry. The conviction of God so overwhelmed me, I had to get out of bed and begin to pray. I prayed all night long in this spirit of conviction. I kept praying through the next whole day. It was so strong upon me that I was not able to stop.

Not only could I not stop praying, but I had no desire for physical food. It wasn't as if I decided not to eat, it was because I could not eat. The only thing I could do was drink water and pray. This went on one whole day. After the first day it did not lift, but instead it increased. I went two days; then three days. This continued for the next forty days and nights. All I could basically do was pray and fast.

I do not want you to be led to believe that I did not drive my car, preach in the pulpit, check the mail, or do the necessary natural things; I did all those things. However, the Spirit of God was on me in a mighty way. Right after God dealt with me this way, we had a wonderful move of God in our home and church.

My little children, of whom I travail in birth again until Christ be formed in you (Galatians 4:19).

My Neck Was in the Guillotine

I had been pastoring in Gettysburg, Pennsylvania for approximately three years (1986). To be honest with you, if I had my preferences as to where to pastor, it would've never been here in Gettysburg. Even statistically, there are many places which are much more open to the things of God than this religious, stiff-necked, hard to deal with the area. Gettysburg has come to be known as the ghost capital of America because of their ghost walks, spiritual séances, and fortune-telling. I am not talking about the Holy Ghost, either. Nor does this include all of the the religious spirits that are in the area, evidenced by their cold, dead seminaries and religious colleges.

I know that there are many who think that where they are laboring is extremely difficult. They may very well be right. For over 30 years, my family and I have labored in this field, seeing very little results, and yet when I go to other areas, God truly shows up. Please don't misunderstand me, yes we have had many moves of God, many healed, many signs and wonders, and yet seen very little enduring fruit. People get healed, delivered, set free and then leave to go to some lukewarm, seeker-friendly atmosphere. You might ask, "Why are you here then?" Because this is where God has called us to labor in His vineyard.

Back to my story: So, I had been pastoring for about three years in this area, when one night I went to sleep as I normally did. This time; however, I had a very frightening and real dream. This dream was not just a figment of my imagination or some kind of stomach disorder caused by something disagreeable that I ate.

In this dream, I was confronted by one of the major ruling spiritual principalities and powers in this area. Here I was sleeping soundly, when suddenly in this dream, I was in a very large mansion. I could tell that it was a historical mansion built in the style of the late 1800s. I found myself in a very large dining room with fancy woodwork, chairs, and other furniture that one would expect in a very wealthy man's house. I could tell that I was on the west side of the house looking towards the east when a young lady came walking through a set of very fancy, wooden, double doors.

Right away I could tell that there was something wrong with this picture and felt in my heart that I was in great danger, so I began to look around for a way of escape. Right behind me was a single, wooden door that exited the dining room.

I immediately ran for this door, entering into a large kitchen with cooking equipment. The floor of this room was made up of large white and black tiles with tables aligned from east to west in a long row used for food preparation. To my right were sinks with old-style faucets and other cooking equipment. To my left were cabinets, meat hooks, large cooking pots and kitchen supplies.

What immediately caught my attention though was that right in front of me, approximately 20 feet away, was the most frighteningly tall and skinny man that I had ever seen. I knew in my heart right away that this was a ruling principality and power in this geographical area. He had on a three-piece suit, dark in color, with some kind of checkered shirt covered by a leather vest. He was also wearing an old-style bow tie that was common in the 1800s. His face was long, ugly and skinny, yet highly educated and intelligent.

Evil radiated from him almost like an invisible aroma that filled the air with a terrible, wicked stench. He was smiling at me with a very large, grotesque grin, almost like the Joker from the Batman genre. Immediately fear, overwhelming fear filled my heart. I had just run from the dining room, escaping the dangerous young lady. Now, as I looked upon this evil spirit, I completely forgot about the young lady in the other room. My instincts were to flee. I turned around to go back through the door I had just come through to escape this wicked, sophisticated, evil and twisted demon.

As I ran back into the dining room, the young lady was still standing there, but now she had taken off her top blouse and was standing there with just a black bra on in a very enticing way. When I saw her, I was hit with a double dose of fear. Sweat began to bead upon my forehead causing me to spin around and head back to the kitchen from which I came. Turning, I confronted the tall, skinny, sophisticated demon as he is coming through the kitchen door. He was laughing uncontrollably, looking directly at me. I was stuck right in the middle between this devil and the partly undressed demoness.

At that very moment, I woke up sitting up in my bed, shivering and shaking with fear and apprehension. This dream began to torment me for some months, not fully comprehending what it could mean until it finally dissipated into my unconsciousness. I never did tell my wife about this dream because it was so frightening and demonic. I did not want to tell anybody about it since I didn't understand what it meant.

About five years had come and gone since I had had this frightening and terrible dream. In the interim, our new church building had been completed. Not only had we built a new church but a new parsonage as well, where my family and I were living. My wife and I had three sons and one daughter.

Everything was so hectic in our house that it was necessary for us to find someone to stay with us to help with the children. My sister Deborah had been doing this, but she had moved away. We took in an ordinary, young lady who attended our church to help with the children, laundry, and other family activities. Everything seemed to be going along just fine, but there was an undercurrent that began to erode away slowly our family unity.

This young lady began to become a part of our family, laughing and joking, all of us teasing one another. Unbeknownst to me, things began to happen slowly but surely like a frog being slow-boiled. I began to have wrong thoughts and desires creep into my mind. In the beginning, I cast them down, taking authority over them. We had an above ground swimming pool in the backyard of our parsonage where my wife, this young lady and my children would swim. We would all end up laughing together, splashing and just acting silly. I began to find myself getting carried away with acting like an idiot.

My wife noticed this and tried to talk to me about the fact that I was a little bit too friendly. Of course, I vehemently denied this, deceiving myself. I was headed for a major downfall, and the devil was laughing all the way. It finally came to the point where something was about to happen that would destroy myself, my family, the church and everything that God had blessed me with if God did not divinely intervene. The good news is that many times the devil overplays his hand.

I went to bed one night as I normally did, falling into a very deep, deep sleep when, out of the blue, I was back in the very same dream from five years before, back in the very house where I had

169

been previously. Once again, I was in the dining room with the same scenario.

There were the young lady and the other demon laughing at me, over and over. Once again in this dream, my heart filled with fear, my mind, and my soul became overwhelmed with great dread, when suddenly, I heard the voice of God speak to me from heaven: "This is that which you saw in the dream." Immediately, I knew in my heart what was going on in this dream. Up to this moment, I was utterly and completely ignorant of the trap that the devil had set for my destruction. My head was already in the guillotine with the blade ready to drop, and I did not even know it.

I woke up weeping and crying, broken in my heart over the lust that had begun to consume me. I woke up my wife crying and began to confess to her the dream that I previously had five years before. Then I told her what had been going on in my mind towards this young lady, confessing that my wife was right all along and that it was true that lust had become the focus of my heart. (Thank God nothing ever did happen).

I wept, and I cried, then I repented. My wife held me, forgiving me for everything. We prayed together, crying out to Jesus for help, thanking Him for His mercy and His grace. God had rescued me once again from my spiritual blindness and fleshly lusts. Thank God for His mercy and the loving-kindness and forgiveness displayed to us by the Great Shepherd of the sheep, our Savior and Messiah, Jesus Christ!

The Communist Were Waiting To Kill Us

About six months later, I arrived back in the Philippines with one of the men from my church who is now a pastor in the Phoenix, Arizona area. When we arrived in the province of Samar, the brethren informed us that the Communists were aware of us coming and were going to be waiting for us. I did not ask them to explain to me what they meant. I absolutely had no fear in my heart. It is hard to explain to people what it is like when you are operating in a gift of faith. It is not normal faith.

It is faith that makes you know that in Christ you cannot be defeated. In the operation of this faith, there is always overwhelming peace. It is the peace of God that passes all understanding. The minute you lose your peace, you need to stop and asked the Father what is wrong. This is a major way in which God leads and guides us is by his peace.

Isaiah 55:12 For ye shall go out with joy, and be led forth with peace: the mountains and the hills shall break forth before you into singing, and all the trees of the field shall clap their hands.

In order to get to this island, we were first going to have to go by land on a worn out concrete road that had been built right after World War II. We had to travel from Catbalogan City to the town of Catarman . Then from Catarman, we continued our journey another 40 miles to reach our canoes that were going to take us to the island. Altogether the journey was hundred and 14 miles.

Now, this may not sound like a long-distance when it comes to traveling in America, but that is a long way on a rough Filipino road. We finally reached a river called the Pambujan River.

To our dismay, the bridge was out. They were putting in a brand-new bridge which they had only begun. So we had to take a long alternative route to reach another bridge to get across this river. This river was over 300 feet wide. (I only mention this because it's an important part of my journey on the motorcycle) We stayed on this road until it ran into the Philippine ocean. From there we took two large canoes. Each canoe had an outboard motor on the back of them. We would have to traverse on the ocean over a mile to reach Laoang. After all of our equipment and the people were loaded into the first canoe I found myself up front at the very tip of the vessel.

During this time there was great excitement and peace in my heart to see what God was about to do. I was optimistic of God manifesting himself on this island that had been shut off from the gospel for many years.

I knew that God was going to have to perform miracles to keep us alive, and yet there was absolutely no fear within my heart, nothing but overflowing peace. As we were coming closer to the island, I could see that there were men lined up along the beach waiting for us.

There was absolutely no fear in my heart as we approach the island. There were approximately 30 men who were standing there with guns and machetes in their hands. The Filipino brothers who were navigating the canoes kept the engines of the canoes running fast enough so the canoes would drive themselves up a little bit onto the dry shore.

As we approached the shore, I was so excited that I stood up to my feet, getting ready to leap out of this canoe towards these communists. It had to be the spirit of God with in me because no sane man would leap to his death. I almost felt like George Washington's famous painting of him crossing the Delaware River. The moment we hit the beach, I was up and out of that canoe. The Communists were standing there waiting to kill us.

The Spirit of God, the gift of faith, the peace of God was possessing me as I began to walk towards them very rapidly. I headed right for the center of this crowd of gun toting and machete-wielding communist.

As I reached them, something supernatural happened. It was like the Lord splitting the Red Sea, but instead of water, it was men who had murder in their hearts. They separated from left to right and allowed our team of men to walk right through the midst of Them.

172

The Blind See & the Deaf Hear

That night we held a crusade right in the middle of the village. As our worship team was singing, the Communists and pagan religious people were marching through our meeting. We simply ignored them and kept on with the meeting. There seemed to be a very large crowd that night, probably because they wanted to see a white man.

It was very seldom when Americans or Europeans came into this area. The tourists flock to Manila and Mindanao. It had been 10 years since anybody had dared come to this island to preach Christianity. The last missionaries they had murdered. Now here I was about to preach the gospel of Jesus Christ that saves, heals and delivers just like it did in the days when Jesus walked in his earthly ministry.

After the singing it was my opportunity to preach. It literally felt like the spirit of God was flowing through me like a mighty river of electricity and power. I preached under the unction of the Holy Ghost, to a great extent not thinking at all what to say, but letting the spirit have his way.

When I was done preaching, there was barely enough light to make out the crowd in front of us. They had lit some torches around the meeting area, trying to bring as much light as possible. Because I could not get down into the crowd to pray for them, I had to speak the word of healing over them. I began to command their bodies to be healed in the name of Jesus Christ of Nazareth. Every time I would speak something in the name of Jesus, the interpreter would copy me in their language.

Miracles began to happen. One old lady who had been blind in one eye could now see. A little boy who had been deaf could now hear. It was too dark out for us to tell how many miracles happened that night, but to this day I have been told there is a thriving church there because of this meeting.

Surrounded by the NPA

The precious brothers we worked with had arranged for us to be put into a two-story house. We would be on the second floor, while they were going to be on the first floor. I know why they did this! They were going to make the Communists have to kill them before they would let the NPA get to us. These were the kind of men that would give their lives without hesitation for the sake of the gospel.

It was really late by the time we went to bed. They gave my friend and I some type of straw mats to lie on. We threw these mats on the wooden floor, and tried to go to sleep. During the night we could hear the Communists outside making a racket. The communist had surrounded our house with groups of men, had started little bonfires around the house where we were staying. As I went to sleep, I saw two large angels like pillars of fire in a dream with swords drawn standing over the top of the house we were in. When we woke up in the morning, it was very peaceful. And the Communists were gone.

The Spirit of the Lord is upon me, because he hath anointed me to preach the gospel to the poor; he hath sent me to heal the brokenhearted, to preach deliverance to the captives, and recovering of sight to the blind, to set at liberty them that are bruised, to preach the acceptable year of the Lord (Luke 4:18-19).

CHAPTER EIGHT

Driving under the Influence of Holy Ghost

We had left the island in the morning, and we were now holding meetings in a town called Pambujan, which was about 19 miles away. God was moving in a wonderful way. The Philippine brother who was over all of the work in this area is named Danny. He also had two other brothers, Jonathan and Hurley, who are also ministers of the gospel. (You can friend them on Facebook if you like). I personally knew their father, Reese Monte's (who has since gone home to be with the Lord), who was an amazing man of God who was instrumental in starting over five hundred churches throughout the Philippines islands.

The name of the organization was "Faith Tabernacle. These men are all apostolic in nature. If I understand correctly, Danny has been instrumental in starting over seventy churches. Now here I was ministering with Danny. Danny came to me late one night and said he was really homesick. He had never been away from his wife this long. We were approximately 32 miles from his home in Catarman.

This may not sound like a long-distance to you, but believe me with the road conditions, the weather, and the communist it was quite a distance, especially if you are going to travel in the night. Actually, in this area, I never saw any vehicles out on the road after the sunset.

Now I had earned a reputation for being good on a motorcycle. In all reality, though I wasn't very good on a motorcycle at all. It is simply that the Spirit of God would quicken me as I would take a motorcycle up into the mountains to preach the gospel to the natives. I'm kind of hyperactive, so in between Crusades and conferences. When everyone else was taking a siesta, I would find someone who was willing to go with me to interpret for me, and I would head up into the mountains.

We were deep in a heavily populated area where there was known to be anti-government radicals, Communists, the NPA, and it was extremely dangerous to be there and especially at night. Brother Danny came to me though one night asking me if I would be willing to take him home on a motorcycle that someone had driven who was on our team. It was a very rainy and foggy night. Now the motorcycle that was available was an old machine—I believe it was a Kawasaki 250. This motorcycle had some issues though. The headlights were very dim, and at times the shifting mechanism would fall off if you were not very careful.

When Danny asked me to take him home, the Spirit of God quickened my heart and said: take him. It was like when David had said he was thirsty for the waters of the well in Bethlehem. Three of his mighty men broke through the host of the Philistines and drew water out of the well in Bethlehem for David to drink. This quickening in my heart was so strong that without any hesitation I told Danny I would take him home to see his precious wife and children.

Danny informed me with almost a whisper that we must not stop along the way no matter what because the Communists would be out in full force. He also said we would have to to be very careful because the Communists (if they heard us coming) would stretch a thin cable wire across the road in order to kill us. I saw a video one time where this is exactly what they had done, and it was captured on film. The motorcyclist was cut right in half. It was not a very pretty image.

He also informed me that if they got their hands on us, we would be dead men. Even with this dire warning from Daniel, I had total and perfect peace. Actually, there was a divine excitement within my heart to go on this journey. This is not something you can explain to a person who has never experienced the quickening, moving, empowering presence of the Holy Ghost.
As we began this journey, we had made one major mistake. We forgot that there was road construction all along the way and that the main bridge was out. If we would have remembered, then we would've taken a long way around. As it was, we took the regular route that would've been the shortest route to Danny's home.

Now as I was driving the motorcycle, I could barely see where I was going. The rain and the fog were coding the shield of my helmet. The headlight was very dim almost nonexistent. I had to keep reaching up with my left hand to wipe my face shield to see where I was going. Danny was sitting behind me holding on tight as I was driving. I believe I was driving at approximately forty-five to fifty miles an hour.

After we had been on this rough construction road for several miles, I thought that I could see something very dark and threatening in the pathway ahead of us. In my mind it seemed to me to be an enemy and waiting, and yet I had total peace. I should have slowed down, but I just kept on going. The next thing I knew, Danny was yelling very loud in my ear with a great warning, "watch out."

I yelled back at Danny: Hold on, we are going to go through it! Whatever this object was, we slammed into it doing about 50 miles an hour. As it turned out, it was a very large pile of gravel and road material. We hit this very large pile of construction material which was almost vertically straight up. The bike without hesitation raced to the top of this pile of construction material and launched us up into the void of the night. During this event, Danny took his head and put it underneath my left forearm, under my armpit.

It turns out he had been in a terrible motorcycle accident before, and now he was trying to protect himself as much as he could from the disaster which was unfolding. In every scenario, this was going to be a major catastrophe. Not only would-would be killed or extremely hurt when we hit the concrete road but then the communist would be upon us. There was no hospitals or help that would be available for us. We Surely Were Dead Men!

Here we were launched up into the darkness of the night. As I was up in the air on the back of this motorcycle, it the truly felt like I was just sailing through the sky like when I used to fly airplanes. During this experience, I was supernaturally engulfed in an amazing bubble of peace and joy. I had absolutely no fear or anxiety whatsoever. I was operating in the REALM of the spiritual. It seemed like for the longest time we were not going to come down.

WE WERE TOSSED INTO THE VELVET BLACKNESS OF THE NIGHT AS WE HIT AN ALMOST VERTICAL HUGE PILE OF GRAVEL!

We were suspended in the heavens. Of course, we must've been sailing through the skies in an upward and downward flow. It was obvious when we hit the wet concrete roadway below us, that something would have to give. But when we make contact with the road, it was so smooth, so nonresistant, that it almost felt like putting on a pair of comfortable old bedroom slippers. This is the only way I can describe it. We did not skid, bounce, or slide in any sense of the word.

The only thing negative that happened when we met the road is that the gear shifter fell off the motorcycle. We were stuck in the Top Gear as we headed down the road. We had to stop and go back and look for it.

We went all the way back to the pile of gravel we had hit and started from the pile working our way out in order to find the shifter. I did not think to measure the distance of our jump. We looked and looked, and looked with the dim headlight of the motorcycle. By this time, Danny was very concerned about the Communists seeing the headlight of the motorcycle and hearing its engine running, so we decided to leave the motorbike in top gear and leave.

As we were headed down the road at about four hundred feet away from the pile of road gravel, I saw something gleaming on the road in front of us in the rain. We stopped, and there was the shifting mechanism! We put it back on the bike and went our way. How far we flew through the night sky that night, only God Knows! Now if you think this sounds incredulous, weight two ye hear about the next part of this journey. Danny Monte's can verify every bit of this journey.

But they that wait upon the LORD shall renew their strength; they shall mount up with wings as eagles; they shall run, and not be weary; and they shall walk, and not faint (Isaiah 40:31).

Evil Knievel would be Jealous

Over a 300' River We Go on Wet Slimy Planks in the Fog and Rain at Night, surrounded by communist!

Here we were on this unreliable motorcycle driving through the rain and the fog in the middle of the night. It seemed as if we had been on the road for an hour when we came upon the river. This river was over three hundred feet wide. It was a very deep and fast-moving river that flowed into the Philippine Sea. We forgot we had taken another way to get to Pambujan. The reason we had to take another way is that the bridge was out. I believe God's hand was in this.

They had driven wooden pilings down into the bed of the river. It looked like they had placed rough sawn planks upon these pilings. These planks were approximately eighteen inches wide and were loosely attached on these pilings. This footbridge appeared to be four to five feet above the river. These planks were wet and slimy. I would not have wanted to walk on them in the daylight, let alone on a wet and extremely foggy night.

To get to the beginning of the planks we would have to to go down a muddy and slimy embankment. Then we had to go up a steep muddy dirt pile in order to get to the planks and unstable walking bridge.

There was just no way we could walk that motorcycle across this river. It was not wide enough to walk alongside other motorcycle and push it. There's no way somebody could stand in front of the motorcycle to control the handlebars, while somebody pushed behind. Even if we could it was too dark, wet, slimy, and foggy. If there is any communist around they could easily pick us off with a gun within that 300 feet to the other side.

Danny asked, "What are we going to do?" The Spirit of God was upon me in the most indescribable way. I do not believe up to that moment I had ever experienced God's presence so manifested in my flesh. There was absolutely not an ounce of fear or inadequacy in me at that moment. This was not pride, conceit, or self-confidence in my ability to drive this motorcycle. It was the spirit of the living God rushing through my veins, my mind and my body.

I shouted to Danny you over the sound of the motorcycle engine, and the rain, "Hold on Danny!" I am sure that at that moment Danny Montes had no idea what as of about to do. I gave him the opportunity to try to stop me. He wrapped his arms tight around my waist as a revved the engine of the motorcycle.

With that declaration, I shifted into first gear, and release the clutch. I took off, shifting into second gear and then shifting into third gear going down the muddy bank. Then I went up the muddy embankment they had built to get to the planks. Remember this was only designed for foot traffic during the day. It was not designed to be used across at night, or for that matter to people on a motorcycle.

I came up onto the first plank. I gunned the throttle and drove the motorcycle onto the first wet, slimy, loose plank—not slipping one time. I still can remember the dim headlight of the motorcycle reflecting off of the wet planks. The friend will of the motorcycle staying right in the middle of the narrow planks one after another. The rushing deep dark river about 5 feet below us. Just one slip, one miscalculation, one turning of the handlebars in the slightest direction, and we would've been swallowed up by the river never to be seen or heard from again.

Over 300 feet of the slimy plank in the rain, with fog, with a very dim headlight! THIS WAS GOD ALL THE WAY! If I would've gone to the left or to the right, either way, half of foot, we would have plummeted into the raging river. It was the Spirit of God that took us across that three-hundred-foot river in the rain and fog, over a precarious bridge that was only made for foot traffic during the daytime. To make a long story short, the Lord saw us safely to Danny's house.

Years later I went on the internet to look at this river I had crossed. The internet image had been updated in 2010. The new bridge they were just beginning to build at that time has been completed. You can see the alternative road we had to take as another route until the new bridge had been built. I am overwhelmed at the amazing things I have watched God do.

I know after that experience Pastor Danny Montes named his next child Michael and his following daughter Kathleen which is my wife's name. A kind of always thought that maybe he did that because of the experience we had that night. Maybe someday he'll tell me if that's true or not.

For with God nothing shall be impossible. And Mary said,
Behold the handmaid of the Lord; be it unto me according to thy
word. And the angel departed from her (Luke 1:37-38).

Because we needed to contact the airline three days in advance before we were to leave, we had to have someone in Manila let them know the date we were leaving. Our tickets were open ended, meaning we could leave anytime we wanted to, we just had to let them know three days in advance. This particular minister, who seemed to be enamored with our lack of fear, was headed back to Manila. We asked him if he would please let the airlines know when we were going to be leaving. He said he would be glad to do that for us. We gave him the dates that we were leaving.

There was unrest in my soul as we said goodbye to him. There was just something about him that made me extremely hesitant to trust him. When we were finished with our meetings in Samar, we caught a plane ride back to Manila. We called this minister, and he came and picked us up in his car at the airport. When we got into his vehicle, he began to talk right away about the meetings he had lined up for us. I asked him, "What meetings are you talking about? We are to be leaving tomorrow." I asked him whether or not he had contacted the airlines for us. He informed us in a hesitant murmuring way that he had not.

The red lights began to flash in my heart right away. It's like I heard the Lord say, get on a plane tomorrow, and get out of this nation. This man has set you up to be murdered. I leaned over and told my friend what the Spirit had spoken to me. He agreed with me one hundred percent. I told him that we were sorry, but that we could not accommodate him since we were leaving the next day. He looked back at us, and basically said that's impossible. You have to give a three-day notice. You might as well go ahead and minister at the meetings I have set up.

We discovered later that he had been making outrageous statements about us, making it sound like we were there to challenge the Communists and were not afraid to die. Of course, the

NPA would come to kill us, not because we were preaching Jesus Christ, but because this man made it sound like we were challenging them and their movement. I did not argue with this man any longer. We stayed at his house that night.

Early in the morning, we woke up and got ready to go to the airport. We discovered he had not taken us seriously about taking us to catch a flight. We insisted that he take us immediately. Finally, he grudgingly agreed. We had him drop us off at the airport and told him he could go home. He said he would wait for us because he knew it was impossible for us to leave. We went to the main office of the airline.

They informed us that our tickets could not be changed because we were flying economy and their plane had already been booked to capacity for the day. I very politely asked if there was someone higher up we could speak to. He took us to a gentleman. We explained to him we needed to leave. When he asked why, I informed him we could not give him a direct answer to his question, but we simply needed to leave. He asked us to wait a little bit for an answer. We stepped out of his office into the foyer.

After a little while, he called us back in. He told us that they were going to do it. Amazingly, they had bought us tickets from a much more expensive airline. He handed us two new tickets and told us that we better hurry to catch the flight, which was boarding at that very moment. As we ran to catch a flight, we saw the minister standing behind the rope line waiting for us. We waved goodbye to him as we headed to catch our flight home.

I know thy works: behold, I have set before thee an open door, and no man can shut it: for thou hast a little strength, and hast kept my word, and hast not denied my name (Revelation 3:8).

Healed When I Slammed My Broken Foot Down the 5ᵗʰ Time

One day I had to climb our 250 foot AM radio tower in order to change the light bulb on the main beacon. However, in order to climb the tower, I had to first find the keys; which I never did. Since I could not find the keys to get the fence open, I did the next best thing—I simply climbed over the fence.

This idea turned out not to be such a wonderful idea after all! With all of my climbing gear hanging from my waist, I climbed the fence to the very top. At this point, my rope gear became entangled in the fencing. As I tried to get free, I lost my balance and fell backwards off the fence. Trying to break my fall, I got my right foot down underneath me. I hit the ground with my foot being turned on its side and I felt something snap in the ankle. I knew instantly I had a broken foot, my ankle.

Most normal people would have climbed back over the fence, go set up a doctor's appointment, have their foot x rayed, and then placed into a cast. But I am not a normal-thinking person, at least according to the standards of the modern day church. When I broke my foot, I followed my routine of confessing my stupidity to God, and asking Him to forgive me for my stupidity.

Moreover, then I spoke to my foot and commanded it to be healed in the name of Jesus Christ of Nazareth. When I had finished speaking to my foot, commanding it to be healed, and then praising and thanking God for the healing, there seem to be no change what so ever in its condition.

The Scripture that came to my heart was where Jesus declared, *"The kingdom of heaven suffereth violence, and the violent take it by force!"* Based completely upon this scripture, I decided to climb the tower by faith, with a broken foot mind you. Please do not misunderstand, my foot hurt so bad I could hardly stand it. And yet, I had declared that I believed I was healed.

184

There were three men watching me as I took the Word of God by faith. I told them what I was about to do, and they looked at me like as if I had lost my mind. I began to climb the 250-foot tower, one painful step at a time.

My foot hurt so bad that I was hyperventilating within just twenty to thirty feet up the tower. It literally felt like I was going to pass out from shock at any moment. Whenever I got to the point of fainting, I would connect my climbing ropes to the tower, stop and take a breather, crying out to Jesus to help me. It seemed to take me forever to get to the top.

Even so, I finally did reach the very top of the tower and replaced the light bulb that had gone out. Usually I can come down that tower within 10 minutes, because I would press my feet against the tower rods, and then slide down, just using my hands and arms to lower myself at a very fast pace.

However, in this situation, my foot could not handle the pressure of being pushed up against the steel. Consequently, I had to work my way down very slowly. After I was down, I slowly climbed over the fence one more time. I hobbled my way over to my vehicle, and drove up to the church office. The men who had been watching this unfold, were right behind me.

I hobbled my way into the front office; which is directly across the street from the radio tower. I informed the personnel that I had broken my foot, showing them my black and blue, extremely swollen foot. It did not help that I had climbed with it! I told them that I was going home to rest. At the same time, however, I told them that I believed I was healed.

Going to my house, which is directly across from the main office of the church parking lot, I made my way slowly up the stairs to our bedroom. I found my wife in the bedroom putting away our clothes. Slowly and painfully I pulled the shoe and sock off of the broken foot.

What a mess! It was fat, swollen, black and blue all over. I put a pillow down at the end of the bed, and carefully pulled myself up onto the bed. Lying on my back, I tenderly placed my broken, black and blue, swollen foot onto the pillow. No matter how I positioned it, the pain did not cease. I just laid there squirming, moaning and sighing.

As I was lying there trying to overcome the shock that kept hitting my body, I heard the audible voice of God. He said to me: "What are you doing in bed? God really got my attention when I heard him with my natural ears. My wife would testify that she heard nothing. Immediately in my heart I said: Lord I'm just resting. Then He spoke to my heart with the still small voice very clearly, Do you always rest at this time of day? No, Lord, I replied. (It was about 3 o'clock in the afternoon)

He spoke to my heart again and said: I thought you said you were healed?

At that very moment the gift of faith exploded inside of me. I said, "Lord, I am healed! Immediately, I pushed myself up off of the bed, grabbed my sock and shoe, and struggled to put them back on. What a tremendous struggle it was! My foot was so swollen that it did not want to go into the shoe. My wife was watching me as I fought to complete this task.

You might wonder what my wife was doing this whole time as I was fighting this battle of faith. She was doing what she always does, just watching me and shaking her head. I finally got the shoe on my swollen, black and blue foot. I put my foot down on the floor and began to put my body weight upon it. When I did, I almost passed out. At that moment, a holy anger exploded on the inside of me. I declared out loud, "I am healed in the name of Jesus Christ of Nazareth!" With that declaration, I took my right (broken) foot, and slammed it down to the floor as hard as I possibly could.

When I did that, I felt the bones of my foot break even more. Like the Fourth of July, an explosion of blue, purple, red, and white, black exploded in my brain and I passed out. I came to lying on my bed. Afterward, my wife informed me that every time I passed out, it was for about ten to twenty seconds.

The moment I came to, I jumped right back up out of bed. The gift of faith was working in me mightily. I got back up and followed the same process again, "In the name of Jesus Christ of Nazareth I am healed," and slammed my foot down once more as hard as I could! For a second time, I could feel the damage in my foot increasing. My mind was once again wrapped in an explosion of colors and pain as I blacked out.

When I regained consciousness, I immediately got up once again, repeating the same process. After the third time of this happening I came to with my wife leaning over the top of me. I remember my wife saying as she looked at me, "You're making me sick. I can't watch you do this." She promptly walked out of our bedroom, and went downstairs.

The fourth time I got up declaring, "In the name of Jesus Christ of Nazareth I am healed," and slammed my foot even harder! Once more, multiple colors of intense pain hit my brain. I passed out again! I got up the fifth time, angrier than ever. This was not a demonic or proud anger.

This was a divine gift of violent I-will-not-take-no-for-an-answer type of faith. I slammed my foot down the fifth time, "In the name of Jesus Christ of Nazareth I am healed!" The minute my foot slammed into the floor, for the fifth time, the power of God hit my foot. I literally stood there under the quickening power of God, and watched my foot shrink and become normal.

All of the pain was completely and totally gone. I pulled back my sock, and watched the black and blue in my foot disappear to normal flesh color. I was healed! Praise God, I was made whole! I went back to the office, giving glory to the Lord and showing the staff my healed foot.

Casting out a Devil easily

As many of the congregation were laughing, shouting, crying I heard a laughter that seemed to be out of sync. Now, I really cannot claim that I can play any instruments, though I did take drum lessons, and I did at one time try to learn to play the guitar. If you strum the strings of the guitar even if you're not a Musician many times you will be able to tell when one of the strings is completely out of tune. As I'm standing in the front of the congregation, I heard one of the strings that seemed to be off.

I looked over to my left and there was one of the young men in our church. He was approximately 20 years old. This was a wonderful young man of God. I looked at him and he was laughing uncontrollably to the point to where his face had completely turned beet red. As I looked at him the Holy Spirit said to me: this laughter is not of me.

You need to cast the devil out of him! This is very important that you hear this. There are many people laughing, and yet this man's laughter was not of God. This young man needed deliverance. The problem with many ministers today is they really do not know God to the place where they can discern what's of the Lord and what's not. If we are not mature in the things of the spirit, and if we do not know the voice of God we can do much damage.

We can do damage in two ways. #1 by ignoring manifestations that are not of God. If we let them continue, it will bring death and destruction for the flesh profited nothing. #2 the second way we can do much damage is if we do not deal with this situation with love and wisdom. In my heart, I knew exactly what needed to be done.

I did not take the microphone and say to the congregation! Now, you all watch what I'm about to do. I am about to cast the devil out of brother so and so. Neither did I stop the service, and become paranoid over everybody else laughing. Just because one man's laughter was not of God did not mean that everybody's laughter was not of God.

As this young man was laying on the floor laughing hysterically, with his face completely beet red, I simply walked up to him. I put my hand on his body. I leaned down and very quietly with an authoritative voice I said: you Foul Unclean Spirit Come Out of him NOW in the name of Jesus! After I spoke this over him, I straightened up and backed off.

You see I knew, that I knew, that I knew this spirit had to come out of this young man. That I did not have to make a big show like Ed Sullivan. That I have authority with Christ because I was submitted to Christ! People who are not submitted to God will not be able to exercise this kind of authority. It is not that I'm super spiritual, but I just simply knew within my heart in every area of my life as far as I knew I was submitted to God.

I backed away from this young man about 10 feet. He was still laughing uncontrollably when suddenly by the gift of discernment I saw the spirit leave them. Immediately he stopped laughing. The beet red from his face completely disappeared. At that moment he began to weep uncontrollably.

He began to cry out to God, repenting from whatever sin he had been involved in. Tears filled my eyes as I watched this precious young man become delivered from an unclean spirit. Nobody in the congregation knew what was happening. I never said anything over the pulpit about this situation. Here it is over 20 years later when I am finally sharing this story. This young man went on to serve God. I never pulled him aside and told him we needed to go through generational deliverance. I never even said a word to him about what happened that day. I never asked him what sins he was involved in?

There is a natural tendency of people wanting to make a big to do out of deliverance. It is the Holy Ghost and the anointing of the spirit of the Lord that will set people free. Yes, we do need our minds renewed, but we do not need hours and hours of deliverance. When you exalt the devil, he will love to come. If we will exalt Jesus Christ the Holy Ghost will come flooding in like a mighty River, or like a mighty wind, or like a consuming fire! All glory and praise to God.

Do Not Leave Naomi Alone in a Car Seat

(1998) A True and Tragic Story of how our little girl Naomi got hurt!

This story is very difficult for me to share. I love to share the positive things that have happened in my life since I have been with Christ but there are also tragedies because of my disobedience or ignorance. This is one of those tragic stories. I was in prayer one day crying out to God when the Spirit of the Lord quickened me and said, **"Do not leave your daughter Naomi alone in her car seat or else she will be seriously injured."**

It was so strong in my heart that I went straight to my wife weeping and in tears. I told her not to leave Naomi alone in the car seat because the Lord told me that she would be seriously hurt if we did. During this time, my wife was struggling with confidence in me because I had made many decisions which were out of the will of God.

One major issue was that she did not want to live in the monstrous house that I had built. But, I had hardened my heart and would not listen to her. The car seat we were using for our daughter had been given to us by one of our parishioners. There seemed to be something seriously wrong with this child seat. My wife was cleaning it and working on it as she cried in frustration. I remember her saying that there was something wrong with this particular seat. We have no idea why, on God's green earth, we did not discard it. Unbeknownst to us, a major part of the chair was missing.

Approximately two weeks later, our little girl (Naomi) was hung by the straps in this chair. She was 18 months old at the time, our youngest daughter. I was not at home at the time of this incident, when Naomi got hurt. That particular morning, the Spirit had quickened my heart to go home from the office to be with my wife and children. But I disobeyed and went out and ate with a local pastor instead. I received a phone call from the office at the restaurant telling me that an ambulance was going to my house because something tragic had happened to our little girl; informing me that she had been accidentally hung in her car seat.

I truly believe that if I would have been there before the medical world got involved, then things would've been different. The physicians told us that our little girl was brain dead, but we prayed, believed and knew in our heart that she was not. This was the beginning of a nightmare that seemed to continue for about 4 to 5 years. And then, in the year 2000, she went home to be with the Lord!

Remove the Life-Support Equipment Now

We were staying at the Ronald McDonald House where our little girl Naomi was taken to Hershey Medical Center. Thank God for people who want to help people in need. Our daughter was in the intensive care unit. My wife and I were told that she was brain dead as they constantly tried to convince us to donate her organs.

We are not talking about just once or twice but on a consistent daily basis. They kept insisting that her organs could help others who were in critical need of a transplant. We had walked into a living nightmare. My wife and I kept crying out to God. After about a month, one night, as I was walking the floor at the Ronald McDonald House at about three o'clock in the morning, the Spirit of the Lord arrested me.

He told me that I was ashamed of the gospel of Christ. I asked, "Lord, what do you mean?" He informed me that I needed to go in and take authority; that the doctors and the medical staff were not my God. You need to go in and take charge, I was commanded.

The Spirit of God informed me that our daughter did not need to be on life-support because she could breathe on her own. Furthermore, I learned that many of the symptoms that she was experiencing was from the medication that they had overdosed her on. Early the following morning, I told my wife to get ready because it was going to be a rough day. I walked in that morning with my minister's collar with which I usually conduct official business.

Because I have a PhD and a Doctor of Divinity, I always required that the medical personnel address me as Dr. Yeager. I went in and confronted the person who oversaw the hospital floor. I insisted for them to remove the breathing tube. They informed me that they could not because she could not live without it. I told the charge nurse that I wanted to speak to the next higher up.

Granted, I did get loud, but I was not ignorant, ungodly, or nasty. Finally, after numerous interviews, the head doctor came. I told him enough is enough; take that equipment off my daughter! He finally agreed to do this. You need to understand that all this time they had been harassing us to donate her organs. The love of money is the root of all evil! When the man who was over the life-support equipment came, I stood by as he extubated her. He let slip a revealing statement.

He said this equipment should have been removed weeks ago. I said, what? He said yes, she does not need this equipment. When they removed the breathing equipment, she breathed easily on her own. As I retell the story, it is almost like it happened just yesterday.

I hope that as I continue to relate what happened, that it will be able to bring understanding to you about why things happen the way they do. I desire for the reader to realize that it is not always God's will for us to endure all of the things that we go through, rather it is because of our disobedience, lack of knowledge, and not hearing from heaven.

Shocking visitation
I Had a Revelation of My Selfish Heart!

One night at about 3 AM as I was walking the floor with Naomi in prayer, a bright light shone upon me. To me, it was literal and real. Immediately, I had a revelation of the selfishness in my heart. I saw myself in my true spiritual condition. I felt as guilty as the day is long.

The Spirit of God began to deal with my heart about how I had disobeyed him and how I had opened the door for all of these tragedies to take place. He also informed me that the house I was living in was an Ishmael; that I needed to forsake it. Previously, when I had walked the land that I had built this house upon, I had heard the voice of God telling me not to build it. But one act of disobedience leads to another. This had also led me into preaching and teaching a seeker-friendly message that would not produce within God's people the image of Christ.

The true message of the gospel is: Thy Kingdom Come Thy Will Be Done on Earth as It Is in Heaven! (Not My Will but His Be Done) When I had this visitation, it filled me with shock and amazement. I cried out to God and repented. I stood before the church the next Sunday morning and acknowledged my sins.

We, as spiritual leaders in the body of Christ, can only take people where we have trod. If we are self-loving, self-serving, and self-seeking then that is exactly where we will lead our flock. We can only reproduce that which we are! If we as leaders are covetous and materialistic then that is exactly what we will produce. God deliver and help us all!

Jeremiah 17:9 The heart is deceitful above all things, and desperately wicked: who can know it?

When The Whirlwind of God Came!

One Sunday, as I was preaching, the Holy Ghost began to pour through me in a mighty way. The spirit of the Lord was present in a powerful way to bring conviction to his people. Those present began to be convicted of their sins. As I was preaching the power of God came through the midst of the congregation like a mighty whirlwind. There was almost three hundred members there.

In the Spirit I saw two whirlwinds come through the right side and left side back of the Sanctuary! When these invisible whirl winds reached the congregation something really strange happened! People were actually being picked up out of their chairs and tossed around as if a miniature tornado was coming through the sanctuary.

After this experience I had one of the sisters come to me saying that she literally felt herself being picked up and tossed across the room. I remember watching her fly through the air.

Not one person that was tossed around had any type of injury or bruises. Some might doubt if this was really God, but it's because they are strangers to who God really is. I have seen this same phenomenon on numerous occasions through the years as I have been preaching the word of the Lord. It is not because I'm preaching condemnation or legalism, but it is the mighty hand of Who is an awesome God.

Weeping and waling exploded over the whole congregation. It seemed like every one was weeping Loudly! They could no longer hear what I was Preaching because they were experiencing the Holy Presence and Fear of the Lord!

As the fear of the Lord came upon the congregation I walked away from the pulpit! I went to my office to lie on my face. After the service people came and told me that many stood up and confessed their sins. No one had encouraged them to do this. But the spirit of God was upon them in such a mighty way that they could not help themselves. When true revival comes you will see many of those who confess they wanted revival, running to preserve their fleshly lives.

During this time the church went through a time of great purging and cleansing. But we discovered very quickly that we did not have a very solid foundation. People could not deal with the convicting power of God. Many of them had never experienced the fear of the Lord. Paul the apostle declared, knowing the terror of the Lord we persuade men!

He also declared, working out your own salvation with fear and trembling for it is God which worketh in you both to will and to do of his good pleasure. God was calling us into his image and likeness, to be holy as He is holy! But the process is too painful for many of those who claim to love to know Christ.

Sixteen Hours On My Face for my Son Would Not die from rabies

My son Daniel when he was 16 years old (in 2000) brought home a baby raccoon. He wanted to keep this raccoon as a pet. Immediately people began to inform me that this was illegal in the state of Pennsylvania. That in order to have a raccoon in Pennsylvania you had to purchase one from someone who was licensed by the state to sell them. The reason for this was the high rate of rabies carried among them. But stubbornness rose up in my heart against what they were telling me.

You see I had a raccoon when I was a child. Her mother had been killed on the Highway, and she had left behind a litter of her little ones. I had taken one of the little ones and bottle-fed it, naming her candy. I had a lot of fond memories of this raccoon, so when my son wanted this raccoon, against better judgment, against the law of the land, I said okay.

I did not realize that baby raccoons can have the rabies virus lying dormant in them for months before it will be manifested. I knew in my heart at the time that I was wrong to let him keep this raccoon, but like so many when we are out of the will of God we justify ourselves.

We do not realize the price that we will have to pay because of our rebellion and disobedience. Daniel named his little raccoon rascal, and he was a rascal because he was constantly getting into everything. A number of months went by, and one day my son Daniel told me he had a frightening dream. I should've known right then and there that he needed to get rid of this raccoon. He said he had a dream where rascal grew up and became big like a bear, and that it attacked him and devoured him.

Some time went by and my son Daniel began to get sick, running a high fever. One morning he came down telling me that something was majorly wrong with rascal. He said that he was wobbling all over the place, and bumping into stuff. Immediately the alarm bells went off.

I asked him where his raccoon was. He informed me that rascal was in his bedroom. Immediately I went upstairs to his room, opening his bedroom door, and their rascal was acting extremely strange. He was bumping into everything, with spittle coming from his mouth. Immediately my heart was filled with great dread. I had grown up around wildlife and farm animals, and I had run into animals with rabies before.

No ifs and's or buts, this raccoon had rabies. I immediately went to Danny asking him if the raccoon had bitten him, or if he had gotten any of rascal saliva in his wounds? He showed me his hands where he had cuts on them, informing me that he had been letting rascal lick these wounds. He had even allowed rascal to lick his mouth. Daniel did not look well, and he was running a high-grade fever and informed me that he felt dizzy.

I knew in my heart we were in terrible trouble. I immediately called up the local forest ranger. They put me on the line with one of their personnel that had a lot of expertise in this area. When I informed him of what was going on, he asked me I did not know that it was illegal to take in a wild raccoon. I told him I did know, and that I had chosen to ignore the law.

He said that he would come immediately over to our house to examine this raccoon and if necessary to take it with him. I had placed rascal in a cage, making sure I did not touch him. When the forest ranger arrived I had the cage sitting in the driveway. He examined the raccoon without touching it. You could tell that he was quite concerned about the condition of this raccoon.

He looked at me with deep regret informing me that if he had ever seen an animal with rabies that according to his almost 30 years in wildlife service, this raccoon definitely had rabies. He asked me if there was anyone who had been in contact with this raccoon with any symptoms of sickness. I informed him that for the last couple days my son Daniel had not been feeling well. Matter of fact he was quite sick.

When I told him the symptoms that Daniel was experiencing he was obviously shaken and upset. He told me that anybody who had been in contact with this raccoon would have to receive shots and that from the description of what my son Daniel was going through, and for how long, that it was too late for him! He literally told me he felt from his experience that there was no hope for my son, and he would die from rabies.

He loaded the raccoon up in the back of his truck, leaving me standing in my driveway weeping. He said that he would get back to me as soon as they had the test results and that I should get ready for state officials to descend upon myself, my family and our church.

I cannot express to you at that moment the hopelessness and despair that had struck my heart. Just earlier in the spring, our little girl Naomi had passed on to be with the Lord at 4 ½ years old, and now my second son Daniel was dying from rabies. Both of these situations could've been prevented if I would have simply listened to the Spirit of God! Immediately I gathered together my wife, my first son Michael, my third son Steven, and my daughter Stephanie.

We all gathered around Daniels bed and began to cry out to God. We wept, cried, and prayed crying out to God. I was repenting and asking God for mercy. Daniel, as he was lying on the bed running a high fever and almost delirious, informed me that he was dying, and he was barely hanging on to consciousness. He knew in his heart he said that he was dying! That he was going to Hell because he was living a lukewarm life. I begged him to repent. He told me he could not because it would not be sincere! I began to WEEP because I did not want him to go to Hell or Die!

After everyone disbursed from his bed with great overwhelming sorrow, I went into our family room where we had a wood stove. I opened up the wood stove which still had a lot of cold old wood ashes from the winter. Handful after handful of ashes I scooped out of the stove pouring it over my head, saturating my body, with weeping and tears of repentance and sorrow running down my face, and then I laid in the ashes.

The ashes got into my eyes, mouth, and nose and into my lungs, making me quite sick. I did not care, all that mattered was that I needed God to have mercy on us, and spare my son, and all our loved ones from the rabies virus.

As I lay on the floor in the ashes, crying out to God with all I had within me, you could hear the house was filled with weeping, crying and praying family members. All night long I wept and prayed, asking God to please have mercy on my stupidity. I prayed that He would #1 remove the rabies virus from my son. #2 That HE would remove it from everyone else that had been in contact with this raccoon.

#3 I also asked God to remove the virus from the raccoon otherwise every one have to vaccinations including my associate pastors eight-month pregnant wife!. I continued in this state of weeping and great agony and prayer all night till early in the morning. After about sixteen hours suddenly the light of heaven shined upon my soul. Great peace that passes understanding overwhelmed me, I got up with victory in my heart and soul. Now, tears of joy overwhelmed me!

I KNEW GOD HAD ANSWERED MY CRY FOR MERCY!

I went upstairs to check on my son Daniel. When I walked into his bedroom the presence of God was all over him. The fever had broken, and he was resting peacefully. Our whole house was filled with the tangible presence of God. From that minute forward he was completely healed.

A couple days later I was contacted by the state informing me that to their amazement they could find nothing wrong with the raccoon. God had supernaturally removed the rabies virus not only from my son, and those in contact with rascal but from the raccoon itself. Thank God that the Lord's mercy endures forever!

PS: They did give me a fine which I was glad to pay!.

CHAPTER NINE

Men, Women, Children, New-borns COULD NOT MOVE or SPEAK for 2 1/2 Hours

My family and I travelled out West ministering in different churches and visiting relatives in Wisconsin. We were invited to speak at a church in Minneapolis, Minnesota. The pastor actually had two different churches that he pastored. One of these churches was in the suburbs, and the other one was in the heart of Minneapolis.

The larger of the two churches was in the suburbs. I was to minister at the larger church first, and then immediately go to his other church downtown. The whole congregation was in the same service that morning. There were approximately 140 to 160 people including women, men, children, and babies in the sanctuary.

As I began to speak, I found myself unexpectedly speaking on the subject of: The year that King Uzia died, I saw the Lord high and lifted up, and his glory filled the Temple, which is found in the book of Isaiah!

The unction of the Holy Ghost was upon me so strong, that it just flowed out of my belly like rivers of living water. To this day I do not remember everything that I said. As I was speaking, I sensed an amazing heavenly touch of God's presence on myself and on everyone in the sanctuary.

The spirit of God was on me in a mighty way, and yet I was aware of the time factor. In order to get to Pastor Bill's sister church downtown Minnesota, I was not going to have time to lay hands on, or pray for anyone. If God was going to confirm his word with signs following, then he would have to do it without me being there.

It turns out that is exactly what God wanted to do! When I was at the limit of the amount of the time allotted to me, I quickly closed with a prayer. I did not say anything to the pastor or anyone else as I grabbed my Bible to leave the sanctuary. My family was already loaded up and waiting for me in our vehicle. As I ran out the door I perceived something strange, awesome and wonderful was beginning to happen to the congregation. There was a heavy, amazing and holy hush that had come upon them.

By the time I arrived at the other church, their worship had already begun. As I stood up in the pulpit to Minister God's word, the Holy Spirit began to speak to me again, with a completely, totally different message. God did wonderful things in the sister church downtown that afternoon as I preached a message on being radically sold out and committed to Christ. Everyone ended up falling out of their chairs to the floor on their faces, weeping and crying before the Lord.

This is not something I have ever encouraged any congregation to do. I have seen this happen numerous times where I simply have to stop preaching because the presence of God is so strong, and so real that people cannot stay in their seats. I would stop preaching, get on my face, and just wait on God, as he moved on the people's hearts.

After that service we went back to our fifth wheel trailer at the local campgrounds where we were camping. Later in the day, I received a phone call from this pastor. He was acting rather strange and speaking very softly in a very hushed manner.

He asked me with a whisper: does that always happen after you are done preaching? I said to him, tell me what happened. He said, "As you were headed out the door, I began to melt to the floor, I could not keep standing, and I found myself pinned to the floor of the sanctuary.

I could not move or speak." Now all the children (including babies) were in the sanctuary with the rest of the congregation. He said he personally could not move for two and a half hours. During this whole experience he did not hear another sound in the facility.

For over two and a half hours he just simply laid there not being able to move or speak a word under the presence and mighty hand of God. After two and a half hours Pastor Bill was able to finally move, and to get up.

He had thought for sure that he was the only one still left in the church. Everybody must have gone home a long time ago, and that he was there by himself. But to his complete shock and amazement everybody was still there, laying on the floor. Nobody could move or speak for over two and a half hours! Men, women, children and even the babies were still lying on the floor, not moving, talking, or crying! God was in the house! The tangible, overwhelming, solemn, presence, and holiness of God had come!

Pastor Bill asked me to come over to his house so we could talk about what happened that day in his church service. My family and I arrived. He invited us inside. He asked if this normally happens wherever I went. I informed him, no, but many wonderful and strange things do take place. It did not always happen, except when I get myself in a place of complete, absolute surrender and submission to Jesus Christ.

This submission included not putting ANYTHING else but the WORD of God into my heart. When I simply seek the face of God, by praying, giving myself completely to the word, meditation, singing and worship, intimacy with the Father, Son and Holy Ghost, this was the result! God is not a respecter of people, what he does for one, he will do for others!

Saved from a Terrible Death at the Mississippi

Many times in my life I have had vivid experiences, perceiving that God is about to do something or that something is about to take place right before it happens! Here is just one example.

On August 1, 2007 my wife, three sons, daughter and I were traveling on Highway I 35 West. We were in our Toyota crew cab pickup truck, pulling a 35 foot fifth wheel trailer. We were on vacation and headed for Yellowstone National Park. At the time, we were headed towards the downtown area of Minneapolis, Minnesota.

As I was driving, I sensed in my heart that we needed to get off this highway even though our GPS was taking us the shortest route to where we were headed. I have discovered and personally experienced 20 major ways that God leads and guides. All 20 of these specific ways in which God leads and guides can be discovered in the Scriptures. What I felt is what I call a Divine unction of the Holy Ghost. It is more than a perception or a feeling. It is more like an overwhelming urgency that flows up out of your belly.

I informed my family that something definitely was wrong, that there was an urgency in my heart and we needed to get off this highway I 35 W. immediately. This is the only time that I have experienced the urgency to get off a road or highway like this. I took the nearest exit and went north towards Canada. After a while, we connected to another highway and headed west. Later in the day, we pulled into a store to take a break from driving. As we entered this facility, we noticed that there were people gathered around the TV.

We could see that some major disaster had taken place. The viewer's informed us that a bridge had collapsed over the Mississippi River earlier in the day with lots of traffic that was loaded on top of it. We could see cars, trucks, buses everywhere that had fallen into the Mississippi.

Amazingly it was the highway the spirit of God Quicken my heart to get off of, it was I 35 W! If I had not left the highway, we would have been on that bridge when it collapsed into the Mississippi River. Thirteen people died that day and (145) were seriously injured. Not including all of the terrible destruction, and horrible nightmare that took place with all of those who were a part of this tragedy. Only God knows if we would've died or not if I had not been obedient to that Holy Ghost unction.

2 Timothy 4:17 Notwithstanding the Lord stood with me, and strengthened me; that by me the preaching might be fully known, and that all the Gentiles might hear: and I was delivered out of the mouth of the lion.

The Dam at Wisconsin Dell Lake Broke

If I had not heard from God, my family and I would have been swept away when the dam broke at Dell Lake in Wisconsin!

On June 8, 2008 my family and I were in Wisconsin at Dell Lake ministering in special meetings for an Indian tribe called the Ho-Chunk Nation. We were there by their invitation. They had provided the facility, and all the advertisements. We had been having some wonderful services.

It was the second night of these meetings. At the end of the service out of the blue I heard the voice of God say: pack up your camper and leave tonight! It had been a long day and my flesh sure did not want to leave, but I know the voice of God. I told the sponsors of the meetings that I was sorry but I would have to go back to Pennsylvania, tonight. I could tell they were extremely disappointed. They tried to convince me to stay because God was moving in such a wonderful way, but I know the voice of God.

My family members were also disappointed. They asked me why we were leaving. They reminded me that I have never canceled or shortened my commitments. I told them I understood this. But we had to leave tonight. I did not know why. I heard the Lord tell me we must leave tonight, so tonight we will leave. We arrived back at the Dell Lake camp grounds. It was beginning to rain extremely hard.

My family asked if we could simply wait until the next morning because it was late, dark and raining heavily. I said no, we must go now! I backed my truck up to the fifth wheel trailer. I saw the spirit of God come upon my 2nd son Daniel, who does not like to get wet or even really work, begin to work frantically. I mean he really began to move like in the supernatural hurry. My boys and I connected up the 5th wheel camper, we picked up all of our equipment and drew in the extended sides of the trailer.

Everybody was wet and tired as we loaded into the crew cab Toyota truck. Then, we were on our way. I noticed as I drove past the Dell Lake dam that water was rushing by like a little river on both sides of the road. Some parts of the road were already flooded.

We drove through the night. There were times we had to crawl because the rain was coming down so hard, fog and strong winds. All the way through Wisconsin, Illinois and Indiana, Ohio the rain came. The wind was extremely strong. We saw 18 wheelers turned over. Lots of car accidents. Trees and debris were blowing everywhere. And yet God was protecting us.

The next day when we had finally arrived back in Pennsylvania, we discovered some shocking news. There had been hundreds of twisters and tornadoes right behind us which caused a huge amount of devastation. But that wasn't the only news. The dam at Dell Lake, Wisconsin had completely and totally collapsed. Dell Lake is the largest man-made lake in Wisconsin, and this had never happened before in all of its history. The whole lake rushed out over the town. We would have been washed away in the storm. There is video footage of this disaster on the Internet.

Psalm 124:1 If it had not been the Lord who was on our side, now may Israel say;2 If it had not been the Lord who was on our side, when men rose up against us:3 then they had swallowed us up quick, when their wrath was kindled against us:

Supernatural Download about faith

I was up early one morning in prayer, simply speaking to the Lord and praying in the spirit, when suddenly the heavens were opened to me. Within three minutes the Spirit of God downloaded into my mind forty major dimensions and aspects of faith. My mind was filled with a Revelation of faith that I had never had before. For over thirty years I have studied the subject of faith, and yet within those three minutes I perceived things about faith I had never heard, even though I had sat underneath renowned men of faith, and attended a school that majored on faith.

Now each of these forty major dimensions of faith had many truths. Some of them have up to twenty eight points. Immediately I grabbed a pen and paper. As I sat at my dining room table I did not have to think what to write, I simply put down on paper what the Lord quickened me. Many of the things the Lord showed me I had never been taught. For instance the Lord showed me that faith comes twenty eight different ways.

What he gave me in three minutes, took over three days to write down. Every dimension of faith the Lord showed me I have gone to the Scriptures to make sure it is absolute truth. Even dealing with the twenty eight ways that faith comes, I wanted to see it in the word. Sure enough faith does come by at least twenty eight ways. Every dimension of faith he spoke to my heart is in perfect agreement with the Bible.

This event took place in 2008 and ever since then, revelation keeps flowing to me on this subject. I am writing a book just to share eighteen ways that faith comes. The other aspects of faith would have to be a library of books. Over 95% of what the Lord had quickened to my heart was downloaded in me within three minutes or less. Now I understand how the prophets of old penned the prophetic words of the Old Testament. It was by the Holy Ghost. We still have the same Holy Ghost.

God is not giving us any new revelation, he is simply causing the Revelation that is in his word to come forth. Oh Lord let it come forth!!!

JESUS is to be The CENTRAL Theme of every message

One day as I was in prayer, I asked the Lord why we were not getting the same results as the early church did. Instead of coming right out and answering my question, the spirit of God put a prompting in my heart, challenging me to study specific words of the New Testament, and how many times these words were used. Below is a list of these words with a number of times they were spoken in the New Testament:

Faith - 245, Love - 180, Grace - 127, Believe - 124, Hope - 53, Trust - 27, Salvation - 43, Forgive - 28, Repent - 24, Spirit - 261, Holy - 181, Truth - 119, Sin - 112, and Anointing – 18. *These are just some of the words I looked up and studied!*

Then the Lord spoke to me very specifically. The Holy Spirit told me to look up every time Jesus Christ was mentioned, not just by name, but in a personal way! By the time I accomplished this task, I was completely flabbergasted and amazed! I discovered that Jesus Christ is revealed to us in a personal way over 9000 times.

After I had completed this task, the Lord spoke to my heart and said: they are not preaching the same gospel that the early church fathers did. This is why you are not getting the same results! In the early church, Jesus Christ was emphasized above all else. Now many of those who are teaching my word, emphasize many other subjects, but very rarely ever exalt MY Son Jesus Christ!

After I heard the Father say this, I began to listen to many, even well-known ministers and discovered they spoke much more on the anointing, power, authority, prosperity, the cross, grace, love …etc, but very rarely ever spoke about Jesus Christ in a continual and personal intimate way.

NEW TESTAMENT STATISTICS:
Number of books: 27
Chapters: 260
Verses: 7,957
Words: 180,552
Letters: 838,380
Jesus revealed personally: almost 10,000 times!

The Lord had me take a 1611 King James Version of the Bible, highlighting in bold every time Christ is mentioned in a personal way. He is the very center, heart, soul, mind and message that God the father has given to the human race. There are Scriptures that clearly declare that there is a transformation, metamorphosis that takes place in the human heart when they look upon, recognize, and have a revelation of Jesus Christ, and what He has accomplished for his beloved bride! If Jesus is not the central theme of every message, we are preaching another gospel!

This task was difficult in some regards, because of the oneness of Christ and his Father. There were many times, especially in the epistles when it was hard to discern who it was speaking about, whether it was the Heavenly Father, or His Son the Lord Jesus Christ! And yet the word of God has not been changed in the least. By the way, the Gospel is Jesus Christ!

Pastor Healed of Terrible Fungus

I Saw Through His Shoes And There Was Fungus On His Feet!

My wife and I were ministering at a church in the Harrisburg, Pennsylvania, area. I had finished ministering the message that God had laid on my heart and was beginning to move in the gifts of the Holy Spirit. God began to confirm His Word with some wonderful signs and wonders. The word of knowledge, wisdom and the discerning of spirits were manifested as I surrendered and yielded to the Spirit of God. New wine began to flow as people were being touched by the Holy Ghost. As I was finishing up with one of the people we were praying for, I looked over at the pastor who was sitting on the front row of chairs, with his wife.

This pastor is a rather large man, in height and in weight. The Holy Spirit drew my attention to his feet. Because he is also involved in the farming industry, he was wearing a heavy-duty pair of shoes. As I was looking at the shoes, all of a sudden, I could see right through them. It actually shocked me, to some extent.

I could very clearly see his feet and toes. This experience was so real that it pulled me right over to him. I stood in front of this pastor, looking at his feet, and with a look of surprise on my face. I pointed down at his feet and said: "What is going on with your toes?" He said: "What?" I repeated my question.

I could see they were completely covered in fungus. I saw that even the nails of his toes were either gone, or completely covered in a black, yellow, nasty fungus. I told him: "Fungus! Your toes and your feet are completely covered in fungus!" He answered: "Yes. They have been like that for many years. When I used to play football (must have been about forty-years earlier) somehow, I contracted this fungus and I have never been able to get rid of it."

209

I fell to my knees, right then and there, putting my hands on his shoes. I spoke to the fungus on his toes and feet and commanded that in the name of Jesus Christ, it had to go. I told the spirit of infirmity to leave his feet now in the name of Jesus. As I spoke the Word of God, I knew in my heart, by a gift of faith, and the gift of healing, he was healed. I told him: "It is gone! In the name of Jesus, it is gone and you are healed!" I got up from off the floor and by the Spirit of God, I continued to minister to others.

About a month later, I was back in this man's church ministering. I asked him: "Brother, how's your feet?" He told me the fungus was completely gone! After all those years he was now free. By the gifts of the Holy Ghost, Jesus Christ had revealed this need and caused him to be completely healed.

My Busted Broken Finger Healed!

We all do stupid things; that is just a part of our humanity. The question is: Will God still heal us in spite of our stupidity? I have discovered many times that the answer to this question is yes! Here is another example of something stupid I did and God was still there for me.

One day I walked into my son Daniel's house. He was in his front room playing a videogame. It's something called PlayStation Move, where he was playing a game called Sports Champion. He held a wand in his hand, thrusting it and waving it back and forth aggressively. As he was doing this, there was another man on the big screen TV following his moves as a fighting opponent.

Right then and there I should have turned around and walked out, but curiosity got the better of me. He asked me if I wanted to play a game with him because you could have two players at one time fighting each other. I thought about it for a while and decided, yes I would play. So he handed me another wand, showing me how to activate it. The object of the game was to wave and thrust the sword on the video by waving the wand in my hand. The man on the screen would follow my movements and fight for me.

He started the game console and we began. Of course, I had never played this game before nor do I make a habit of playing video games, so he was winning. I began to get more aggressive trying to win the game but no matter how much I tried, my son seems to be able to score points against me. I totally gave into my flesh and began to wave, stab and wave my make-believe sword everywhere.

I mean I really aggressively got into this thing. In the process of trying with everything inside me to win this game I did not notice that I had gotten close to hitting a heavy duty metal case that he had in his front room. Before I knew what I did, I was sweeping the sword to the right down away from me with all my might, and slammed my right hand into the corner of this metal cabinet.

I am telling you that I really slammed my hand extremely hard. My son Daniel said I hit the cabinet so hard that it put a dent in the cabinet. The minute I hit that cabinet with all my might, pain exploded through my body. I looked at my index finger and it was all mangled and twisted. Immediately, it swelled up turning black and blue and was twisted. Just looking at my busted up index finger made me sick.

I began to jump around holding my finger with my other hand. And this is what I was crying out to God as I was jumping and screaming, "Lord, please forgive me for being so stupid. Lord, I will never play this game again. I'm so sorry, Father God, in the name of Jesus I repent. I kept jumping around holding onto my finger crying out to God saying: I repent, I repent, I repent. Forgive me, Lord!"

My son Daniel looked at the finger and said dad you broke it, you are going to have to go to the doctor. With my finger so full of pain and my other hand holding it, I told him I did not need a doctor that I had Jesus Christ and he is the great physician. After I made sure that I had sufficient repentance, I spoke to my finger. I commanded my bones to be knit back together and for my finger to be made completely whole. And then I began to thank God that I was healed. I just kept praising the Lord that my finger was made whole no matter how it felt or how it looked.

The spirit of God must have spoken through me at that moment because I told my three sons that by tomorrow morning my finger would be completely well and you would not be able to tell that I had ever slammed it by being so stupid. When I was finished making this declaration of faith, I walked away from them holding onto my finger. Even though the pain was throbbing through my body, I just kept thanking God that I was healed.

My son Daniel still remembers very vividly how busted, twisted, broken, black and blue my finger was. I believe that he thinks it was rather funny how I was jumping around confessing and repenting and promising God to never do this again. I went to bed that night and fell asleep holding onto my finger, thanking God that I was healed. I was meditating on the Word and confessing that what Jesus did for me when he had taken the stripes on his back had the ability to completely make me whole from stupid accidents that were my fault.

The next morning when I woke up early to pray and seek God, I had completely forgotten about my finger. And then it hit me that there was no pain. I looked at my index finger and you could not even tell that I had busted, broken and bruised it. I was completely healed! I went and showed my three sons what God had done for me in spite of my own stupidity.

God is so awesome and amazing. All we have to do is cry out to Him and He will answer and deliver us from every situation if we simply trust, repent and obey him; giving praise and thanks no matter how it looks. How long do we keep thanking and praising God? We are to keep on knocking and to keep on asking until we receive the full manifestation of that which we believe for!

Matthew 21:14, And the blind and the lame came to him in the temple; and he healed them.

Heated Church for over two months on empty LP tank

On Monday, March 9th, 2015 I sat down to count the finances from Sunday, and some money that had come in by other sources. Our Sunday morning service had in attendance about 37 people, which I considered wonderful since everyone had lost about an hour of sleep with the time change. (it is one of our smallest attended services) so our offering was very small!

There in front of me sat a small bundle of $20s, along with some other size bills, and checks. Now, this is where it begins to get very interesting. The stack of $20 dollar bills in front of me was not very high, and I did not have a great expectation of there being very many $20 bills in this pile. In order to make this job as quick as possible, I decided that I would count out the $20 bills in piles of five which would equal $100 on each stack.

I picked up the pile of $20s bills and very quickly counted out five $20 bills. Then I counted out another pile of $20 bills which I laid in the opposite direction on top of the first pile. Then I counted out five more $20 bills and placed them in the same direction of the first pile of that stack. I was already kind of amazed because I did not think there was $300 in this pile of $20 bills.

I thought okay I guess I was wrong, here we go again. As I looked at the stack of money in my hand it seemed to me that it was not getting any smaller. By the time I had counted out 10 stacks of $20 bills I knew that I was experiencing a miracle of multiplication before my eyes.

My wife was sitting right next to me doing something on her computer, but I did not say anything to her because I thought that she would think I was nuts. Then I went through another five of the

213

$20s, and my heart began to beat faster in my chest. I got to thinking: will I be able to just keep counting this stack of $20 bills until we had the $120,000.00 we needed to get out of debt? I kept on counting pile after pile, after pile of $20 bills.

Okay, Lord, I prayed in my heart let it just keep on happening. I counted out another pile of five of these $20 bills. It did not look like the pile was getting any smaller.

In the past, I have had similar experiences with money and even gasoline in our vehicle, and LP fuel in our fuel tank. About 3 years ago our 1000 gallon LP tank ran out of gas behind the church. We had no money so I went out early Sunday morning in the winter, laid my hands on that tank, and ask God either to provide the money or to cause the gas to keep flowing from this empty tank.

I went into the church, and simply turned on the heater's(we have been smelling the garlic in the LP, and that meant the tank was empty) simply saying okay Lord here we go. Surprisingly the heaters came on with that lovely blue-yellow flame. For the next 2 ½ months (everybody in the church would march out on Sunday mornings and look at the empty gauge on the tank) our church was heated by an empty LP tank.

So now here I was counting $20s on Monday morning, and they just kept on coming. I counted out another stack of 5 of these $20 bills. And then I counted out another stack of 5 of these $20 bills, and then I counted out another stack of 5 of these $20 bills. Hallelujah thank you, Jesus, God is so wonderful.

I guess the Lord figured I was putting too much hope in a stack of $20s, so eventually, it simply ran out. By the time I was done counting this small stack of $20s I had over $2200 sitting there in front of me. Praise God, Jesus is so wonderful.

Multiplication of Money

Many times when we have made deposits at our local bank, our deposit slip is almost always wrong! Actually about 90% of the time there is more than what we calculated.

On one particular Monday morning when we normally make the deposit, I asked another brother at the church to help me. I told him: let us see what God will do today. I explained to him how every time I went to make a deposit, almost every time I had more cash than what I had counted. Now I am not real good at counting, but surely I could count sufficiently and not be wrong almost every time. I told Jesse that he could count the cash, and then I would count the cash. We both came up with the same amount. I told him: let's do it again. Sure enough we both came up with the same amount.

When we were done making the deposit slip, I went to the bank. I gave the teller the money bag. I jokingly said to the girl at the window; let's see if we got it right today. She laughed, because it was a running joke at the bank that I was never able to get the right amount of cash on the deposit slips.

After a brief period, the teller came back to the window and informed me that we were wrong as usual. I asked her if it was to the good or to the bad. She informed me that we had more cash on hand, than what was on the deposit slip. I asked her how much extra there was. She informed me that we had $400 more cash on hand, than what was on a deposit slip! Wow, God really did want us to understand that He is still in the business of doing miracles of multiplication.

The Song of Heaven in harmony

Amazing Dream of Creation Held Together by a Divine Song!

I had an amazing dream. It's very hard to describe in human terms. I was sleeping peacefully when, at about three o'clock in the morning, I was suddenly smack dab in the middle of heaven, close to the throne of God. It was so real and tangible; it literally felt as if I was in heaven physically. God gave me eyes to see all of existence. It was as if I was omnipresent. All of creation lay before me. My mind and emotions, and all five of my senses perceived all things. I embraced everything at one time.

It was the most amazing experience you could imagine. It was so beautiful and magnificent that it is beyond precise description. It could be likened to being in the eye of a storm with everything spinning around you. With this supernatural, imparted ability I could perceive the spiritual and angelic.

I saw angels of all types and ranks. I saw and felt the nature and the physical realms. I saw the planets, moons, stars, solar systems, and the whole universe. I saw animal life, plant life, oceans, seas, lakes, and rivers. I even saw the microscopic molecular realm. God supernaturally expanded my capacity mentally and emotionally to perceive all things. If it had not happened to me personally, I would be skeptical myself of someone saying these things.

In the midst of this experience I began to be overtaken by an absolute sense of incredible harmony. It was a unity and oneness of a mind-boggling proportion. It resonated through my whole being. I could feel it in my bones, flesh, emotions, and mind. My heart resonated with His harmony. My whole being was engulfed in this unbelievable symphony.

All creation, the universe, and spiritual realm was in complete and total harmony and unity. Instantly I perceived everything was at one with God. Not one molecule, not one atom or proton was out of sync with God. As I was looking at creation, suddenly I perceived an invisible force permeating and saturating all of it.

God literally gave me eyes to see this invisible force. I could see it moving, flowing, and penetrating everything. With this ability to see, He also gave me spiritual understanding. I realized at that moment that it was this incredible invisible force which was causing all things to exist and flow and move as one living, breathing creation.

What I am sharing with you was a progressive revelation unfolding before me like a flower blossoming. In the midst of this experience my ears opened, and I heard the most incredible music, a breathtaking song. This invisible force was literally a song that was being sung. Instantly I perceived that it was this music, this song, which was holding all of creation together. This song was permeating every animate and inanimate thing together.

Not only was it holding everything together but also everything was singing along with it. It was the most incredible music and song you could ever imagine. Actually it is beyond comprehension or human ability to describe this song and what it was doing. All of creation was being upheld and kept together by this song. I could see it and feel it. It was inside of me. I was a part of it. No maestro, psalmist, no Beethoven or Mozart could ever produce such a majestic masterpiece.

As I watched and listened, I was overwhelmed with the reality that it was this song that was causing everything to be in harmony and unity. It was this song causing everything to live, move, exist, and have being. During this experience a curiosity took a hold of me. I began to wonder, where is this music, this song, coming from?

I began to look high and low, trying to discover where this

song had originated. I finally looked behind me, and on a higher elevation I saw God sitting upon His throne. I did not see the clarity of God's form or face. He was covered in a glistening mist, somewhat like fog. But as I looked upon His form, it was as if my eyes zoomed in on His mouth. I was looking intently at the mouth of God. Out of His mouth was coming this amazing, beautiful, awesome song.

This song that God was singing was holding everything together and in perfect harmony. God the Father was making everything one with Himself through this song, this music coming out of His mouth. I literally could see, feel, and experience the song coming out of God's mouth. In my heart I said to the Father, "Father, how long will You sing this song?" And He spoke to me in my heart, "Throughout eternity, My voice will never cease to sing. My voice will never cease to be heard."

I could see letters streaming from God's mouth. Words were coming forth from His mouth. They were swimming in a river of transparent life, like fish swimming in a river. These words seemed to be alive. They were spreading throughout the entire universe, causing everything to exist and to be in harmony. They were permeating all of creation, visible and invisible, spiritual and natural.

I knew in my heart that this was the Word of God, the divinely inspired Scriptures. The Word was swimming as if in an invisible transparent river. I knew that this river was a living, quickening force. I knew that it was this river which was causing the Word of God to be alive. The Word of God was being carried forth by this river. I said to the Father, "Father, what is this river that the Word is flowing, swimming, and living in?" And He said to my heart, "It is the Holy Ghost!"

I was stunned into silence. After a while I repeated my question. Once again He said to me, "It is the Holy Ghost. It is the breath of My mouth coming from the voice of My lips. And this voice is My Son, Jesus Christ. My voice is My Son, Jesus Christ. And out of His voice comes the Holy Ghost and My

Word."

Further He said to me, "My Word would not sustain, heal, deliver, or bring life unless it is quickened and made alive by My Spirit." Then the Father confirmed this to me by quoting the Scripture where Jesus said, "My Words are Spirit, and they are life." (See John 6:63.) The Father spoke to me again and said, "You can quote, memorize, and declare the whole Bible, but it will be dead and lifeless until you yield, surrender, move, flow, and come into complete harmony with the Word of God and the Holy Ghost."

This I believe, to some extent, reveals God's eternal purpose for you and I: To be in complete oneness and harmony with God, the Father, the Son, and the Holy Ghost!

One dream can change the whole perspective of your life

It can open your eyes to truths and realities that you could never obtained by worldly knowledge or wisdom.

Completely Engulfed in a Consuming Fire

Back in 1980 I began to memorize and meditate on Scriptures declaring that fire cannot consume me.

Isaiah 43:2, "When thou passest through the waters, I will be with thee; and through the rivers, they shall not overflow thee: when thou walkest through the fire, thou shalt not be burned ; neither shall the flame kindle upon thee."

I meditated on the scriptures because I kept burning myself with our woodstove. Through the years, I have maintained these scriptures in my heart. In the summer of 2011, I had an amazing experience when God used these scriptures to come to my rescue, otherwise I would have been burned to death.

This particular morning, I woke up lost, totally DRUNK in the Holy Ghost. I mean, my mind and my heart was so caught up in God, I was totally **intoxicated** in the spirit. I was so heavenly minded at the time that you could even say I was not really much earthly good. In this condition I decided it was a good day to burn the large pile of brush that we had on our property.

This very large brush pile which was way over my head, and needed to be burned. It was a very, very hot day. I am sure it was over 90° outside! I took a 2-gallon plastic gas container to this pile of brush with the full intention of lighting the brush on fire. When I took the cap off this container, the container was so hot you could see the visible fumes pouring of the gasoline in the air. I had with me one of those long stemmed lighters that you can pick up at any hardware store.

I stepped into this pile of very dry brush which was higher than my head by about ten feet. I took the gas container and began to spread gasoline over the pile by splashing it out of the container all over the brush and wood pile. The liquid gasoline was up to the edge of my feet. Realize I am completely drunk in the Spirit.

At the time I was not at all thinking about what I was doing, I was simply meditating on the WORD of God Lost in the Holy Ghost. My son Daniel had come out of our house and was walking toward me. He saw me put the gas container in my left hand, with long stem Lighter in my right hand. The fumes were visible as they were radiating out of this container. I took the long stem lighter in my right hand and reached down to light the gas.

My son Daniel saw what I was about to do and started yelling at the top of his lungs, **DAD DONT**! I only heard him partly because I was so lost in the spirit, drunk, intoxicated. I pulled the trigger of the long stemmed lighter and instantly there was an explosion of fire all around me and I was totally engulfed in the flames of this explosion of fire.

I was completely surrounded with fire. My son Daniel said that he could not see me because the fire had swallowed me up. Daniel thought was burning to death, and there was nothing he could do about it! The FIRE was so hot he could not reach me to pull me out!

I remember being in the flames of this fire and it seemed as if there was this shimmering invisible force field around me, and the heat and the flames could not penetrate this invisible force field. This force field sparkled like glistening fog. Its color was light blue, silver, gold, and glistening white!

I remember standing being surrounded completely by fire thinking **WOW, this is Awesome**. And immediately at the same time something clicked in my head: You're in the **fire dummy**! You need to get out of this fire!

Immediately, I began to backtrack away from the fire walking backwards through the flames with the gas container still in my right hand! When I was out of the fire about 30 feet, I looked down at my body and my clothes and not a flame had kindled upon me. The gas container in my left hand alone should have exploded, because of the fumes that were coming out of it. I can truly say that not once did I feel the heat!

Once again God had miraculously delivered me from my stupidity. My son Daniel can attest to this story for he saw the whole thing. We rejoiced in God for His great mercy! Of course, my son Daniel was extremely upset with me and was in a state of shock and amazement because he saw me engulfed in the fire.

He thought surely I was a dead man! He also was traumatized because he could not get anywhere near the flames to rescue me. I told him years later that there was nothing he could have done. At the time it happened he did not realize that God was shielding me from the flames and **1500° degree heat!**

The most commonly known flammable liquid is gasoline. It has a flash point of about -50° F (-65° C). The ignition temperature is about 495° E (232° C), a comparatively low figure. Burning gasoline has a temperature above 1500° E (945° C)

Dan 3:24 Then Nebuchadnezzar the king was astonied, and rose up in haste, and spake, and said unto his counsellors, Did not we cast three men bound into the midst of the fire? They answered and said unto the king, True, O king. 25 He answered and said, Lo, I see four men loose, walking in the midst of the fire, and they have no hurt; and the form of the fourth is like the Son of God.

Saw by the Spirit He Was a Pedophile

I have a house where I rent at a very low price to single men. These men are either on assistance, getting out of jail, or even homeless. My whole purpose is to help them get back on their feet, or to help them assimilate back into society. Now to rent from me, there are certain criteria that you have to meet.

My house is in a residential area so I never rent to anybody who I would consider a danger to the community. There was an older gentleman who came to me who wanted to rent a room. I **perceived** in my heart that he was a pedophile. I asked him straight out if he was on Megan's list or if he had ever committed a sexual crime! He assured me that he was not on Megan's list; neither had he ever committed a sexual crime. Once again I asked him very bluntly. He very energetically declared that no, he had never committed a sexual crime. I should have gone with that which I had **perceived** by the Spirit of God. Sometimes our natural thinking kicks in, and the enemy blinds us.

Now we also had a house that was close to our church that we would rent rooms to those who seem to be hungry for God. This older gentleman wanted to attend our church and move down to this house to be close to the church. Something in my heart was not enthusiastic about this man moving upon the church's property. In spite of the red flags, I set up an appointment for him to come and look at one of the rooms that we had available. When he arrived at our property my son Daniel was standing there with me. The minute he saw this gentleman, Dan became extremely upset. I told this man to go ahead into the house and I would be with him in a minute.

I asked my son what was wrong. He said, "Dad: I just had a vision of this man!" (This is one way that God speaks to us) I said: "Okay, tell me what you saw." He said, "Dad: this man is a pedophile!" I said, "Dan you've got to be wrong." I told him that I also had **perceived** there was something wrong with him in this area, but I told my son that I had already asked him repeatedly point-blank if he was on Megan's list, or if he had ever messed around with children. He very vocally declared that he had not. Dan told me that he had an open vision, and in this open vision, he saw this man chasing a little girl who was around six years old.

My son Daniel continued to insist that what he saw was of God, and I needed to check it out. I told him: okay, let me go talk to him. I went into the house where this man was looking at one of the rooms. I came right out and said to him, "Harvey I asked you before if you had ever committed a sexual crime, or if you were on Megan's list. You need to tell me the truth right now. I am asking you again: have you ever committed a sexual crime?" He hung his head down, and whispered: I lied, I do have a record of committing a sexual crime.

Because of my son's open vision, I asked him: who was it? With his head hung down, he said: my six-year-old niece. Now you might say, Pastor isn't there forgiveness for sexual crimes? Yes, there is! But from my experience of almost forty years of pastoring, there is such a strong demonic spirit involved in this act, that unless a person truly repents with all of their heart, and cries out to God for complete deliverance, they never get free. Yes we forgive, but we must also protect our loved ones. May God give us spiritual discernment!

CHAPTER TEN

God Moves upon Rapist & Murderers

My 2nd son Daniel and I went to minister in a little country called Suriname (this little nation's population is basically of African slavery descent). While we were there we were invited to a men's high-security prison. They wanted us to speak to young men who had been incarcerated for the serious crimes of murder, rape, and terrible deeds. We agreed to do this. There was a godly young mother who had a burden for these young boys. They were prisoners from 12 years old up to 18. She told us that she had not seen a hardly results even though she had been pouring her life and much prayer into this endeavor. This particular day her prayers finally paid off.

My son Daniel was to be the one to minister to them because he was in his 20s. This precious lady felt that if they heard a young man speak, it might touch them. As my son spoke, he was sharing about his life, but it did not seem like it was having much of, if any effect upon them whatsoever. He finally turned the service over to me.

I began to share my life experience, and how God had delivered me from drugs, alcohol, violence, and running with a gang outside of Chicago. As I was speaking, I happen to look over at my son Daniel, and I saw and perceived that the spirit of God was moving upon him in a mighty way. The hair on the back of my neck literally stood up, the spirit of the Lord was upon him so powerfully. Intermediately I turned this meeting back over to him.

A tremendous prophetic word began to come forth out of his mouth. I can tell you without a shadow of a doubt it was not my son speaking, but the spirit of the living God. He began to talk about a young man named Joseph, and how Joseph had ended up in prison wrongfully. But that he had maintained a spirit of integrity and love for God. That even in prison he never became bitter or angry at God or others. He just kept pressing in and taking a hold of the Lord no matter what his condition or situation was.

Because of Joseph's godly disposition and seeking the Lord that eventually Joseph was put second in charge over all of the land of Egypt (which was the most powerful nation on the world at the time) literally overnight. He told them that no matter why they were there, or their present condition, that if they would truly cry out to God with all of their hearts, turning their lives over to Jesus they could become a Joseph.

As my son preached underneath this heavy anointing, the spirit of God fell upon these young men. I sat there in utter amazement as I watched an amazing transformation before my eyes as they surrendered their lives to Christ on the spot! When my son was done, the spirit of the Lord had me to have all of them shout in English: I am a Joseph! (English is their primary language) They shouted this phrase over and over.

I will never forget this amazing meeting where the Spirit of God was so tangible that you could cut it with a knife. Now they could not pronounce Joseph the way we do, so they ended up shouting: I Am a YOSEPH! Over and over they shouted: I Am a YOSEPH! The whole prison shook as these approximately 40 young men declaring with all of their hearts and vocal abilities by the spirit of the Lord: I Am a YOSEPH! I Am a YOSEPH! I Am a YOSEPH!

I will never forget that day as long as I live! Both my son and I began to weep for these young men as the spirit of God overwhelmed them. Then my son Daniel and I took every one of those young men one at a time into our arms weeping and praying for them that they would become a Joseph even as they had boldly proclaimed. We all stood there in amazement, and tears as GOD had stepped down from heaven to be with us at that moment!

Weeping, wailing in Surinam

I was ministering in a little country called Suriname, which is located right below Brazil across the Amazon River. A precious brother and pastor from the Baltimore Christian center had arranged for me to be speaking in small gatherings. In these meetings a precious apostolic sister by the name of Rinia Refos, heard me speak. The Lord touched her in such a wonderful way that she wanted me to meet her apostle, who is over one of the largest churches in this nation. She took me to this precious Elderly Apostle. I gave her one of my books about my experience of going to hell. And shared with her some of my testimony.

After we had left this meeting, I think approximately a day later sister Rinia Refos informed me that her apostle would love to have me speak at the next Sunday morning service. I agreed to this request. It came into my heart to begin to prepare for this particular service. I informed my son Daniel and the peoples whose house where I was staying that I would not be eating for a number of days, in order to get the mind of Christ.

It came into my heart that I was to share from memory the book of James. God has allowed me to memorize 10 books of the New Testament including many Scriptures. All I did for approximately 3 days was quote the book of James over and over to myself slowly, meditating upon its wonderful truths.

Back in 1997 when I had originally memorized this book I had informed my congregation that I would be sharing it on a Sunday night. That I would be preaching the book of James from beginning to end by memory. I still remember that amazing night. There were literally hundreds of people who had showed up to watch me proclaim this message. As I was ministering, I could sense a mighty move of God beginning to take place. When I gave the altar call well over 100 people (believers) came running for the altar weeping and wailing. God did a wonderful work that night!

Here I was once again meditating, praying and pondering, musing upon the book of James. The Sunday morning I was to speak finally came. As I entered into the sanctuary, which I believe sits about 3000, it was almost filled to capacity. Now in the natural I'm a little bit nearsighted. This building was narrow and very deep. The stage was about 3 to 4 feet high. The very 1st row of chairs I think was probably about 30 feet away. When I stood upon the stage I could see the 1st couple rolls of people, but from there back it was very blurry.

Now to say that I was pumped up, would not be sufficient to declare how I felt at this moment. I had been fasting and quoting the book of James for 3 days from morning to night. My heart had been filled with the fire of heaven. The lady who was to interpret for me stood by the pulpit. Now this is where I really messed up. I was so pumped up that I was standing on the very edge of the stage as if I was trying to get out to the people.

I am sure they were expecting me to stand right there next to the pulpit. The precious lady who was to interpret for me was behind my back. I had a microphone in my hand, waiting to be released upon these precious people with the truths of the book of James burning in my heart. I have a terrible habit of speaking fast as it is, but now I had to have it interpreted into their language. As I began to speak, rapidly this precious lady kept trying to get me to slow down.

It also seemed to me that the apostle sitting on the front row of chairs, was not very happy with what was going on. In my heart I began to get frustrated with myself, because I felt like I was really messing up. As I continued to preach the book of James from my heart, it seem like things were going from bad to worse. The interpreter kept trying to get me to slow up, turn around and speak to where she could see my lips. I knew that my time was running out, and I really wanted to get to chapter 3 and chapter 4. As I was speaking I saw that there was a lot of motion taking place in the congregation. It seemed to me that people were not wanting to stay in their chairs. I could not really see very well because of my nearsightedness.

I finally came to the place where I knew I had run out of time. I finished up speaking a little bit out of chapter 3 and chapter 4. I felt as if in my heart that if I did not stop soon, they would drag me off of the stage. So in my heart, with utter defeat, I gave the altar call. During this whole time there had been movement going on in the congregation. I thought within my mind that they were leaving out of frustration of me speaking so fast, and the interpreter not being able to interpret what I was saying. What a disaster!

When I gave the altar call, something amazing happened. People were running for the front. In a very brief time the whole front of this large sanctuary was filled with people who were weeping and crying. I began to look for workers, altar workers to help with all of these precious people who had come forward. But there was nobody to help. I went down into the mist of them trying to pray for as many as I could. This went on for quite a while. Eventually people began to wander away. In my heart I was so grateful that these people responded to my terrible message, but I still felt like I was a complete failure.

A number of days went by, as I was ministering in other smaller fellowships. The precious sister who had set up these meetings (Rinia Refos) while we were in the car brought up this particular meeting. She said to me: was it not just amazing how God moved in the meeting on Sunday? I was completely baffled by this statement. I asked her to explain what she meant? I told her because of my nearsightedness I could not really tell what was going on.

She told me that as I began to preach and teach from the book of James that literally the power of God had hit the congregation. That as I was preaching people were falling out of their chairs, and being tossed about by the power of God. I could not hardly believe what I was hearing. I knew I had seen movement, but I did not know that it was the Holy Ghost moving. And then she said something that was even more amazing! She told me that it was wonderful when you gave the altar call, and all of those people who had come forward. I told her I was blessed with that also, but I asked her where the leaders were.

That's when she informed me that the most amazing thing about the whole meeting was that all of those people who had come running forward weeping and wailing before God, were the leaders of the church. Yes it was the leaders of the church that God had convicted! For judgment must 1st begin in the house of the Lord. This is the reason why there was nobody there to help pray for them. In spite of my over zealousness, and lack of wisdom God had once again showed up to do a mighty work.

Abused Woman instantly Healed

I had to go to a local business place and as I was getting ready to go in, there was a precious African-American lady who was moving really slow. She got to the entrance and there was step up. It was only approximately 4 or 6 inches high. She could not even lift her foot that high. I asked her what was wrong and she informed me that her ex-boyfriend and his buddy had beaten her up the night before. She was bruised, black and blue and stiff from head to toe and could barely move any part of her body.

The Lord had been speaking to me about releasing His power through the spoken word. He had Quicken to my heart that I should leave every word that I spoke would come to pass. That Moses and Samuel had come tool the place were not one word they spoke fell to the ground. And that if I would believe the Scriptures, that said we would give an account of every word we speak, and only speak that which you desire to happen according to the will of the father, it would come to pass.

This particular lady turned her back on me as she tried to continue to lift her foot. At that moment, it was quickened in my heart to speak to her body. There was another gentleman standing there waiting to also enter this building. Without even thinking I pointed my finger at her body towards her back and commanded that in the name of Jesus Christ of Nazareth that all of her afflictions, pains and bruising of the beating to be instantly gone in the name of Jesus. I did not shout or speak loud. I simply spoke it at a normal voice. The minute I spoke I perceived that the spirit of God literally hit her body. Instantly, her foot came up real high as if something had been holding it down but now sprang forth being connected to a bungee cords.

She started moving both of her legs and her feet up and down very rapidly. She spun around and stared at me. This may sound strange but she was as white as a sheet (whatever that means). She asked me with a very astonished quivering, mystified and almost in an angry voice, what just happened to me. I preached Jesus Christ and ministered the truth to her. She was still standing there under the power of God as I left. The gentleman who was right behind me stood there watching all of this. I think he was so strong with amazement that he himself could not say anything!

I Saw the Coming Harvest

I would like to share with you an amazing visitation that I had on February the 20, 2012. On the 18 of February, I celebrated my 56th birthday. The 37th year of being born again.(I v been a pastor since 1977) I set my heart to seek God, trusting to totally separate my mind, my heart, completely free from all knowledge but God's Word, and only that information which I need in order to fulfill the will of God.

From the minute I set my mind and heart to be completely given over to the Lord, great anticipation and expectation began to rise in me. On the third day I went to bed meditating upon God's WORD. The dream I am about to share with you was more than a dream. All of my five senses and physical being experienced that which I am about to share.

In this Dream I found myself standing outside of a small town on top of a grass covered hill. Other saints (some that I am familiar with) were gathered together there with me. (There were seven to a dozen of us). The stars were shining brightly from above. There was no moon this particular night. It was a beautiful warm summer evening. You could hear the night life all around us. The crickets and frogs were joined together in their song. As I was standing there with the gathering of these saints, I sensed in my heart that something astounding was about to happen in the heavens above us.

I perceived that the heavens were about to be shaken. I perceived in my heart that it was necessary for all of us to immediately get on our backs, and look into the heavens. When I shared this with those who were gathered together with me on the Hill, they all agreed and we immediately laid down on our backs. Within just a matter of minutes the heavens above us exploded into activity. It was as if a great battle was unfolding in the heavens. There was destruction happening throughout the sky as if it was in great travail and pain, and yet that there was a birthing, a coming forth of life and a new heaven.

What we watched unfold before us was mind boggling and dumbfounding. Frightening and yet exhilarating. It seemed to go on for hours. And as fast as it had begun, it was over with. All of us present slowly arose to our feet. We were so overwhelmed and dumbfounded with what we saw that none of us could talk.

We were utterly speechless. Our hearts were filled with wonder and amazement. I perceived that all who were present knew that God was revealing himself to the human race in a way He had not previously demonstrated. That God was doing something in the heavens and the earth that humanity had not yet seen or experienced.

We all dispersed from the hilltop slowly going our own separate ways. I found myself on a sidewalk beginning to enter into a small community. The streets were filled with people looking into the heavens. I could see great fear filling the faces on those who were speaking back and forth to one another in whispers about what all of this could mean? I continued to walk down the sidewalk not speaking to anyone. The atmosphere was filled with a sense of great fear and anticipation.

As I entered deeper into this town, once again I sense that something was about to happen. (Now this is where it really begins to get interesting.)The minute I perceived something dramatic was about to happen I stopped. There were tall buildings off to my right and left hand, which you would typically find in a small town. I looked up into the heavens, and it seemed as if to me the heavens were made from a parchment. I watched in amazement as if an invisible hand was rolling up the heavens like they were a newspaper, or a parchment. And then as if the heavens were insignificant, it was set aside as if it were nothing.

The minute this took place behind where the heavens had been there was now an innumerable multitude of the heavenly host. The Saints of all ages dressed in glistening white, were gathered with the angelic armies behind them. In the midst was the Heavenly Father sitting upon a great white throne. God the Father was so huge in size that all else looked small in comparison. All of those who were present including the Father seemed to be looking off to my right.

As I looked in the direction in which they were gazing to my amazement there was the Lamb of God. His wool was glistening white as snow. He was lying upon His side as if He had been slain. His backside was away from me, His underside toward me. And out from His rib, it seemed to be His third rib, from his side flowed a stream of bright shimmering living, quickening blood. Directly in front of His body there had formed a pool of this living blood. I knew there was no bottom to this pool of blood. It is hard to explain what I sensed in my heart as I looked upon His, the Lamb of God's precious living blood.

As I was looking upon this pool of precious blood, I felt something manifest itself in my right hand. I looked down, and there in my right hand was a branch, a ROD. (This was the specific word that came to my mind)This was not just any ordinary Rod. It was absolutely straight, and it was made of Olive Wood, seemingly seven feet tall. (These are things I just knew to be true)

Immediately I knew what I was to do with this Rod in my right hand. I lifted this Rod towards the pool of blood in the heavens. To my amazement it seemed to be just the right length to reach into the blood. This blood was in the heavens, and yet this seven foot Rod was able to reach the precious blood of Jesus.

I put the end of the Rod right into this pool of living blood. The blood immediately flowed to the end of the Rod. This living blood wrapped itself around the end of the Rod as if it was in absolute oneness with the Rod. Then with my right hand I pulled the Rod back towards me. Once the Rod was back into my Realm (I do not know how else to explain it). I directed the end of the Rod towards my mouth. It looked as if the blood was going to fall off from the end of the Rod. But not a drop fell to the ground.

I opened my mouth wide, and stuck the end of the Rod with the Living Blood into my mouth. I drank all of the blood which had been on the Rod. The very moment that I drank the blood, it was as if Power exploded inside of me, knocking me flat on my back like a dead man. It slammed me violently to the ground. I cannot properly express how drastic and violent the power of God hit me.

As I lay on the ground, my sight had become slightly dim. I saw a figure of a man walking towards me from the left. He seemed to be wearing the brown robes of a Prophet. I knew in my heart he was a Prophet. I could not see his face because there was a foggy glow that was emanating from his face.

A bright light was shining from behind him. He stopped in front of me. And he said to me, **Stand upon Thy Feet O Son of Man**. The minute these words left his mouth it was like as if someone grabbed me violently by my shirt collar, and jerked me to my feet. My whole body was trembling and weak.

After I was on my feet, this Prophet held out a small wooden bowl made of acacia wood. (This word came to me in my mind) I can still see the bold white and brown grains swirling around that bowl inside and out. The Prophet commanded me to eat of its contents. I looked into the bowl, and there in the bottom were approximately a dozen almonds.

They were sliced long ways in very thin strips. They were moist and slightly green. I reached forth my right hand, because the Rod was now in my left hand. I scraped up about half of these almonds strips and stuck them into my mouth. As I completed this task the unknown Prophet turned his back on me, and walked away.

As I chewed these almonds strips they released a very bitter taste in my mouth. And as I chewed these almonds and swallowed, all that was around me suddenly disappeared. I found myself looking into the heavens again. But now there was nothing but darkness above me. The heavens were totally empty of all-stars and lights. Nothing but empty blackness as far as my eyes could see. I noticed a motion off to my right.

I saw like a small seed of light beginning to be formed. As it began to grow, I saw that it was a letter. The Letter was an H. as the letter H. continued to grow, blood was covering it, flowing into it, out of it, and through it. It was filled with the brilliant shimmering living, quickening blood of Jesus Christ. I knew that it was the blood which I had drank. This H. was living, active and growing.

I also noticed a motion off to my left. There in the darkness was another H. forming and growing. But this letter H. had a sense of evil and darkness about it. It was covered and dripping in a putrid, dead and stinking blood. As each one of these letters continued to grow, there was a separation taking place. They were growing farther and farther apart from one another. The letter H. to my right was filling the heavens with light, love and life. But the H. to my left was filled with deception, death and misery.

As I continued to watch this unfold before my eyes, suddenly the voice of God came thundering from the heavens. This is what I Heard Him Say to me:

My Holy Church! - I knew he was speaking pertaining to the H. on my right hand side. After a pause he said

The Harlot Church! - This he was speaking pertaining to the H. on my left hand side.

I began to weep uncontrollably in my dream. I knew in my heart that it was 3 AM in the morning. As I opened my eyes, (wide awake) tears were rolling down my face. It was 3:12 in the morning. *Let him that has an ear, hear what the Spirit is saying to His Holy church!*

Atheist Saved, Healed, Delivered

Vicky had come to me (being her pastor) with great concern about her sister C....... Her sister was not only an atheist, but she had begun to dabble into satanic activities and was also experiencing great physical afflictions. On numerous occasions, Vicky came to the front of the church after service and I prayed with her pertaining to her sister. After one service I perceived in my heart that if God did not divinely intervene in her sister's life in the very near future that not only would Connie lose her soul, but that she was headed for a very tragic death.

I encouraged Vicky to go even deeper in prayer for her sister, and that I would join her. Up to this time, I had never met C......, but the Lord had laid her upon my heart in a very real way. The next time Sunday when I saw sister Vicky, I encouraged her to get her sister to come to one of our services. That I believed if God could get her sister to come up from West Virginia, HE would do something amazing for her. V..... began to strongly encourage her sister to attend one of our church services, but she strongly resisted all of V.....'s encouragements.

One Sunday Vicky came to me, informing me that her sister C..... had to be hospitalized for surgery. While she was in the hospital for surgery, she contracted a very deadly infection called MRSA.

MRSA stands for methicillin-resistant Staphylococcus aureus. It is a "staph" germ that does not get better with many of antibiotics that usually cure staph infections. Most staph germs are spread by skin-to-skin contact (touching). A doctor, nurse, other health care provider, or visitors to a hospital may have staph germs on their body that can spread to a patient. Once the staph germ enters the body, it can spread to bones, joints, the blood, or any organ, such as the lungs, heart, or brain. Serious staph infections are more common in people with chronic (long-term) medical problems. Each year, 90,000 Americans suffer from invasive MRSA infection, and about 20,000 die.

The MRSA was so bad that the doctors had to put a stint in her chest where they could administer antibiotics a couple times a day directly into her main arteries. When she finally was released from the hospital, a doctor from the CDC would actually go to her house several times a week. In the midst of all of this terrible situation, the spirit of the Lord was able to finally move upon C......'s heart.

She told her sister Vicky that she was going to come to one of our church services no matter how difficult it was for her to come. She wanted to have pastor mike pray for her.

C....... drove up from West Virginia to her sister Vicky's house one Sunday morning. That wonderful Sunday morning Vicky C....., and her sister Linda, all walked in together as that the service had already begun. God did an amazing miracle in C........s life that morning.

Vicky said: as we walked into the church, GODS presence was so strong that L.... and I started weeping right away. We all three sat down as everyone in the congregation was praying for each other and it looked like everybody was weeping in the service because of the presence of God. The spirit of the Lord was so strong in this service that I do not even remember Pastor Mike preaching. I simply remember everybody praying and worshiping the Lord.

During the service my sister C..... had her eyes closed as she was praying and sincerely crying out to the Lord. The atheism that she had clung to, simply seem to melt off of her as if it had never existed. C...... later informed me and Linda that as she had her eyes closed praying she had heard a voice say: Get on Your Knees. She said in her heart that she could not do this because both of her kneecaps had been replaced with metal. She said the voice said to her again: Get on Your Knees.

This voice was so strong within her heart that she decided to do what she had heard no matter what it took. At that very moment C..... literally bent her legs and got down on her knees. As she went to her knees C..... said that someone laid hands on her and was praying for her, she thought it was pastor Mike at the time.

Vicky later on said that she had seen her sister go to her knees, but that no one was there praying over her. We now believe that it was Jesus himself laying his hands upon her sick, fevered, germ infested and broken body.

At that very moment, Jesus completely healed C..... from the MRCA. Not only did the Lord deliver her from the staph infection, but healed her knees to where when she walked out of the church she threw away her cane.

That morning C..... gave her heart to Jesus, and was filled with the Holy Ghost. When C..... later went back to the hospital for bloodwork because of the MRCA, they kept testing her because they could not find the infection. Nine times they tested her for the MRCA, but praise the Lord it was gone. The doctors were completely shocked by this discovery! She was also delivered from her drug and alcohol addictions. Suicidal desires and manic depression also left her!

For the last update about C...... we were told that she is now teaching a Sunday school class in the church in West Virginia.

Vision of a Plowed Field, Filled with Diamonds

In August of 2012 my wife and I were returning early Saturday morning from a ministers conference that we had attended in West Lafayette, Indiana. My wife was sleeping peacefully at about 3 AM as I was driving in talking to the Lord headed back to Gettysburg, Pennsylvania. I was having a wonderful time of fellowship with the Lord when out of the blue I had an open vision!

This open vision appeared outside of the front windshield of our car. I could still see the road in front of me, but super imposed over the highway in front of me I saw a plowed dirt field which seemed to be freshly overturned. In the mist of all of this dirt I saw diamonds of different sizes sparkling, and scattered everywhere. As I was looking at these diamonds in the plowed field in this open vision I heard the voice of God say to me: PICK THEM UP!

Immediately my eyes swelled up with tears, as I said: Yes Lord, but What Are They? And He said to me: They are my ministers who have endured much tribulation, and testing. They Are Ready to Come! Then the vision was over, but from that moment, to the time I arrived home, too early Sunday morning the Lord began to give to me instructions and Revelation of what he wanted me to do.

He specifically spoke to my heart informing me that we would begin to have four services every day. 6 AM we were to have prayer, 10 AM, 2 PM, and 7 PM we would have ministry of the word, worship, and praying for the sick. The gift of faith took a hold of my heart knowing that this was the will of God. The Lord also instructed me that I was to have a different minister to speak at every service except for Sundays. This meant that we were going to be having over 70 different ministers a month speaking in the church.

I perceived in my heart that I needed to ask each minister to come just once a month to minister. That there was going to be no financial gift for their involvement, but that I was to let them know they would be carried on our TV network. These ministers were to be full gospel, Holy Ghost, Spirit Filled, Pentecostal preachers. Where were all these ministers going to come from? The Lord had told me that they were ready, and they would come.

The Lord also spoke to my heart that this was going to be a practice run of a coming revival. That when this revival came it would not be just a small handful of ministers ministering like in previous revivals. That it would be the whole body of Jesus Christ participating. Now, because each minister would only be speaking once a month when the revival hit, they would not be filled with pride, or get worn out from the demands that would be placed upon them.

I shared this vision, this divine direction with our congregation Sunday morning. When Monday morning came I simply picked up the phone, and began to call ministers that I knew in the local community that would meet the criteria the Lord had given me. As I began to share the vision, many of these ministers literally started to shout or cry over the phone. Some of them got extremely excited, and informed me they wanted to be involved, and at the same time giving me the names of others. Within a matter of weeks we had over 200 ministers, Holy Ghost spirit filled preachers who said they wanted to be involved.

These meetings began September 1, 2012, and continued every day for almost 2 years. Before these meetings began we had a joint ministers gathering where over 100 ministers came and participated in communion, prayer, worship, and foot washing. What an amazing and wonderful move of the Holy Ghost that we had. I do not think there was one dry eye in the whole gathering. I believe with all my heart that this was God preparing us for a coming great Holy Ghost movement.

As a result of these meetings that we had for almost 2 years we discovered the ministers that God would have us to work with when the revival hits. Out of almost 300 ministers that we were able to get to know personally, we found precious diamonds who had been out in the harvest field, the plowed fields of life. We have kept in good relationship with many of these ministers, and are simply waiting for the final outpouring of the early and the latter rain of the Holy Ghost.

Pastor Healed Instantly of Cancer

Pastor Healed of Cancer When She Was Called out with the Word of Knowledge! **In Her Own Words**: In the Month of February 2013, I was diagnosed with a large lesion in the upper left Chest area. Pastor Mike I came to your fellowship, Jesus is Lord Ministries that Sunday Morning, I had The X-ray results from the study on my chair. I was praying that somehow that Father God would give ME an opportunity to share with you, and ask you to pray for me.

Well, do you know that during the time that you were delivering the message you stopped preaching, and asked me to stand to my feet because God had revealed to you exactly what I was dealing! This was without me telling you anything. You pointed directly to the Left side of my chest and said: I see a growth in your lungs. You then called me forward to be prayed for. You anointed my forehead with oil and asked me to place my hand on my left chest, you began to pray for me, the power of God hit me, and we both jumped, and you said. "I'm waiting for the praise report" I was scheduled for a CT SCAN of my chest the following Saturday.

The report from that study read: **THERE IS NO LESION FOUND IN LEFT LUNG AREA"** I did return to Jesus is Lord Church and shared my miracle testimony with you, and the congregation. I want to thank you man of God for every time I've fellowship with your Precious Church family, I always get restored, refreshed and watered to overflowing.

I've always known that this is a "Well of refreshing water for me". I'm grateful to Jesus for your prayers, intercession, loving kindness towards me, and Joy overflowing in my soul! Pastor Lauretta Melendez. Owings Mills, MD.

Pastor Mike's side of the story: as I was preaching the word of God, and looking over the congregation, something supernatural took place. As I was looking at Pastor Lauretta (at the time I did not know her or that she was a pastor - the Lord supernaturally told me that she was a pastor, which she confirmed later.) I had a very strong picture or image that floated up from my heart into my mind. I could literally see that there was a growth in her left lungs. As I saw this by the word of wisdom and the gift of faith, I knew, that I knew God was going to healer this morning.

I stopped preaching, pointed my finger at her, and told her what the Lord said to me. She began to immediately rejoice because that is exactly why she had come to our service. I called her up front, anointed her with oil, and laying my hands upon her. I cursed the growth in her lungs in the name of Jesus and commanded the growth and cancer to be gone. Then I told her by the Holy Ghost that she needed to go back to the doctors, and get it confirmed.

Praise God, I obeyed what the Lord said to me, she responded accordingly, and God healed her. She came and showed us the x-ray's that the growth was gone! Jesus Christ is the same yesterday today and forever!

Divine Manifestation of Frankincense & Myrrh

We were having a woman's conference in our main sanctuary. In this particular gathering something wonderful and supernatural happened when all of a sudden a divine and wonderful fragrance of frankincense and myrrh came rushing into the service. The subject of the conference was on offering up our lives as a sweet fragrance in the nostrils of God. My wife and I had gone all the way to Lancaster in order to purchase the original incense (frankincense and myrrh) that the high priest used to burn in the holy of holy s. The ladies who were putting on the conference had wanted this incense to burn at just the right moment in the meeting.

I was in the back with the audio and video people, waiting to light the incense when we were instructed to. Sister Joanna (daughter of Jack Coe) was ministering up front at the time. This special incense was sitting in a brass basin which we had bought, and was designed specifically for the burning of this incense. Everything was prepared for this event, with the matches sitting next to the basin.

As sister Joanna was ministering something amazing and wonderful took place. All of a sudden the sanctuary began to be filled with the fragrance of the incense. I mean the smell of this fragrance was so strong that Sister Joanna up front literally stopped preaching. She looked back at me with what looked to be a look of consternation. You could tell in her facial expressions that she was wondering what in the world I was doing. Why in the world would Pastor Mike light the incense before I told him to? She had specifically told me to wait until she gave me the signal to light it.

The fragrance was growing stronger and stronger as it flooded the sanctuary. She finally said over the PA system: Pastor Mike I told you to wait until I specifically told you to light the incense. At that moment I picked up the bowl of incense in my hand, lifting it for all to see. I said: Sister Joanna I did not light the incense.

The fragrance that you are smelling is not coming from this bowl of incense. Before we had begun this meeting, we had burned a little bit of the incense to see what it smelled like. Here we were smelling that exact same fragrance which had flooded our sanctuary. I was standing there with the basin full of incense unlit.

Myself and some of the personnel took a walk through the building, and outside to try to discover where this strong heavenly smell of frankincense and myrrh was coming from. We came back, reporting that we could not find the source of it.

As the realization that this was all divine manifestation, the women began to excitedly praise and worship the Lord. There were tears flowing down many cheeks at that moment. We were all overcome with a very strong sense of God's presence and holiness. From that moment forward that woman's conference entered into a much deeper realm of the spirit. God was in the house. Remember that God **Confirms His Word with Signs Following.**

Our Prius Was Hit by a Logging Chain

My wife and I went to her mother's house too install a small satellite dish system, with the receiver. Her mother was filled with great anticipation to watch our network on the small dish (WBNTV). After we had installed the system, we ate lunch, and headed back home to Gettysburg Pennsylvania. We took route 994 from Cassville, through three Springs, to Orbisonia, PA.

When we entered Orbisonia, we turned right onto Route 522 towards McConnell burg, Pennsylvania. My wife and I were having a wonderful time just sharing and talking about the goodness of God, while at the same time obeying the speed limit.

As we were coming around a rather sharp turn, I saw on the other side of the road a logging truck just coming around this curve, and coming way to fast.

This logging truck definitely was coming around that corner way faster than what it should have been. Not only was this 18 Wheeler Going Way to fast, but it was fully loaded with logs to the very top of its steel racks. At that very moment out of the corner of my left eye I seem to see something flying loose at the very end of the truck.

This truck was going so fast that as it roared past us the wind of its passage literally began to push our little Toyota Prius right off of the road. Then suddenly out of the blue, I saw something heading for our windshield, and towards the front of the car. My wife also saw this object coming towards us, automatically threw her hands and arms up in front of her face to try to protect herself. Right before this object hit us though there was a gigantic burst of a bright white light. This fluffy white cloud got between us and the oncoming object.

At that very moment something struck our windshield and our vehicle so hard, that Our vehicle shook so violently that it felt like we were going to be flipped end over end. This all happened extremely fast because we were doing approximately 55 miles an hour, with the logging truck going past us going in the opposite direction faster than the speed limit.

My wife at that moment per her hands over her ears because we heard a horrendous crashing sound hitting our little Prius. Now as fast as it happened it was over. My wife yelled as the logging truck continued on its way, never slowing down even for one moment: "what was that!"

Oh I can tell you that we are so blessed to be alive! We couldn't believe that the windshield was still whole in front of us, with not even one crack or chip! I immediately pulled the vehicle off to the edge of the road and stopped in order to take a look at the damage. Surely whatever had hit us must have taken out the whole front part of the car, including its left side.

I got out of the vehicle, and exam that car very carefully from top to bottom. Amazingly we found not even one scratch or dent on the Prius! As I got back into the vehicle, and drove down the road my wife and I both declared that we had just beheld a wonderful and marvelous angelic miracle.

We are now convinced that an angel got between us and a loose flying logging chain from the logging truck. We both saw a flash of white light that enveloped the whole front of the vehicle a split second before we were hit, and the car shook with a loud crashing sound. This logging chain, without God's divine intervention, would have cut through our car like a guillotine, or a red-hot knife on a stick of soft butter.

It would have taken off the top of our car, cutting both my wife and I into half. What an amazing and wonderful God that we serve. Once again he had sent his angelic beings to protect us. We are so thankful for the goodness of God and His angelic protection!

The Violent Take It by FORCE

I was lying in bed back in 2013 when I heard the audible voice of God, and he said to me: the violent take it by force! For a while now this has been marinating in my soul. Sometimes when God speaks to me, it takes time for it to become a reality.

It could be four years later or maybe decades as the spirit of God will be at work on my inside. You could say that it is like a woman when she gets pregnant, life is growing inside of her womb. Even so, faith begins as a seed, and must grow within us, in our hearts. We have a lot to do with that faith growing, expanding, enlarging and becoming mature.

Please understand everybody has faith, everybody was born with a measure, a proportion of faith. When Jesus shared the parables about the ten virgins who were asleep, they all woke up when the trumpet sounded, but Jesus said there were five foolish and five wise. The Five that were wise had enough oil to take them to the arrival of their husband to be. I believe that the oil that Jesus was speaking about is the oil of faith; I believe it's faith in God and Jesus Christ.

People who do not have sufficient faith in this time period are going to have it rough. They're going to try to find somebody that has faith, but it will be too late. Then there are those who have faith which has been in hibernation. Faith can be lying dormant inside of you for many years, and then suddenly something supernatural happens, and it begins to come forth like a bear coming out of hibernation!

Faith can be lying dormant inside of you for many years, and then suddenly something supernatural happens, and it begins to come forth like a bear coming out of hibernation!

Hebrews 11:32 And what shall I more say? for the time would fail me to tell of Gedeon, and of Barak, and of Samson, and of Jephthae; of David also, and Samuel, and of the prophets:33 Who through faith subdued kingdoms, wrought righteousness, obtained promises, stopped the mouths of lions.34 Quenched the violence of fire, escaped the edge of the sword, out of weakness were made strong, waxed valiant in fight, turned to flight the armies of the aliens.

RAISING THE DEAD AT LONG HORN

My wife, Kathleen Yeager, and Joanna Herndon (the late great Jack Coes daughter) were on their way to Hanover, Pennsylvania. Joanna had told Kathleen that she wanted to take her to a special place to eat. This was a few years ago here in Hanover, Pennsylvania. She was going to take her to Longhorn steakhouse. Joanna had her purse full of coupons that could be used at the Longhorn steakhouse to make the experience less expensive.

They would've been at Longhorn steakhouse earlier in the day but the idea came to Joanna to take Kathleen to get their nails and feet done before they went to eat. This was going to be a girl's day out. They got their nails and their feet completed a little bit later than what they had been expecting. But God was even involved in this. He does everything in his own timing

They finally arrived at the Longhorn steakhouse. As they walked into the restaurant something big was coming down. They saw one of the waitresses running, but nobody was at the front desk of the restaurant which was highly unusual. Finally, a lady came and informed them that they just could not help them right now. That they had a major emergency happening.

Joanna and Kathleen decided to seat themselves. As they came around the corner there was a lady standing in the middle of the restaurant screaming hysterical, she was shaking all over. As my wife and Joanna walked up to this lady, they asked her what was wrong? At the same time, Joanna and Kathleen looked into the booth with his lady was standing.

Now, there right before them was a lady slumped over in the booth with her head all the way back. This lady looked like a ghost. Her face was all white, and she was not breathing. There were four ladies all together in this party, with this one lady slumped backward with her head laid back. It was to them that she had died. Joanna and my wife immediately jumped into action. Without thinking they ran over to her, working their way into the booth, and laying their hands upon this precious dead ladies carcass.

They began to speak in the Name of Jesus, commanding her to be healed. Both ladies also were speaking in tongues because when you know not how to pray this is the perfect language. During this whole event, the lady who had obviously died was not moving, breathing or doing anything. From all indications, she had been like this for maybe 15 minutes.

Finally, an ENT guy who was in the restaurant walked over to the ladies. He began to try to get a pulse. He watched Joanna and my wife Kathleen speaking the name of Jesus over this woman. It turns out that he must've been a believer because he began to agree with them in their prayers and in their speaking over this lady's dead body.

It turns out that he had been a medic in the Army at one time, and that he was not retired. He could not find a pulse. Joanna relates in retelling the story that she thought maybe the woman had choked on something. Maybe we need to give her that Heimlich maneuver. She told us how she did not know how to do it, but she thought well maybe that she had choked on something and no one noticed.

Joanna asked the ladies exactly what had happened before she slumped over? They said: well we were talking to her and then in less than a second she was simply gone. Yes, just like that she was just gone. The girls asked her what her name was. They informed Joanna and my wife that her name was Diane. The ladies put their hands back on Diane and began to speak to her. This is what they said: **Diane Wherever You Went, You Get Back In His Body Right Now In Jesus Name**. You come back now in Jesus name!

They kept commanding Diane to come back into her body in Jesus name. As they were speaking In the Name of Jesus, suddenly, they saw one of Diane's eyes again to twitch. Joanna boldly said: She's Back. But she was not yet moving. Joanna told Diane to move her hand to prove to her friends that she was back.

This time she did move her hand. She then began to move her head. When Diane moved her head, her friends began to talk to her at 90 mph. When Diane was finally able to get a word in she said: what's wrong with you all? Here Diane had not even realized that she had died. Now, they did not have a doctor there to prove 100% that she was dead. Yet, without any doubt, she was gone. When you die, you mess all over yourself, and she had already eliminated her bodily fluids. Her bowels had let loose.

She had been gone for maybe 15 minutes before the ladies had shown up and commanded her to come back to her body from wherever she was. Finally, the medics showed up. They pushed the girls out of the way to get to this lady. She kept telling these medics: I don't need anything. I don't need to go anywhere. I don't need anything. But they said, you still must go with us to the hospital. The last time the girls saw her she was getting into an ambulance.

Joanna and Kathleen were able to finally sit down to eat their meal. When they went to pay for the meal, the manager came over and informed them that the meal was on the house. That they had seen how God raised that lady from the dead. From what I understand some days later once again Joanna and Kathleen went to eat at the same restaurant. When they walked into the restaurant a waitress pointed them out. She told some people that she had seen a lady die. But that because of the prayers of these ladies God had raised that woman from the dead.

Of course, it was Jesus Christ who had raised that lady from the dead as the girls said simply cried out, and used the authority that we discover in Jesus. Jesus Christ is the same Yesterday, today, and forever!

CHAPTER ELEVEN

I Was Totally Engulfed in a Gasoline Tar Fire!

Everything around me exploded into fire! (Tears are filling my eyes as I share this incredible story of God's protection in the midst of my stupidity.) It all began as I was stirring gasoline into a five-gallon bucket of black tar, thinning it to be spread on our Churches Steal roof! We had a thirty gallon galvanized garbage can with a LP torch under this container melting the tar! The fumes ignited and this massive wave of fire came rushing from about 20 feet away completely engulfing me.

I mean I am completely swallowed up in this gasoline and black tar fire. The two buckets of gasoline are burning at my feet. The bucket of tar and gasoline I was stirring is on fire. I myself had been using an excessive amount of gas to keep my hands, arms and face free from tar. Gasoline is the only thing that would clean the black tar off me. My clothes are completely saturated in gasoline, as well as my hands, arms and face. I'm standing there in the midst of all of this fire with no fear in my heart. Just utter peace, but still knowing that I was in big trouble.

Back in 1980 I began to memorize and meditate on Scriptures declaring that fire cannot consume me.

Isaiah 43:2, "When thou passest through the waters, I will be with thee; and through the rivers, they shall not overflow thee: when thou walkest through the fire, thou shalt not be burned ; neither shall the flame kindle upon thee."

I meditated on the scriptures because I kept burning myself with our woodstove. Through the years, I have maintained these scriptures in my heart. In the summer of 2011, I had an amazing experience when God used these scriptures to come to my rescue, otherwise I would have been burned to death.

I can honestly tell you that I did not feel the heat, flames or the fire upon me. I grabbed a metal canister and put it over the top of the one bucket of gas that was burning. I quickly found another canister that I could put over the other bucket. During this time, I'm literally running in and out of the fire.

I'm not thinking, I'm just moving knowing that our gymnasium and our whole church could go up in flames at any moment. We are right up against the gymnasium with a house trailer right there. The apartment and the stairs to the apartment above our gymnasium were right there. I had to get the fire out, and I mean fast! Everything was on fire including the ground where we had spilled tar and gas.

The whole place is nothing but an infernal. During this time, Jesse had made his way around the flames nurturing his burnt arm, which he had received standing outside of the flames! He was trying to find a water hose we had laying there to water a small garden. I'm still running in and out of the flames trying to put out this raging fire. Jesse had been through a terrible fire in the past, being seriously hurt. I could see that he was in the midst of some shock from the fire and the heat.

Right before my very eyes, the bucket that was filled with tar and gasoline had melted at my feet to less than 8 inches high.

Now the flames were getting worse, they were reaching high into the sky. The men who have been spreading the mixture of tar and Gasoline come running seeing the flames on top of our Church Sanctuary. The whole thing was nothing but a massive blaze. During this time, brother Mark, who lives in the apartment up above, comes running out onto the deck of his apartment. He sees everything that is happening.

Brother Jesse is wrestling with the water hose, trying to disconnect it from another hose in order that we can use it to fight the fire. I ran over and began to help him. And then I took the hoses from him, heading back into the fire. Praise God the water did the job even with gasoline and burning tar everywhere. We were able to douse the flames. Praise God, praise God, praise God the fire was out.

Things happened so fast at the time that I did not even realize exactly the events that had transpired. But God in His grace and in His mercy once again protected me from my own massive stupidity. Jesse did receive burns on his right forearm. Amazingly, I did not receive one burn, not one singed hair or even the smell of smoke on me. All of the gas that was on me, my hands, my face and my clothes never ignited. God is so good! His Mercy Endures Forever!

Dream about Obama

Bye-Bye Obama, Bye-Bye Obama, Bye-Bye Obama!

I had an amazing dream NOVEMBER 13, 2014. In this amazingly vivid dream my wife and I were in a very large outdoor meeting. A Minister I know was just finishing his message. A holy hush fell upon this large gathering of thousands of believers. As we were all waiting upon God for what was to happen next, my wife Kathleen who is at my side, stood to her feet, got out of our aisle and went to the front of the gathering.

She stood behind the podium and began to speak in a wonderful heavenly language (this is a spiritual gift called diversity of tongues). In the midst of her speaking in this tongues scattered throughout the tongues were the words Bye-Bye Obama, Bye-Bye Obama, Bye-Bye Obama. On three different occasions she would stop speaking in tongues and say: Bye-Bye Obama, Bye-Bye Obama, Bye-Bye Obama.

To be honest in this dream I became extremely intimidated with what my wife was doing, because I knew that I was going to have to give the interpretation. When she finished with this tongues, immediately I sensed a very strong quickening of my spirit. A divine boldness came upon me and I stood to my feet.

I stepped out of the row of people I was in and went up front. My wife had stepped aside, and I boldly stepped behind the pulpit and began to give the interpretation. As I gave this interpretation my physical, and voice inflections matched that which my wife had spoken as she was flowing in the gift of the diversity of tongues. At the exact same place in her tongues were she had said Bye-Bye Obama, Bye-Bye Obama, Bye-Bye Obama I spoke the exact same thing.

I watched myself give this interpretation in this dream, and I was amazed at what I heard the spirit of the Lord saying to his people. I cannot exactly give you word for word everything that was spoken, but the meaning was that Obama was leaving. I am not speaking about him being impeached, but that he will be leaving at the end of 2 years, is my understanding from the interpretation of the tongues.

Many conservatives, well-known people, believers and even so-called profits have been saying that Obama would declare martial law and stay in office longer than normal. If you did a search on Google about Obama, and martial law, you would see thousands of posts. Even well-known people like Dr. Ben Carson believes that this might be the case. Dr. Ben Carson is a very well-known black neurosurgeon, who has repeatedly stated that he believes there is a chance that the 2016 elections may not be held at all.

Many believe that widespread anarchy gripping the country could be reason enough for the Obama administration to announce the implementation of martial law and the suspension of some, if not all, of Americans' constitutionally protected rights — including the right to vote and hold national elections. People's hearts are being filled with fear that Obama is going to orchestrate some type of disaster in order to stay in power. As a result of this divine dream I had, I no longer fear this.

In the mist of this interpretation I heard the Lord say that Obama was like a Nebuchadnezzar that had God had used to bring judgment to America. That everything that was shaken and going to be shaken was in order to separate those who truly love Christ, from those who did not. That the division that was and is happening in our nation right now was simply the revealing of people's hearts.

That now those who put their trust in God, and those who put their trust in Man has been revealed. That from here on out our nation will never be the same, but that this dividing between light and darkness will grow ever wider. The revealing and manifestation of this spiritual war and division has begun.

Daniel 12:10 Many shall be purified, and made white, and tried; but the wicked shall do wickedly: and none of the wicked shall understand; but the wise shall understand.

Mountain Man Completely Healed & Restored

Vicki and Linda, two sisters who attend the church I pastor, informed me that their father (in his late 70s) had suffered a terrible stroke. It was the Sunday before Thanksgiving, and they were attending our Sunday morning service. That is when I was informed that their father had a devastating and terrible stroke. The minute they told me, I knew in my heart that I had to get to the Chambersburg Hospital to pray for him. I told them that as soon as I could, I would get up to the hospital, even today.

It was approximately 2 PM when I arrived at the hospital. As I walked down the hospital hallway, entering the hospital elevator, and pushed the button for the third-floor, I was in deep prayer. There was great expectation in my heart that God was about to do something wonderful. When I found the hospital room, the door was hanging slightly open. I entered the room where their father was located. The room was full of family members who were obviously quite upset. On the bed laid this tall, husky, full white bearded man. He actually look like a mountain man that you would read about in the old-time books.

The doctor was standing next to the bed and giving a report to the family. It was obvious that he was not giving them a good report. He was telling them that he could not guarantee their father would ever recover from this terrible stroke. Their father seemed to in a coma,(not that he was) for he was neither here nor there. His eyes were coated with a dull looking white color.

The Doctor told them that their father was blind and he did not know if their father would ever recover his eyesight even if he recovered from the stroke. Everything the doctor said was negative. There were tears flowing in that hospital room that day. I just stood there quietly waiting for the doctor to finish, and then to leave. I knew that what his doctor was saying was true in the natural, but we have access to the one who created all things. I believed in my heart that day that the great physician was going to pay them a house call.

Something was stirring in my heart, and I knew what it was. It was the gift of faith that produces immediate results, causing there to be excitement and joy in believers hearts. After the doctor walked out, I walked over to the hospital bed where William was lying in a state of what looked like death. I spoke up drawing everybody's attention to me. I told them: don't be afraid, Bill is going to be okay. I told them by the word of wisdom that his eyesight was going to come back. I told them that his mind was going to be quickened by the spirit of God, and that the Lord was going to raise him up again.

One of the family members asked me: are you sure? I said: **absolutely**. Now, Thanksgiving was only about four days away. I told them: I believe that he will be home for Thanksgiving! Faith rose up in all of the family members who were there. Instead of tears of sorrow, now flowed tears of great joy.

Some of them began to cry out right. I said to them: now let's lay hands on William, and take care of this problem. They gathered around Williams bed, laying hands upon him. I did not pray real loud, but I prayed with authority. In the **Name of Jesus** I commanded him to be healed, and we all agreed. I commanded for his eyesight, his mind, his reasoning, and his body functions to come back to normal In the **Name of Jesus**!

When I was done praying, with everybody in total agreement, I said: now let us praise God for Bills complete recovery. We all began to quietly praise the Lord for answered prayer. The hospital room was now filled with great joy, and peace. As I left I told them that I was expecting a good report. I encouraged them to have a wonderful Thanksgiving, and that I would be in touch with them.

About three days later I was contacted by one of the daughters of William. They were extremely excited because her father had made a complete and absolute recovery. His eyesight had come back, and his brain, mental awareness had completely returned. That Thanksgiving he was home eating turkey with the rest of the family.

To the writing of this book he is still doing wonderful. Every day his children walk with him down the paths and the roads of the forest they live in, right outside of Chambersburg Pennsylvania. God still answers prayer when we pray in faith, believing. That was in 2015, and here it is 2018, and I'm doing the marriage for one of his grandsons. Up to this time he is healthy and strong, still walking every day.

Young Girls Prayers Snatch me Out of Hell

(9 years later she became my Wife!)

As I share this experience, tears are filling my eyes. May this story help you to never underestimate what God can do when you pray! One day, not too long ago, I was in the sanctuary of the church I pastor praying. I was walking back and forth in the very front, by the altar. My heart was filled with overwhelming thankfulness and gratefulness for God saving my wretched and miserable soul. You see at one time I was extremely lost, in bondage to drugs, alcohol, and immorality.

On my 19th birthday, February 18, 1975, at about 3 o'clock in the afternoon I was in the process of committing suicide. I was a manic depressant and simply wanted to die. I had a large survival knife that I was using, getting ready to cut my wrist. As I was weeping full of self-pity, with the sharp blade pressed up against my wrist, something supernatural and amazing happened to me.

A blanket of God's divine fear fell upon my heart. At that very moment, I knew that I knew that I deserved hell, and I was headed there. This reality was so real that it shook me be to my innermost being. I dropped the knife into the sink and fell to my knees crying out to Jesus Christ in prayer. At that very instant, I was gloriously born again. Jesus set me free from the drugs, alcohol, perversions, depression, tobacco, worldly music all at one time.

Now here I was, over 40 years later thanking God for my glorious and amazing salvation. All those years I have shared with people about my salvation experience, telling them as far as I knew my salvation was a sovereign move of God. I had not known any believers or anyone who had been praying for me. In my heart, I always assumed that it was simply that God had a plan for me.

That God had simply by his sovereign will, and his mercy stepped into my life, snatched me out of the hands of the enemy, saved my soul, and put me into the ministry.

As I had my hands lifted towards heaven praising God that I was rescued from a life sin and perversion, I had an open vision. Now, an open vision is one in which your eyes are open, but you see into another realm. To share with you exactly how this works would take too long. I suggest you get my book called "How God Leads and Guides".

In this open vision, I saw this slender young girl who was approximately 10 years old. She had long blonde, strawberry colored hair. I saw this young girl standing with her hands reached out to heaven. The vision almost seemed a little grainy like it was from an old movie back in the 60s. This vision was so realistic that it almost took away my breath. This is how God moves. One moment everything is normal, and the next minute you're into the supernatural.

This young girl had her hands reached out towards heaven. She was crying out and praying to God for something. And then I heard her prayer. I could hardly believe my ears. She was crying out for her husband to be. She literally was reaching into the future asking God to prepare the man who would be her husband. As I heard her sincere and desperate prayer tears began to roll down my face. It was like the glory of God was shot down upon her. I knew the Lord was hearing her.

1 Peter 3:12 For the eyes of the Lord are over the righteous, and his ears are open unto their prayers:

As I'm standing in the sanctuary of our church with my heart transfixed upon this vision, I said to the Lord: Lord what is this? He said to me: because of her, I was able To Rescue You! I said to the Lord: WHAT? The Lord said to me: It is because of this girl's prayers I was able to save your soul. I stood there in complete shock and amazement. With the trembling lip, I said: Lord who is this? He said to me: This is your wife, Kathleen! She cried out for your soul as a young girl praying for her husband to be.

When I heard, the Lord say this, my heart literally broke. (I'm not exaggerating) I began to weep with a heavy sob. All these years I had assumed that my salvation was based simply on God's sovereignty. He had rescued by soul because He had a wonderful job for me to perform. Now here I was 40 years later discovering that my whole salvation had depended upon a young girl crying out to God for her future husband. Oh, how I wept, and rejoice in the fact that God hears and answers prayers. I had loved my wife before this experience, but not my soul was bursting with new found love for my precious wife of 37 years.

Later that afternoon I went home specifically to see my wife. I said to her with almost a tremble in my voice. Baby doll when you were a young girl, did you cry out to God for your husband to be? She looked at me with utter sincerity. She replied: Yes. She told me that she prayed all the time that God's hand would be upon her husband. She did not tell me exactly what she prayed, but I had heard her praying for her husband in this open vision. I thanked her profusely for her prayers. I believe it is because of her prayers that I am her husband today and a minister of the gospel.

Do not ever doubt for even a moment that God does not hear your prayers. My wife Kathleen reached into the future, and nine years later it rescued my soul. Many times, when I should've died in between those years, God was using her prayers to keep me from dying like many of my friends in the gang I used to run with. Even those years before I got saved there were many times and I was amazed that I did not die in accidents and tomfooleries. Thank You, Jesus, For the Faithful Prayers of your Saints.

Raising the Dead in Cracker Barrel!

One morning in the middle of November of 2016, my wife asked me to take her to breakfast at Cracker Barrel. "Normally we only eat at Cracker Barrel when Joanna and Randy Herndon (Joanna is the daughter of the late great Jack Coe) are staying at our church." I agreed to her request, informing her that I would love to go eat breakfast with her at Cracker Barrel. From where we pastor in Gettysburg, PA, it is about a 20-minute drive.

We arrived at Cracker Barrel around 10 AM. One of the waitresses took us to our table which was in about the middle of the restaurant. We were sitting and simply discussing the how good and wonderful God has been to us. We ordered our breakfast meal. Eventually, the food arrived, and we held hands thanking God for our food, and for his divine guidance in our lives.

We ate our food leisurely enjoying each other's company. When out of the blue two waitresses began to walk briskly down the length of the restaurant urgently asking if there was any doctor or nurse available. The way they were calling out you could tell that something urgent and tragic was going on.

In most of these similar situations, I would be immediately upon my feet heading to the problem area. One time I was at (in about 1996) Lowe's with my family shopping when a similar situation happened. One of the tellers had gone into an epileptic seizure. I immediately ran over to the counter informing them that I was a doctor (Ph.D. in biblical theology) and that I could help. In that situation, I simply leaned over the counter and laid my hands on the girl who was having a seizure and was thrashing about. I took authority very quietly commanding the devil to let her go. Immediately the seizure stopped, and she jumped up to her feet.

Now here I was in a seemingly similar situation. What is so strange though is that I did not sense any urgency in my heart to go help at that moment. It did not occur to me until after this event that for some reason I had not acted in my regular routine method. Now that I look back, I believe that God was in this. My wife and I simply sat there, talking back and forth a little bit, and finishing our meal.

Approximately 10 minutes later we simply got to our feet and began to walk towards the front of the restaurant. As we got to the opening of the entrance to the restaurant we noticed a small crowd had gathered. As we walked up to this crowd I could see that there is a woman who was leaning over the top of a rather large lady who was laying on her left side, on the floor with her body completely extended.

This lady who was laying out on the floor was completely still. There was no movement from her whatsoever. There was a very heavy blanket of silence over the whole crowd, with nobody talking. Everybody's eyes were upon the lady who was laying on the hardwood floor completely still.

When I saw this lady laid out upon the floor the compassion of God rose up in my heart, and immediately overwhelmed me. When the love of God begins the flood when your heart to this extent, the best thing to do is simply to surrender to the divine impulse at work inside of you. In my heart, it was as if the lady laying on the floor was a very personal person to me.

I had to do something and at that very moment, I was motivated to get involved. I walked over to the crowd and very gently pushed my way through. I spoke up informing them that I was a local pastor and that I would like to help. I did not have to push my way through, they simply made room for me to come through.

The woman who was bending over this lady on the floor informed me that she was a nurse. She had a hold of one of the hands of the lady on the floor. I could see that she had her fingers on her wrist, looking for a heartbeat. I knelt down next to her. This lady who was laying on the floor looked to be in her mid to late-60s. She was laying on her left side completely still. Tears began to fill my eyes, and I reached forth my hand and place it upon her cheek. I discovered that her cheek was extremely cold to my touch.

I have learned in over 40 years of moving in the spirit that you do not have to pray aloud prayer or shout at the enemy. (Them that do know their God shall be strong and do exploits) With the love of God flowing in my heart, I prayed a very simple prayer in Jesus name. I commanded the spirit of infirmity to go and began speaking life over her very quietly in Jesus name.

As I'm praying for this lady, tears were filling my eyes. I felt as if I knew her personally and that she was someone who was important to me. This is how the Holy Spirit works. God has shed His love abroad in our hearts by the Holy Ghost. It is in this realm that the gift of faith will begin to operate. You're not leaning on the understanding of your mind, or operating in simple human sympathy.

In probably less than a minute as I was praying the nurse spoke up very excitedly and made this statement: She Has a Pulse! As I thought about this later it became obvious to me that this lady up to that moment had lost her pulse. I continue to pray softly, as I still had my right hand on her cheek very softly. The next thing I knew this lady who was laying on the floor began to stir, and she reached up her right hand and put it on my hand squeezing it.

I knew in my heart that my job was done. The spirit of Christ had touched this precious lady, raising her from the dead. There were no fireworks, explosions, or loud shouting, but simply the gentle moving of the Spirit of Christ. The resurrection power of God manifested without people even realizing it.

I got up from my kneeling position, walking back to the crowd. My wife was simply waiting for me to complete the task. As we walked out the door of Cracker Barrel, the ambulance was coming around the corner, with its lights flashing. We simply walked out to our car and got into it. We took a minute to thank

God once again for confirmed the authority and power that we have in the Name of Jesus, with signs following.

The Holy Ghost Fell on Her and Then...

This morning as I was speaking on Revival, the When, the Where, and the Why, the Holy Ghost showed up.

What a wonderful move the Holy Ghost this morning (October 7, 2018) at our 10 AM service.
The worship service brought people to the front worshiping God their hands lifted up, some on their faces without an invitation.

I felt extremely invigorated and energized during the time of preaching. We were focusing on being obsessed, possessed, and consumed with loving Jesus Christ.

At the end, we began to worship God once again. Without any invitation, people began to come to the front to once again glorify Christ. I gave an invitation to all of those who want to be consumed in love for Jesus to come forward.

I began to lay hands upon people, asking God to give them a revelation of who Jesus really is. The first person in line was an older sister who had decided to come to our service. When I laid hands on her, the power of God came upon her mightily. She began to shake and swoon under the power of the Holy Spirit. She found herself on the floor under the mighty hand of God.

The rest of the service was amazing. Prophetic words, healing's, great freedom in the Holy Spirit.

People began to slowly leave the service. There was maybe

about a dozen or less of us standing around just being saturated by God. I noticed this older sister was back at our book table. She had a number of books in her hand, and she was looking in order to pay someone.

I walked to the back of the sanctuary which she was waiting. Sister Beverley was there trying to assist her. I walked up to her, and she handed the money to me for two of the books. Then she began to inform me that she had basically given up on the church. That she was within walking distance in Gettysburg of a Pentecostal church. She had gone there but was extremely disappointed. She was so disappointed that she had been staying home and doing nothing but watching Jimmy Swaggart on TV.

It came into our heart to come to our church service. She said she was mightily touched of God by the spirit, and that she wanted to come back. Then she began to tell me that many years ago she had been prayed for to receive the baptism of the Holy Ghost. She said she thought that she had spoken a little bit in tongues, but she wasn't really quite sure. She almost seemed like as if she wasn't sure if she had even received the Holy Ghost.

I told her that I would like her to get some more information before I laid hands on her for the Holy Ghost. (But God's plans are not our plans). I gave her one of my books for free on"Why We Pray in the Spirit". She wanted to pay me for it, but I told her I wanted her to have it as a gift.

Then she said she would like to come back to the night service, but she could not drive at night because she had some kind of affliction in her eyes. Instantly the Holy Ghost told me to put my thumbs on her eyelids, and tell that infirmity to come out of her. I told her: let's take care of that. With her glasses still on, I put my thumbs over her eyelids. I began to speak healing into her eyes in the name of Jesus.

Like a streak of lightning, the Holy Ghost fell upon her. I had to hold her up as the Holy Ghost overwhelmed her. Instantly out of her mouth came the manifestation of the gift of tongues. It completely overwhelmed her. Beverly got behind her as I tried to hold her up. She was speaking in tongues about a hundred miles an hour.

We held her up for a little longer until we finally Laid her gently to the floor. I asked Beverly to continue to minister to her. As I walked away to minister to somebody else, she was drunk in the Holy Ghost on the floor, speaking in tongues. Oh, how God loves us! I love it when the Holy Ghost has his way.

Amazing Testimony of God's Intervention
4/1/2019

I received a phone call from one of my parishioners Patty by name. Her 35-year-old son had been riding his bike down the main road in York Pennsylvania with no helmet. A young lady who was preoccupied on her phone did not even see him. She hit this young man Jason doing at least 45 miles an hour. She dragged him for 50 feet before she realized what happened. I'm not quite sure if the body of this man was under her car.

But thank God she immediately called 911. When they arrived he had already been dead for seven minutes. They immediately using a Defibrillator on him to bring him back to life.

Defibrillation is a treatment that delivers a dose of electric current (often called a counter shock) to the heart. This has the ability to shock the human heart back into once again pumping blood.

Immediately they rushed him to the hospital by ambulance. All of the reports were bad. He had extreme head damage, with his head swelling to a very large size, cuts, deep scrapings, and damage on the front of his head and in the back. Plus his brain had been without oxygen for at least seven minutes.

She shared with the congregation Sunday but how bad it was. The women gathered around her and prayed for her and her son with great passion. I told Patty that I would come up on Monday morning to York Hospital, and pray for her son, anointing him with oil according to the word of God.

I invited one of the pastors from my staff to join me in going to the hospital. Pastor Pete agreed to go along with me. When we got into York Pennsylvania we called Patty and told her we would meet her at the hospital. She met us in the main lobby.

Brother Pete and I had been praying and believing that God was going to do a miracle. When we entered the ICU, there was no one in his hospital room. He was all hooked up to equipment, including a breathing machine. The swelling had gone down to some extent, but they told Patty they did not know if he would ever come out of this coma. He had been in the coma ever since the young lady had ran him over. The doctors told Patty that he was still in grave danger of dying.

Patty, her sister, Brother Pete, and I took the anointing oil and anointed Jason's head. We prayed with passion, love, and faith that God would completely restore him. During that whole time, there was no sign that God had heard our prayers. But by faith, we simply believed.

After we had prayed for Patty and her sister, we said our goodbyes. Patty contacted me to tell me the exciting miracle they witnessed. Right after Brother Pete and I left through the double doors, Jason opened up his eyes. Yes, he opened up his eyes and squeezed his mother's hand as she was holding his hand.

He is now headed for a complete and total recovery. He is no longer on the breathing machine. And the operation that they thought they were going to have to do, they say is no longer necessary. Let us continue to pray, believe, and thank God for this wonderful miracle, and that it will be completed in Jesus name.

Patty shared with the congregation this last Sunday that he is going to be moved out of the intensive care unit, to a recovery room.

She testified that the medical personnel are completely baffled and shocked at how he has been restored because they had given him no hope to survive this terrible accident. God is still in the business of performing supernatural miracles. Thank you Jesus!

How to Live in the Miraculous!

This is a quick explanation of how to live and move in the realm of the miraculous. Seeing divine interventions of God is not something that just spontaneously happens because you have been born-again. There are certain biblical principles and truths that must be evident in your life. This is a very basic list of some of these truths and laws:

1. You must give Jesus Christ your whole heart. You cannot be lackadaisical in this endeavour. Being lukewarm in your walk with God is repulsive to the Lord. He wants 100% commitment. Jesus gave His all, now it is our turn to give our all. He loved us 100%. Now we must love Him 100%.

My son, give me thine heart, and let thine eyes observe my ways (Proverbs 23:26).

So then because thou art lukewarm, and neither cold nor hot, I will spew thee out of my mouth (Revelation 3:16).

2. There must be a complete agreement with God's Word. We must be in harmony with the Lord in our attitude, actions, thoughts, and deeds. Whatever the Word of God declares in the New Testament is what we wholeheartedly agree with.

Can two walk together, except they be agreed? (Amos 3:3).

For the eyes of the LORD run to and fro throughout the whole earth, to shew himself strong in the behalf of them whose heart is perfect toward him (2 Chronicles 16:9).

3. Obey and do the Word from the heart, from the simplest to the most complicated request or command. No matter what the Word says to do, do it! Here are some simple examples: Lift your hands in praise, in everything give thanks, forgive instantly, gather together with the saints, and give offerings to the Lord, and so on.

I can of mine own self do nothing: as I hear, I judge: and my judgment is just; because I seek not mine own will, but the will of the Father which hath sent me (John 5:30).

4. Make Jesus the highest priority of your life. Everything you do, do not do it as unto men, but do it as unto God.

If ye then be risen with Christ, seek those things which are above, where Christ sitteth on the right hand of God. Set your affection on things above, not on things on the earth (Colossians 3:1-2).

5. Die to self! The old man says, "My will be done!" The new man says, "God's will be done!"

I am crucified with Christ: nevertheless I live; yet not I, but Christ liveth in me: and the life which I now live in the flesh I live by the faith of the Son of God, who loved me, and gave himself for me (Galatians 2:20).

Now if we be dead with Christ, we believe that we shall also live with him (Romans 6:8).

6. Repent the minute you get out of God's will—no matter how minor, or small the sin may seem.

(Revelation 3:19).

As many as I love, I rebuke and chasten: be zealous therefore, and repent.

7. Take one step at a time. God will test you (not to do evil) to see

if you will obey him. *Whatever He tells you to do: by His Word, by His Spirit, or within your conscience, do it.* He will never tell you to do something contrary to His nature or His Word!

> *For whosoever shall do the will of my Father which is in heaven, the same is my brother, and sister, and mother (Matthew 12:50).*

> *Then went he down, and dipped himself seven times in Jordan, according to the saying of the man of God: and his flesh came again like unto the flesh of a little child, and he was clean (2 Kings 5:14).*

ABOUT THE AUTHOR

Michael met and married his wonderful wife (Kathleen) in 1978. As a direct result of the Author and his wife's personal, amazing experiences with God, they have had the privilege to serve as pastors/apostles, missionaries, evangelist, broadcasters, and authors for over four decades. By Gods Divine enablement's and Grace, Doc Yeager has written over 80 books, ministered over 10,000 Sermons, and having helped to start over 25 churches. His books are filled with hundreds of their amazing testimonies of Gods protection, provision, healing's, miracles, and answered prayers.

Websites Connected to Doc Yeager

www.docyeager.com

www.jilmi.org

www.wbntv.org

<u>Some of the Books Written by Doc Yeager:</u>

"Living in the Realm of the Miraculous #1"
"I need God Cause I'm Stupid"
"The Miracles of Smith Wigglesworth"
"How Faith Comes 28 WAYS"
"Horrors of Hell, Splendors of Heaven"
"The Coming Great Awakening"
"Sinners in The Hands of an Angry GOD", (modernized)
"Brain Parasite Epidemic"
"My JOURNEY to HELL" - illustrated for teenagers
"Divine Revelation of Jesus Christ"
"My Daily Meditations"
"Holy Bible of JESUS CHRIST"
"War In The Heavenlies - (Chronicles of Micah)"
"Living in the Realm of the Miraculous #2"
"My Legal Rights to Witness"
"Why We (MUST) Gather! - 30 Biblical Reasons"
"My Incredible, Supernatural, Divine Experiences"
"Living in the Realm of the Miraculous #3"
"How GOD Leads & Guides! - 20 Ways"
"Weapons of Our Warfare"
"How You Can Be Healed"
"God Still Heals"
"God Still Provides"
"God Still Protects"

Made in United States
Troutdale, OR
03/30/2024

18834392R00156